Jeff Apter is the author of more than 20 music biographies, many of them bestsellers. His subjects include Johnny O'Keefe, Keith Urban, John Farnham, the Bee Gees, the Finn brothers and Angus Young of AC/DC. As a ghostwriter, he has worked with Kasey Chambers, Mark Evans (of AC/DC) and Richard Clapton. Jeff was on staff at *Rolling Stone* for several years and has written about legends such as Aretha Franklin, Patti Smith, Robbie Robertson, Bob Dylan, Chrissie Hynde and Lucinda Williams. In 2015, he worked on the Helpmann award–nominated live show *A State of Grace: The Music of Jeff and Tim Buckley*. Away from music, Jeff has also worked on books with soldiers and diplomats and sports greats such as Michael Slater and Tim Cahill. He lives in Wollongong, New South Wales, with his wife, two children and a cat that's so damned cool it needs no name. www.jeffapter.com.au

THE BOOK OF DANIEL

OF DANIEL

FROM SILVERCHAIR TO DREAMS

JEFF APTER

ALLEN&UNWIN
SYDNEY•MELBOURNE•AUCKLAND•LONDON

First published in 2018

Allen & Unwin
83 Alexander Street
Crows Nest NSW 2065
Australia
Phone: (61 2) 8425 0100
Email: info@allenandunwin.com
Web: www.allenandunwin.com

 A catalogue record for this book is available from the National Library of Australia

ISBN 978 1 76029 629 2

Internal photographs courtesy of Tony Mott
Set in 13.5/18 pt Bodoni BT by Midland Typesetters, Australia
Printed and bound in China by Hang Tai Printing Company Limited

10 9 8 7 6 5

This one's for Christian

INTRODUCTION

I'VE ENCOUNTERED MANY VERSIONS of Daniel Johns, each as fascinating as the next. Like all great, slightly crazy artists, he's a shape shifter, a complicated, driven, frequently brilliant guy who refuses to stand still creatively. Daniel's very human, too. Once too often in these post-Silverchair times he's been snapped looking not-so-elegantly wasted; he's even needed at least one trip to the ER to be patched up after a lively night. Hey, plenty of us have done that, but none of us is Daniel Johns, artiste/public figure/wealthy muso. Perhaps he's just making up for all the teenage years he spent living in the cocoon that was Silverchair.

So, let me break this down.

One Daniel Johns I met was the guy in 2002 suffering the effects of chronic reactive arthritis, a young guy trapped in a broken body. I—insensitive clod that I am sometimes—rang the doorbell of his Merewether home for our scheduled interview and stood there impatiently as I was greeted by nothing but silence, cursing under my breath about the rudeness of rock stars. What I should have been tuned into was the simple fact that it was taking a long, painful time for Daniel, who needed a cane to walk, to cross the floor of his stylish crib and answer my ring. That was the damaged Daniel, a guy whose body had a habit of letting him down. As we spoke that afternoon, looking out from his rock-star eyrie down over his native 'Newie' (Newcastle), I felt genuine concern for the man–child—he wasn't yet 21—who'd lived much of the last half-dozen years in public. He was in a bad way.

Then there was the emotionally fragile Daniel Johns. While with *Rolling Stone*, I snaffled the prized gig of charting the evolution of Silverchair's *Diorama* album, in the studio and elsewhere. (Okay, I was in a position to commission myself to cover the making of what would be my favourite Silverchair record—*but wouldn't you give yourself the gig?*) I spent time with Daniel and his band-mates, Chris Joannou and Ben Gillies, over a period of months in Sydney, Newcastle and Los Angeles. I also got to meet producer David Bottrill, Paul Mac and others. I even got to see the legendary Van Dyke Parks—Daniel's collaborator—in action, conducting an orchestra inside Sydney's Studios 301 (when he wasn't telling dirty jokes). I found Daniel friendly but also a tad wary; I sensed he wasn't in the best psychological health, which turned out to be the case. Sometimes he could be distant, withdrawn, not willing to give too much away. I spent an awkward couple of hours with him in an LA record store. It was there, feeling a bit nervous myself and struggling for conversation, I asked him whether he'd be wearing his glittery mirror jacket on the next tour. He stared at me for a while. 'I'm not thinking about costumes just now,' he slowly replied. Fair enough, too; he was in the midst of a difficult mix of an album that had already presented its share of challenges. Stage gear could wait. And I should have had better questions to ask.

There was also the rock-star Daniel, a bright blazing whirlwind of onstage charisma and energy—and oft-overlooked wit. Again, I saw this Daniel during the *Diorama* period; he and the band were playing a homecoming gig in April 2003, at Newcastle's stately old girl, the Civic Theatre. One loud power chord away was Jewells Tavern, the venue where in June 1994 he and the band had been scouted by the two Johns, O'Donnell and Watson, and the Silverchair odyssey began. Newcastle was the Silver-three's turf; they'd all been raised here and retained strong roots to the working-class centre. Daniel Johns circa 2003 was a wild man; shirtless for much of the latter half of the gig, his pants hanging low on his barely there hips as he cheekily humped the onstage speakers, squeezing notes out of his guitar and testing the very limits of his gear and the audience's hearing. He looked great, lean and sinewy, primal even, his body a mass of tatts. Daniel owned the stage. I wondered how this could be the same guy who only recently had a cane and a limp and a broken body? Afterwards, in the cramped and humid backstage green room, as friends, parents and then band partners Natalie Imbruglia and Sarah McLeod drifted in and out of the conversation, Daniel Johns was a most gracious and affable host, someone who made sure your glass was full and that proper introductions had been made all round. A lovely young man, as my dear mum would say. With pierced nipples.

So which of these was the real Daniel Johns? Or were they simply different parts of the man, someone with so many sides he might well be round? I get the sense Daniel likes to keep at least a little of himself off the record—and off the stage, too, because he's refused to tour since Silverchair's 'indefinite hiatus' began in 2011. But I can say this: he's a writer's dream, a puzzling, challenging, creatively charged chameleon—the leap from 1994's raw *Frogstomp* to 2015's sophisticated *Talk* makes my head spin—who for me has been the standout local figure in my 30 years of writing about music and musicians.

1

They thought they had a crazy son, but after
eighteen months they realised they had a
normal boy like everyone else.
—Daniel Johns

NUMBERS RARELY LIE, so let's begin this story with
some stats. Silverchair, the band fronted by Daniel Johns,
were Australia's most popular rock group of the past twenty
years. Each of their five albums—*Frogstomp*, *Freak Show*,
Neon Ballroom, *Diorama* and *Young Modern*—debuted at
number one on the Australian charts, and they shifted, in
total, more than six million copies worldwide. The band's
fan base stretched from their hometown, Newcastle, to most
parts of the globe; they were the type of band who attracted
true believers—zealots—not just fans. In a golden run
between 1994 and 2007, they had fifteen Top 20 singles
in Australia, including three number ones—'Tomorrow',
'Freak' and 'Straight Lines'—the last, the best pop song
they ever recorded, raced to number one in 2007 and stayed

there for a month; it won an Australasian Performing Right Association (APRA) award for the most-played song of 2008. Daniel Johns also claimed the coveted APRA Songwriter of the Year gong in 2008. By the time the band went into recess during May 2011, after a serious internal falling out, they'd won enough Australian Recording Industry Association (ARIA) awards to fill several mantelpieces—21 in all—with numerous Best Band and Best Album gongs among them, and had very publicly graduated from grungy beach rats to mature men with a real sense of rock-and-roll cool. Daniel Johns's solo debut, *Talk*, peaked at number two in the Oz charts on its May 2015 release, and surprised everyone with its smooth, sleek grooves. Then he shocked everyone all over again with 2018's DREAMS, his most extreme project yet.

Johns is a remarkably ambitious musician, who has morphed from the punked-up grunge of Silverchair's early days to someone who is more than happy to bring in an orchestra when needed, or explore the outer realms of digital-era R&B. But there's more to his story than great songs, frenetic shows and a die-hard following who accepted his every creative step, no matter how radical (although all this has contributed hugely to his success). Johns, now in his late thirties, has lived through any number of personal crises. He's endured a life-threatening eating disorder, crippling arthritis, chronic depression, a divorce and the heavy emotional baggage that comes with a life lived reluctantly in the public eye. The simple fact that a clutch of paparazzi hired a helicopter to hover overhead, angling for a money shot, during his wedding to former *Neighbours* star Natalie Imbruglia in 2003 confirmed his tabloid worth (although Imbruglia had some market value, too). Of late he appears to have been snapped every time he's overindulged and fallen down—he's even been tailed by paps while going about the seemingly mundane task of checking his phone and smoking a cigarette. Privacy is a rare commodity for Daniel Johns. What he's drawn from all this is a batch of passionate, deeply felt songs that have connected powerfully with his fiercely loyal audience. And those myriad personal problems have brought his fans closer: they appreciate the hardships he's endured.

———◄○►———

The timing of Silverchair's emergence was perfect: they surfaced in the mid-1990s as the grunge wave broke, in the wake of Nirvana's era-defining album *Nevermind*—and being all of fifteen at the time, and cheeky as hell, they had an irresistible hook for the music media. It also didn't hurt, of course, that their lead singer was blond, blue-eyed and in desperate need of a hug, or that Johns, drummer Ben Gillies and bassist Chris Joannou grew into strikingly handsome, camera-friendly young men.

Silverchair's rise followed one of rock's worst flat spots. A cursory run through the ten top Oz singles of 1991 and 1992 reveals plenty about the dire state of music in that post-punk, pre-grunge, pre-Silverchair time. The '*Grease* Mega-Mix' was 1991's best seller, with Daryl Braithwaite's slick 'The Horses' and Bryan Adams's even slicker '(Everything I Do) I Do It for You' not far behind. Pop diva Cher and Rod Stewart were selling hefty amounts of records, as was songbird Mariah Carey. The pop charts have always been clogged with fluff, but this period in pop history was especially facile.

The internet hadn't grown sufficiently to help those interested in music who fell between the cracks; downloading wasn't even heard of yet. Streaming was still something urologists discussed with their patients. Mainstream Australia was being force-fed the pub rock of the Baby Animals or the bluster of Jimmy Barnes, whose unstoppable covers album, *Soul Deep*, was such a no-brainer to succeed that the man himself admitted 'a monkey could sing these songs and they'd still be hits'.

Yet during the 1980s, the very same Jimmy Barnes had been at the forefront of a distinctive style of Australian rock and roll—Oz rock—that had made an enormous impact. Cold Chisel, Rose Tattoo, The Angels and Midnight Oil had served apprenticeships in sweaty bloodhouses such as Sydney's Stagedoor Tavern, the Bondi Lifesaver and Melbourne's Bombay Rock. They emerged from this beery baptism to make powerful, era-defining records such as The Angels' *Face to Face*, Cold Chisel's *East* and Midnight Oil's *10, 9, 8, 7, 6, 5, 4, 3, 2, 1*.

Oz rock crowds were rowdy and randy. They were up for big nights of drinking, rooting and fighting. 'Suck more piss' was their call to arms. And these bands—the Oils, the Chisels, the Tatts—supplied the soundtrack to thousands of beer-stained evenings. There were common threads to all of these bands: a blazing guitar riff and a ball-tearing vocal to keep the crowds keen, and if the lyrics could connect to Aussie themes, well, all the better. Songs about Newcastle's Star Hotel, flame trees and bad boys for love, as well as crowd chants of 'no way get fucked fuck off'—the high point of any Angels gig—all hit the spot. The publicans were happy, because the punters drank. The bands got work. It was the best of rock-and-roll times.

The regulations requiring a certain quota of Australian music on radio also meant that local groups were receiving healthy airplay, which quickly led to record sales. In April 1981, Oz rock reached a very public early peak when Cold Chisel caused havoc at the Countdown Awards, smashing the set and nearly frightening the hat clean off Molly Meldrum's head. Within a month, their album *East* had sold more than 200,000 copies.

But Oz rock began to fade by the late 1980s. Noise restrictions and revamped licensing laws meant that venues were closing, while the bigger bands were either splitting up or losing their crowd-pulling appeal. The Angels and Midnight Oil started looking Stateside for a larger audience, with mixed success. The credible, punk-influenced underground bands that had emerged during the tail end of the Oz rock era—Brisbane's The Go-Betweens and The Saints, Perth's The Triffids, the Nick Cave–led The Birthday Party from Melbourne—had all left town.

As the 1990s began, there were ripples of change in the mainstream. Lewd and tattooed Californian punks the

Red Hot Chili Peppers hit big, really big, with their junkies' requiem 'Under the Bridge', and its parent album, *Blood Sugar Sex Magik*, which reached number one in Australia during November 1991 and hung about the charts for an astonishing 61 weeks. American college rockers R.E.M. crossed over into the mainstream in 1991 with their *Out of Time* album and its break-out hit single 'Losing My Religion'. And at the number seventeen spot on the Australian best-selling album chart for 1992 was the record that started the musical and cultural revolution known as 'alternative': Nirvana's *Nevermind*.

So, what was Australia's contribution during this time? Nothing much, just safe local acts such as 1927, Wendy Matthews and the Rockmelons, playing music designed, as one critic put it at the time, 'for people who don't like music'.

Occasionally, underground acts such as Ratcat broke through with a hit, but their success was as brief as the songs they sang. Meanwhile, at the major record labels, artist and repertoire (A&R) talent-spotters such as Sony's John Watson, Polydor's Craig Kamber and Ra's Todd Wagstaff were on the lookout for Australian bands that packed the same anti-everything attitude and rock-and-roll clout as Nirvana. 'Alternative' acts You Am I and Tumbleweed were seen as the bands most likely to shake up the mainstream, but their sales didn't make much of an impression on the Top 40. You Am I's first four albums debuted at number one on the Australian album chart, but none had the staying power to shift serious units; within weeks of release they'd dropped off the chart altogether. What was needed was a band that passed the 'cool test' and also appealed to middle Australia.

———◄◦►———

None of this mattered much in Newcastle, the second-largest city in New South Wales and home to Daniel Johns. Newcastle had been founded in 1804 as a colony for the First Fleet's worst convicts, and in the shadows of World War I it became home to one of BHP's major steelworks. It was a city of industry. For much of the twentieth century it flourished, a rough-and-tumble place where rugby league ruled and beer flowed as freely as the surf at Nobbys Beach. But work in the steel town and its surrounds started to slacken off. The region was hit hard by unemployment, which ran somewhere near 30 per cent by the early 1990s.

Daniel Johns was once asked about growing up in the region. 'One half of Newcastle is real industrial, and the other half is all beach and stuff,' he explained. 'It's [Merewether, the suburb in which he lived] a reasonably small town.' Daniel liked to surf; he loved the beach, just like any other kid from Newie. 'People basically leave us alone, but some call us long-haired louts.' Those name-callers didn't know that these 'long-haired louts' would become Newcastle's most famous exports.

Daniel Paul Johns was born on 22 April 1979. His Silverchair partners, Benjamin David Gillies and Christopher John Joannou, were born on 24 October and 10 November

1979, respectively. Johns was the first of three children for his parents, Greg, who ran a fruit stall in Newcastle, and Julie. Before Daniel's siblings were born, he had an imaginary friend named Robin, who was as good as real in Daniel's mind. If Daniel was being bathed, he'd scream at his parents, 'Don't get shampoo in Robin's eyes!' An extra place was set at the dinner table for Robin. It took his parents a while to adjust, as Daniel would recall. 'They thought they had a crazy son, but after eighteen months they realised they had a normal boy like everyone else.' A normal boy with an imaginary friend, that is. Daniel's younger brother Heath eventually took the place of his invisible friend, but Robin didn't disappear completely from Daniel's thoughts. Sometimes Daniel concentrated deeply, trying hard to bring him back.

Ben was the second child for plumber David Gillies and his wife, Annette. Joannou was one of three kids; he had an older sister as well as a twin sister. David and Sue Joannou operated a dry-cleaning franchise (later the site of Chris Joannou's venue The Edwards, which burned down in June 2018). The Johns, Joannou and Gillies families were typical Novocastrians: unpretentious, dedicated working-class folk, dreaming of maybe one day wiping off the mortgage and not having to work so damned hard.

While in third grade at primary school, Daniel met Ben and Chris, who already knew each other; soon Daniel became especially tight with Ben. Initially, their common bonds were simple and very much a product of their envi-ronment: they loved music, bodyboarding and surfing.

But Oz rock meant little to the Merewether three, with the exception of Midnight Oil; their *10, 9, 8, 7, 6, 5, 4, 3, 2, 1* LP was the first Australian record Daniel bought. He was ten at the time. 'I never got into the pub-rock scene, it didn't appeal to me,' Johns said in March 1999.

Instead, as Johns later revealed, it was their parents' record collections that were their entrée into the world of rock and roll. These were collections heavy with the type of bands—Black Sabbath, Led Zeppelin, etc.—that loved loud guitars, crashing drums and wailing vocals and that would have a huge influence on the early sound of Silverchair. Johns's father, in particular, was a huge hard-rock fan, with a serious collection of Deep Purple vinyl. 'Mum and Dad were really into the whole hippie thing,' Johns told *Rolling Stone*, 'so I grew up listening to Hendrix, Deep Purple, Black Sabbath, Cat Stevens and John Lennon.'

Johns's favourite albums included *Led Zeppelin IV* ('one of the first records I heard, along with Sabbath and Deep Purple') and *Deep Purple in Rock* ('the first rock album I ever bought'). Not a bad education.

The boys' parents—especially their fathers—had dabbled in bands when they were younger. Gillies' father played rhythm guitar and his mother played piano. Joannou's father played bass. Much later, Johns's brother Heath would start his own band—going by the name of the Army of Prawns—with more than a little help from his successful sibling. Heath Johns would eventually score a prized post in the music industry with BMG Australia and manage Daniel's solo career; Joannou's sister also worked in the biz. Music was definitely in all their bloodlines.

Johns, Gillies and Joannou lived within a few blocks of each other in Merewether. With a school friend helping out on keyboards, Johns and Gillies, aged nine, had formed a rap outfit, the Silly Men (yes, Daniel Johns was a rapper). Their repertoire included rhymes about big issues such as the Welsh and food, with 'The Elephant Rap' being the high point of their set. 'An elephant was walking down the street,' the pair would shout. 'And his feet were tapping to the beat/His ears were flapping and his toes were, too/ And he was doing a rap, just for you/Elephant Rap! Doing the Elephant Rap!' (Years later, Gillies and Johns would still bust out these rhymes in the back of the bus when the tedium of touring got to them.)

While Gillies was drumming with the school band—the Marching Koalas—Johns and Joannou had taken trumpet lessons, but the instrument didn't rock their world. Daniel craved an axe. 'I got this little electric guitar for $80 or something for a birthday present,' Johns said of his first six-string. 'It was called the Rock Axe. It looked kind of like a [Fender] Strat[ocaster], but it was really small. And it was all white. I thought it was good at the time, because I could just turn up the amp and go "Yeah!"'

Johns and Gillies jammed in Ben's parents' garage. Johns had taken a year's worth of classical guitar training, so there was some finesse amid the racket the two were making. As Johns told *Guitar School* magazine in February 1996: 'This guy, he just taught me all the main chords and stuff.

And after a year, I thought, I can't be bothered having lessons. So, I just decided to figure out my own stuff.' As to forming a band with Gillies, there was no master plan—Johns once said they only started playing 'if the surf was shit or we had no homework'.

Johns and Gillies tried on—and discarded—a variety of band names. They were the Witchdoctors, then Nine Point Nine on the Richter Scale and Short Elvis. Short Elvis played an actual gig—of Elvis Presley covers, naturally. Then it was back to the garage. Johns fronted for rehearsals trailing his trusty 60-watt Fender amp; Gillies pounded his tattered drum kit with all the gusto his skinny frame could muster. It was fun; they were making a noise. It was a good outlet for whatever frustrations they had, even though both seemed pretty well adjusted, if not overly inspired by school, as their average grades testified.

In 1991, the two twelve-year-olds, who sat somewhere in the middle of their social pecking order—neither wildly popular or intensely disliked—played their debut school concert. They were now called the Innocent Criminals. Silverchair legend has it that Johns spent the entire show facing the back of the stage. He couldn't meet the eyes of the few students who'd gathered to check them out. Gillies, however, had a slightly different recollection of the show. 'I think that's been overexaggerated,' he told me. 'I think he was just looking away, a bit.' What Johns didn't know was that his father, Greg, was watching proudly from the back of the hall, having been invited, on the quiet, by Newcastle High School principal Peter McNair. 'I never really wanted to be a singer,' Johns said in a 1996 interview. 'I just wanted to play guitar. Then one day we had a gig, and we still didn't have a singer. None of us wanted to sing. But I ended up doing it, and from then on I've been the singer.' Simple.

Around this time, Johns and Gillies started jamming with another schoolmate, Tobin Finnane, also playing guitar. The Gillies home had always been the drop-in centre for the boys, including Joannou, who was yet to join the band. It was on the way to school, so they always stopped in. 'You'd eat all the biscuits and keep going,' Joannou remembered, laughing. Now Johns, Gillies and Finnane gathered there to eat biscuits *and* to jam, first in the lounge room, then in Gillies' bedroom and, finally, in the garage (aka The Loft, which would become a ground zero, of sorts, in Silverchair history). Gillies' parents were supportive, although his mother would occasionally poke her head in and tell them to turn the volume down.

One day, a Gillies family friend dropped in, at the request of Annette Gillies, to show the boys how a bass worked, which, up until then, they hadn't realised was an essential part of a rock band. Johns, Gillies and Finnane were thrilled. 'We went "Wow! How cool did that sound?" Then we went on a mission to find a bass player.' Johns and Gillies asked a few schoolmates, but most were keener on playing drums or guitar, the true weapons of choice for any budding teen rocker. But they knew that Chris Joannou's father owned a bass—a copy of a Höfner, no less, just like Paul McCartney had played in The Beatles.

They approached their friend, encouraging him to learn how to play. Within days Joannou started jamming with them.

If volume is any indication of quality, by 1992 the four-piece Innocent Criminals were on their way: Gillies said, 'it just seemed to get louder and louder'. They entered a few local talent comps, playing Black Sabbath covers plus the few originals that Johns, Gillies and Finnane were thrashing out in The Loft. But then Finnane dropped some big news: his parents were leaving Newcastle to live in England for a year.

At this stage, the Innocent Criminals were two pairs of tight buddies: Johns and Gillies; Finnane and Joannou. When Finnane left, the remaining three were unsure what to do next—split the band or kick on as a trio? Would that be disloyal to Finnane? But they soon agreed that they'd gotten this far, so why not keep going? When Johns and Gillies made the proposal to their fast-improving bass man to play as a trio, Joannou was all for it.

Soon after, the Innocent Criminals played their first 'pro' gig at a Newcastle street fair. 'We got ten dollars each to play,' Johns recalled, with a fair dash of teen spirit. 'We got up there and played Deep Purple, Led Zeppelin and Black Sabbath songs.'

The gig didn't last long; a local complained about the volume and threatened to call the cops if they didn't pull the plug. 'They were absolutely dreadful,' the resident grumbled to the *Newcastle Herald*. 'The music was amplified, it was loud and it was really bad.'

'So, we had to stop playing,' laughed Johns. 'But we didn't care, we still got paid.'

2

I didn't really like ['Tomorrow'].
—Daniel Johns

JOHNS, GILLIES AND JOANNOU were working class all the way to their blue-collar roots, and expectations weren't high. They may have loved rock and roll, but the idea of becoming millionaire rock stars was inconceivable. But they were possibly the luckiest teenagers on the planet, or at least the luckiest in Newie. Their principal at Newcastle High, Peter McNair, gave the band more freedom than they could ever have imagined. According to McNair—who took up his post the year Johns, Gillies, Finnane and Joannou started high school—the unofficial school motto among the 1300 students was 'It's cool to be different'. The school prided itself on tolerance and diversity; piercings and coloured hair were permitted; creativity was encouraged. And McNair clearly recognised the trio's potential: he encouraged them to continue playing at lunchtime for their schoolmates.

By charging two bucks admission—not quite in keeping with Board of Education guidelines—the band raised enough cash to rent some lights and a PA, and buy a new amp. Their lunchtime shows became a roaring success. 'I knew there was something special,' McNair recalled of the Innocent Criminals. 'They had a sound that was so raw, so honest. The older kids were jumping around in excitement. Teachers still remember it today.'

The three rockers were smart enough, but school wasn't proving too inspiring for them. Johns admitted he was 'shit in maths and science' and took art as an elective principally because 'it's a bludge'. He said that 'English was my best subject', but only by a simple process of elimination: 'I was crap at everything else'. A lot of Johns's and Gillies' time was soaked up writing songs, which the three mixed with cover versions in their lunchtime sets and garage jams.

Word of these Innocent Criminals made its way to the local newspaper—and this time the response was positive. In late 1993, a small item on the band was noticed by Terry Farrelly, who ran Platinum Sound Studios, located in the Newcastle suburb of Cardiff. He contacted the band and offered them some studio time, at a bargain rate.

Farrelly's offer was generous: not only did it let the trio familiarise themselves with the workings of the studio, but they were also able to record basic versions of four songs, including a six-and-a-half-minute-long version of 'Tomorrow'.

According to Johns, the session 'cost about $75. We weren't in there for more than an hour.' Of the four demo tracks, 'Tomorrow' was the obvious standout.

'Tomorrow' had started to come together in Gillies' bedroom; he and Daniel had been watching the Led Zeppelin concert film *The Song Remains the Same* and were impressed by the sheer length of the song 'Dazed and Confused'. 'I really think we should write a song to it,' Gillies said, nodding towards the screen. 'Let's have a jam.' Johns resisted at first, but a few nights later they reconvened and got to work.

A jam session typically consisted of playing along with their favourite records—or rock film, in this case—chancing on a riff that they heard and liked, and seeing where things went from there. This time, as they jammed, Johns growled the lyric 'You wait 'til tomorrow' and everyone froze. 'Man, that's a cool line,' the others told him. Johns didn't totally agree.

'We just had a jam,' Johns said, 'and I came up with the riff to the chorus. Ben liked it, but I didn't really like it.'

Afterwards, Gillies spoke with Johns on the phone.

'We should make something out of this,' he said.

Johns was still unconvinced.

'Nah, nah,' he repeated, but the others persisted and he was finally talked around. It proved to be a career-making move. Without 'Tomorrow', these Innocent Criminals might never have left the Gillies garage.

In early 1994, a neighbour of the Johns family, Sarah Lawson, noticed that *nomad*, a program on multicultural television network SBS, was running a music competition called Pick Me. The comp's organisers were in search of the best demo recording by an unsigned Australian band; among the prizes was a day's recording at radio station Triple J's Sydney studio, as well as the chance to make a video for the song.

Lawson told the band, who got about as excited as diffident fifteen-year-olds could become. (Lawson was a good source of music for Johns—he joked that he'd try to steal records he liked from her impressive collection.) They submitted the tape of their Platinum Sound Studios session accompanied by a statement—in 25 words or less, as the rules insisted—as to what made the band so special: 'We're not hip-hop or rap,' the three wrote. 'We're rock!'

Out of the 800 entries, 'Tomorrow' was the song that caught the ear of one of the competition judges, Robert Hambling, an SBS freelancer and expatriate British video director. Hambling was destined for a long history with the band, as an archivist, video maker and insider. Hambling was sold on these Innocent Criminals.

'"Tomorrow" had all those things you want out of a great song,' he told me. 'Memorable lyrics, a really good hook. And there was no denying their connection to the Seattle sound. But it never went through my head that they were borrowing; it was just what they were listening to. And my point at the time was that if you're going to pick a competition based on the best entry, this is it; it doesn't get any better than this. Three very young kids, living in Newcastle, playing out of their bedroom—what else do you want?'

During the competition judging, Hambling had called the number supplied with the Innocent Criminals entry to make it known they were on the short list. Unaware at the time of their ages, he spoke with Johns's mother. Even though she told him Johns was at school, Hambling figured that she had to be the singer's wife or girlfriend. It just didn't enter his head that it was a teenager growling those pissed-off lyrics. When he did find out, Hambling placed a call to his friend, producer Nick Launay, to whom he'd played the demo.

'You'll never fucking guess how old they are,' Hambling told him.

Soon after, Hambling called the Johns household again. This time Johns answered. Hambling told him they'd won the right to record 'Tomorrow' at Triple J and have the *nomad* team direct their video. 'We didn't, like, go spastic or anything,' Johns said about hearing the big news, 'but we were pretty happy.'

But when the band convened in Gillies' garage, they dropped the cool charade. According to Joannou: 'Daniel's mum was at my house, and she ran out and said, "They won! They won!" We were just crazy, running around, going so berserk. It was so exciting.' Gillies remembered 'running around my house and yelling at the top of my voice. Then I remember thinking, "Fuck, how long is this going to last?"'

Tracee Hutchison, another of the *nomad* judges, also called Johns, asking him if the song could be cut down to a more serviceable four minutes. She asked Nick Launay to produce the song. He'd already done a rough edit of the demo version. Launay, who'd just relocated from the UK, had quite the track record, having worked with acts such as Public Image Limited, Killing Joke and Midnight Oil—he'd co-produced their *10 . . . 1* album, the first Australian record purchased by Daniel Johns. They seemed destined to work together—although not quite yet.

On the eve of recording 'Tomorrow', Launay fell sick and the production job went to Triple J's in-house producer, Phil McKellar, a veteran of the Triple J programs *Live at the Wireless* and *Australian Music Show*. McKellar and the band, accompanied by their parents, spent roughly eight hours together in the ABC's Sydney studio. Hambling—now incredibly passionate about the band, and professionally involved because of the *nomad* competition—babysat the session.

While Platinum Sound Studios may have been a shoebox with microphones, that experience helped the band make a smooth transition to the marginally more sophisticated ABC facility. McKellar was thrilled by their energy in the studio, and understood that the best way to bottle that was to record essentially live. And when Johns opened his mouth to sing, he was floored.

As McKellar would recall, 'I remember saying to myself, "How good is this?"'

Johns's vocal made the song.

Once the recording was ready, Hambling directed the moody video for 'Tomorrow', which was shot on the streets of Merewether, and in a gaol cell in the old Newcastle police station. The video set *nomad* back a whopping $2000. (A typical US video budget at the time was US$200,000.)

'The only special effect was that we screwed a light bulb into a cord and pushed it—it was all very George Lucas and R2D2,' Hambling recalled.

Wisely, much of the video showed the band actually playing, proof they knew one end of their instruments from the other. There were also clear traces of a Nirvana/'Teen Spirit' influence on the clip: it was dark and moody and menacing. After the shoot, Hutchison interviewed the band in front of Newcastle landmark Fort Scratchley.

A little after 8 p.m. on Thursday, 16 June 1994, during what turned out to be the show's final episode, *nomad* announced that the Innocent Criminals had won the Pick Me competition. They screened the video and aired the interview with the band. While no one knew it at the time, Australian music history had just been created.

———◄○►———

It had been almost three years since Nirvana's 'Smells Like Teen Spirit' had broken out all over, and local music-business taste-makers were still searching for an Australian answer to the grunge phenomenon. Sydney act Ratcat had scored some chart success with their guitar- and hook-heavy sound, but frontman Simon Day didn't wield Kurt Cobain's dysfunctional menace. Instead, he wore striped tops and was cute as a button. Ratcat's 1991 album, *Blind Love*, raced to number one in the local charts, but then their 1992 LP, *Insideout*, sank like a stone, proving just how fickle audiences can be. But Daniel Johns was a way more intriguing character than Day—he not only had an unreasonably sonorous voice that echoed the sound of Seattle, but he could also be enigmatic, sullen and serious, when not goofing off like a typical teenager (egging cars was one of his favourite pastimes). He used the words 'sorta', 'whatever' and 'you know' with extreme prejudice, usually while looking at the ground—most good things were 'sick'. Johns insisted with all due diffidence that they'd only started playing music for something to do when the surf 'sucked'. Still, there was clearly something going on here, even if the kid was barely fifteen.

After the *nomad* announcement, Triple J staffers circulated the 'Tomorrow' video to record-company contacts whom they thought would 'get' the band. Enough interest was building in the Innocent Criminals to entice Sydney-based record company talent-spotters to check them out. The Innocent Criminals were the complete package: they rocked like heathens and had a growling lead singer whose dirty blond hair and razorblade riffs had taste-makers whispering about 'the new Kurt Cobain'—a tag Johns was already growing to dislike. (After one too many Cobain comparisons, he threatened to 'shave my head and look like a punk'.) And young girls swooned when he sang.

Meanwhile, Johns's mother, Julie, was booking the band's shows and dealing with the circling industry sharks. She was protective and more than a little wary.

Ex-rock-and-roll journalist John O'Donnell and Sony's John Watson had a copy of the 'Tomorrow' video, even though neither had seen the *nomad* broadcast. The pair, both in their early thirties, was sharing an office at Sony's Sydney base. O'Donnell was only a week into his new job with Murmur Records, a boutique 'development' label established in June. He had left his post as founding editor of *Juice* magazine (and an editorial post at *Rolling Stone* before that) after Watson recommended him for the Murmur job. Watson, a former musician (he was in a band called the Spliffs, no less), record-shop worker, journalist and manager of Sydney indie band the WhipperSnappers, was then Sony's Director of A&R and international marketing. Their backgrounds were ideal for developing a band such as this: they understood how the media machine operated and were aware of how it could chew up an act. O'Donnell called their working relationship a 'tag team'. They were the 'Two Johns'.

Both had good ears and were big music fans—the Murmur label had been named by O'Donnell as a nod to his favourite R.E.M. record. 'We were listening to all the things they [the Innocent Criminals] were listening to,' says O'Donnell, 'from Pearl Jam to Nirvana to Screaming Trees and Soundgarden, as well as Sabbath and all that stuff they'd grown up around. We were genuine fans of that music.'

O'Donnell needed a hit to make his new job secure. And Watson was both ambitious and frustrated; previously, in his A&R role, he'd tried to sign hot local bands You Am I and Powderfinger but, because of the corporate rigidity of Sony, he couldn't offer them the flexible deals they needed. Both Watson and O'Donnell were impressed by the Innocent Criminals. They were exactly what Murmur needed to get started: a cool rock act—and a homegrown one, no less. And Sony boss Denis Handlin had granted O'Donnell, as head of Murmur, the flexibility to break the company rules, allowing him to offer bands record deals that didn't stitch them up for life.

As Watson recalled in an interview in 1997: 'As A&R manager, I had certain criteria in my head. Silverchair [or the Innocent Criminals, as they were at the time] had it all; with them, all the pieces of the puzzle fit: they played great, had catchy songs, good attitudes and they were fresh, charismatic—and they looked good. They reminded me of why I got into the music business in the first place. When you're that age, you don't make music to get laid or to make money or to see your photo on the cover of a magazine. You make music because you like the noise you make when you bang on your guitar. All great music is born from that.'

Keen to seize the moment, O'Donnell called Julie Johns to find out when the band were next playing. She told him there was a gig on the following Tuesday, but a contingent from Michael Gudinski's Mushroom label had already made inquiries, as had EMI. Curiously enough, it was the older songs on the Platinum Sound Studios demo tape that interested Mushroom, rather than 'Tomorrow'—they thought 'Won't You Be Mine' was the perfect first single, even though it was a song that the band had discarded. O'Donnell and Watson were stuck, because a Sony commitment on the same night forced them to miss the Criminals show.

Mushroom did make the gig, and met with the band and their parents. It looked as though O'Donnell and Watson had missed out. But O'Donnell called Johns's mother again and urged them not to sign with anyone. Not yet, anyway.

On 24 June 1994, the Innocent Criminals played Jewells Tavern, near Newcastle. Because the band were under the legal drinking age, they had to set up and play in the bistro and stay in the tiny band room between sets. O'Donnell and Watson—and some bored bikers who kept yelling for 'Born To Be Wild'—checked out the show, which included early takes on originals 'Acid Rain', 'Stoned' and 'Pure Massacre', as well as Pearl Jam, Hendrix, Kiss and Black Sabbath covers. There may have been only a dozen people in the room—and a few of those seemed keener on the footy screening on the pub television—but the two record-company execs were so impressed that O'Donnell remembered being 'totally speechless. It was like seeing the Beatles at the Cavern before they became stars.' As Watson recalled, 'It was literally the only time I've been to a show where you go, "This can't be happening".'

On the drive back to Sydney, Watson turned to O'Donnell. 'If I ever leave [Sony] to manage a band,' he said, 'this is the one.'

During that drive, they started formulating a career plan for the band, one that would be sensitive to their age rather than use it as a marketing device. As O'Donnell told me, it was a strategy that would ensure 'they would still be going strong when they were twenty and beyond.'

Both Mushroom and Murmur made offers to the Innocent Criminals. Mushroom was keen to capitalise on the teen appeal of the band. The label loved their name—unlike the band themselves—and envisaged them playing concerts in front of a banner that screamed 'Innocent Criminals'. Although Mushroom offered just a little more money up-front, Murmur's long-term plan—the concept of building a proper music career—appealed more strongly to the band and their families. It didn't hurt when O'Donnell and Watson slipped the guys rare Pearl Jam live CDs. And O'Donnell talked rugby league with Johns's father, which also did no damage at all.

The band didn't feel the need to overthink the decision. As the boys were riding their bikes to school soon after, Joannou turned to the others.

'I like the two John guys the best.'

'And if we signed straight to a big label,' Johns said, in defence of Murmur, 'there'll be all this advertising and shit.'

Everyone agreed. Case closed.

The band signed to Murmur for just one album. They became the label's second signing, joining up just a week after Perth alt-rockers Ammonia, who'd support Silverchair during an early tour. The advance paid to the Innocent Criminals—which they would have to recoup through record sales—was modest, less than $100,000. This included the recording budget of their first album. Still, they could buy some new gear, which was all they really craved right now. That and some good waves.

How to deal with Johns's feared 'advertising and shit' was a key part of the Murmur deal. O'Donnell and Watson knew the band were still too green for such serious music press as *Rolling Stone* and *Juice*, but neither did they want the three to be seen grinning from the pages of *Girlfriend* magazine. Accordingly, their first step was to score the band some coverage in the free music press, the 'street press', where they could build cred and gain the right kind of buzz.

O'Donnell and Watson had drilled what they called an 'anti-marketing strategy' into the heads of their young charges. They stressed that all publicity should focus on the band's music; Watson was aware the media could turn them into 'a teeny-bopper band, which would have given them a short shelf-life'. Watson was also concerned about the so-called 'Ratcat syndrome' in which a band explodes and implodes within the course of a couple of years.

This 'cool at all costs' mantra clearly made sense to Daniel Johns, because he repeated it frequently during early interviews. 'If we did teen press and things like that, we would be getting the wrong kind of audience,' Johns said. 'We're not going for the same people that listen to Bon Jovi. We just wanted to reach the alternative press, street press, fanzines, guitar mags and stuff like that.'

The band toasted their signing with what became a legendary gig on 22 October at Sydney's Vulcan Hotel, a venue so tiny and cramped that punters needed to turn sideways to take a breath. They were merely supporting alt-rock acts Nancy Vandal and the Popgun Assassins, but the house was full when they started to play—overly full, because 500 punters were trying to squeeze into the 150-capacity room. It was so full, in fact, that the stage collapsed due to the crush. 'People were crowd-surfing, hanging onto the roof,' said Joannou. 'It was just madness.'

By August 1994, calls started coming in to *Request Fest*, a listener-driven Triple J program, asking for 'Tomorrow', which had initially been played on Richard Kingsmill's *Oz Music Show*. This heavy anthem was striking all the right kind of chords, even if Triple J's music director, Arnold Frolows, wasn't totally sold. 'When it came in,' he told Sydney's *The Daily Telegraph* in 1995, 'we didn't think that much of it. It wasn't like we thought, "Oh God, this is a hit".'

As the airplay increased, a concerned John O'Donnell put in a call to producer Phil McKellar. 'Are there two mixes [of 'Tomorrow']?' he asked. After a little sleuthing work, it turned out that *Request Fest* host Michael Tunn had done his own edit on the song, trimming a part of the instrumental 'breakdown', thereby making it a slightly easier fit for radio. McKellar, every inch the gentleman, quietly suggested that it would be best to stick with his version, and Tunn's was swiftly shelved. 'It was a bit cheeky,' laughed McKellar.

Johns, Gillies and Joannou, meanwhile, were keen to ditch the name Innocent Criminals. As Johns said in September 1994, the band had 'started to get sick of it, and we found it a bit of a kids' name. We wanted something a bit more mature, so people didn't think of us as kids.' Watson and O'Donnell agreed. 'We thought it was a really bad name,' says O'Donnell. 'It threw too much light on the fact that they were a teenage band.' In the salubrious surrounds of a Strathfield pizza joint, the idea for a name change was proposed. But the band's parents thought, quite justifiably, that a lot of goodwill and recognition had built around the name after the *nomad* win. Despite their parents' resistance, the band's unanimous vote meant that they were Innocent Criminals no more.

The story of their new name has a few different versions. The band's standard line at the time was that it came to them one night when the three had gathered at Gillies' parents' home to make calls to Triple J's *Request Fest*. Johns wanted to hear You Am I's 'Berlin Chair', while Gillies opted for Nirvana's 'Sliver'—it was suggested they simply ask for 'Sliverchair'. Joannou transcribed this incorrectly, and the name Silverchair was born.

John Watson, looking back in 2002, had a different recollection: 'It was from the C.S. Lewis Narnia books'. *The Silver Chair* was written by Lewis in 1953, one of seven books in the Narnia series. 'We had literally hundreds of names on a list,' Watson continued—those other names included Grunt Truck and Warm Fish Milkshake. 'Silverchair came from a catalogue in the Johns household. At that stage, nothing was dismissed as a potential band name, and through a process of attrition, that's the one that stayed.' The book title's similarity to the two songs the band loved didn't hurt, either.

So, the band now had a name and a following, but no new music to share with their hungry audience. The band played a Sony music conference in Sydney on 19 August, then returned to Triple J studios, again with producer McKellar, to cut the tracks 'Stoned', 'Blind' and 'Acid Rain'. McKellar was just as impressed as he'd been at their earlier session. 'Like so many young bands, they were very exciting. They just really wanted to play.'

Along with 'Tomorrow', these three songs made up the band's debut release, a four-track EP priced at $9.95—three bucks higher than a regular single—which was released on 16 September. This jacked-up price was part of the marketing plan of O'Donnell and Watson—keep it low-key, make the songs the focus, don't oversell the band—in fact, make them a bit pricier than the competition. As O'Donnell read it, 'We thought if we stopped some young girl buying the record and making it a teen-based thing, great. As it turned out, it didn't hurt sales at all.' Another shrewd move on the part of the two Johns was to hold back on two tracks—'Pure Massacre' and 'Israel's Son'—for their band's upcoming album, rather than add them to the EP. O'Donnell had told McKellar that the songs, especially the former, were 'killers'—and he was right on the money.

As noted in Watson and O'Donnell's (handwritten) marketing plan, the original goal was to sell 6000 copies of 'Tomorrow'; that way, both band and label would be on track to start recouping Sony's investment. Yet something about 'Tomorrow' connected with a lot more than 6000 punters. Despite some clumsy poetry from Johns—'there is no bathroom and there is no sink/the water out of the tap is very hard to drink'—the song's stop-start dynamic and Johns's growling vocal, which packed an unclear but quite palpable discontent, hit pay dirt. Johns's guitar howled like a stuck pig, while the band rocked like a hurricane. It was a song born of grunge, bound to send mosh pits into convulsions.

Exactly what was Johns so angry about? The song was inspired by something he witnessed on the evening news; it wasn't some deeply felt statement. After all, what life experiences did a relatively well-adjusted fifteen-year-old have to draw on?

'There was this poor guy taking a rich guy through a hotel to experience the losses of those less fortunate than him,' Johns explained. 'The rich guy is complaining because he just wants to get out, and the poor guy is saying you have to wait until tomorrow to get out. That's one of our least serious songs, but it still has meaning to it.'

Meanwhile, as the calls kept coming in to Triple J and the Silverchair buzz gathered momentum, Johns and the band were about to understand that popularity is a mixed blessing. In October 1994, a mysterious letter appeared in Melbourne's street-press mag *Beat*, not too long after their first Melbourne shows. A female writer bragged how she and her girlfriends snuck Silverchair back to her house and 'took something away from these innocent boys that they'll never be able to give any other girl'.

Gillies replied by stating: 'That's the biggest load of crap'.

They weren't old enough to drive or drink, they didn't even shave, for God's sake, but already Silverchair were the object of female fantasies. The rumour quickly faded away; it turned out to be a dumb prank.

In November 1994, Silvermania became official, when 'Tomorrow' reached number one on the Top 40 singles chart, going gold the next week and staying on top for six weeks. In the process, the Merewether three had breezed past Kylie Minogue, Tina Arena and Madonna on their way to the top spot. They were the only local rock band inside the Top 30.

Gillies was getting ready for school when his mother hung up the telephone. She told him that 'Tomorrow' was number one.

Gillies didn't quite know what to make of it.

As he recalled, 'My first thought was, "Fuck, what's going on here?" That was really fucking weird.'

By December, 'Tomorrow' had sold 180,000 copies, 30 times more than the two Johns' expectations. And the song not only had legs, but it also proved to be incredibly influential, as Scott Owen of Melbourne band The Living End would tell a reporter. 'It taught kids that if you give it a go you have the chance to take on the world.' Owen was right on the money— trying to tally the number of bands that formed in Australia in the wake of the trailblazing 'Tomorrow' would make your head spin. James Tidswell of Violent Soho backed this up. Once he heard Silverchair's earliest recordings, all Tidswell wanted to do was 'play in a band. I wanted to do nothing else.'

Yet Daniel Johns's expectations for 'Tomorrow' had been even lower than his label's, or so he insisted in a near-perfect example of teen understatement. 'We expected it to sell about 2000. And then when it started going up a bit, we're going, "Oh my God, ha ha ha!" Then when it got to 15,000, we're going, "Hope it doesn't sell any more, we don't want it to sell any more". When it went to number one, we were kind of spewing. They're going "Congratulations", and we're going, "Everyone's going to expect every record to go to number one".'

Taking their cues from the anti-everything attitude of grunge, the band had no desire to be stars, at least not publicly. Eddie Vedder and Kurt Cobain had proclaimed that uncool, and many bands—Silverchair included— treated their every agitated mumble as gospel. It was a strange time to explode; the pervading climate of cool made it hard to enjoy the spoils of success, or at least not get caught doing it.

'We don't want to be very big at all,' Johns said. 'We don't want to be known as the band who think they're rock stars.'

And they did have some principles—and priorities. Multinationals began offering the band crazy amounts of money to play corporate gigs (up to A\$250,000, according to one report), but instead they opted to do shows like a fund-raiser in northern Sydney for the Surfrider Foundation, for which they each received a new surfboard and wetsuit.

By the end of 1994, 'Tomorrow' was still hogging the charts; it had become the ninth-highest-selling single of the year and was voted number five on the taste-making Triple J Hottest 100 chart, just pipped by Nine Inch Nails, The Cranberries and The Offspring (who charted twice). The band then signed on for their first Big Day Out, and the madness was about to truly begin.

3

People give us shit. It's good in some ways . . .
If people hate you, it makes you want to keep
going, 'cause you want to prove them wrong.
—Daniel Johns

KEN WEST AND VIVIAN LEES were savvy promoters
heavily into alternative music. They were well connected
and ambitious in a cool-school, indie-cred kind of way.
Since the late 1980s, they'd promoted such international acts as Billy Bragg, They Might Be Giants and
the Violent Femmes on Australian tours. On 25 January
1992, the Australia Day long weekend, they staged the
first Big Day Out. The event was closely based on Lollapalooza, the annual alternative-rock roadshow that started
to crisscross the USA in 1991, which hosted such cutting-
edge acts as Beck, Smashing Pumpkins, Soundgarden
and Jane's Addiction while promoting political activism and
selling the type of exotic food not found in your typical
strip mall. For punters, Lollapalooza offered the chance to

get seriously rocked *and* join Greenpeace. For bands that made the bill, the exposure guaranteed well-paid shows before big crowds, strong record sales and some lively backstage action.

'As a promoter, I've always tried to do things that were interesting,' West said on the day of the inaugural Big Day Out. 'I get bored with just putting together the same old bills.' To drive home his aversion to the 'same old bills', the first Big Day Out was a musical smorgasbord. Sandwiched between Indigenous rockers Yothu Yindi and undergrad faves the Violent Femmes was Nirvana, whose second album, *Nevermind*, was about to explode in the USA and then all over the world. Playing before 9000 mad-for-it punters in Sydney's Hordern Pavilion, their set, as described by *Rolling Stone* magazine, was 'blistering, intense and wildly received, with the mosh pit drenched in water and a frenzy of stage divers.' (I was there and vividly recall the sight of dozens of one-shoed punters emerging from the mosh— they'd lost footwear in the mayhem.) The verdict was unanimous: Nirvana was the shit, and the Big Day Out was a hit.

The Big Day Out just kept getting bigger. In 1993, the event went national and in 1994, the top five acts on the bill—Soundgarden, The Cruel Sea, Björk, Smashing Pumpkins and Urge Overkill—had albums in the Top 10 within two weeks of the event. Major labels found this commercial knock-on effect very attractive, and lobbied Lees and West to get their bands on the bill. And for local acts with just a whiff of ambition, a spot on any of the four main outdoor stages guaranteed a leg-up for their career— and the chance to hang out with their heroes.

There was really only one band that had 'must see' written all over them at the Big Day Out 1995: Silverchair. O'Donnell approached West in late 1994, slipping him a pre-release copy of the 'Tomorrow' EP and talking up the band. On the urging of Silverchair's booking agent, Owen Orford, West checked out the chaos at the band's Vulcan Hotel show in Sydney and was sold.

'He got it straight away,' says O'Donnell of West. 'They got the band for next to nothing, and it created all this excitement. We needed the band to play the right kind of shows—and with other credible bands.' (Silverchair management refused to name the exact figure they were paid for Big Day Out 1995, but referred to it as the 'bargain of the century'.)

As part of Watson and O'Donnell's softly-softly strategy for the band, Silverchair were booked for a mid-afternoon spot on the outdoor Skate Stage at the Sydney event, a hundred metres away from the main action inside the Hordern Pavilion. At a stretch, 5000 punters could see the band. However, some 15,000 sun- and beer-drenched fans tried to squeeze together, sardine style, to check out this new band of baggy-shorted, T-shirted teen hot shots.

David Fricke, a senior editor from American *Rolling Stone*, was in Australia to see the Big Day Out and register how it stacked up against Lollapalooza. He couldn't quite believe what he witnessed when Silverchair hit the stage, as he wrote in his report of the madness. 'Tsunami-force waves of crowd-surfers repeatedly roll towards the stage, damn near crushing the packs of defiant, cheering teenage girls pressed against the security barrier. Several enterprising fans, determined to get a better view, scramble up a drain-pipe to the roof of an adjacent building, breaking the pipe and yanking part of it off the wall in the process.'

Fricke looked on, more than a little stunned, as one shirtless dude scaled a light pole overlooking the mosh pit, dangling from his precarious perch, four storeys high. (In Melbourne, punters actually jumped off nearby rooftops into the huge mosh pit or trampolined on the tarpaulin hanging over the band.)

It was 3 p.m. when Silverchair exited the Sydney stage. Still to play were Hole and The Offspring, but it was Silverchair that everyone was talking about, Daniel Johns especially. Fricke again: 'Johns sings with a full-blooded voice that belies his age. The madhouse atmosphere is not a Pavlovian reaction to overnight success; the Seattle-fried crunch of "Stoned" and "Pure Massacre" is truly potent stuff.'

The mouthy Courtney Love noticed the attention directed towards the Novocastrian trio. In typical Love fashion, she decided to bring the band, particularly Johns, down a notch or two. 'So, this young guy from Silverchair looks like my dead husband, Kurt, and sings like Eddie Vedder,' she slurred during her set. 'How lame.' Love repeated this observation a few nights later at her band's show at Sydney venue Selina's. Whatever her intention, Love's comments showed that, almost against his will, Daniel Johns and Silverchair were leaving their mark on the rock world beyond Australia. An insult from Love meant that he was definitely on the cool radar.

When the roadshow reached New Zealand, Johns stood and watched as Love emptied a bag full of lingerie in full sight of airport staff and passengers, as she searched for her passport. 'That was pretty much my first introduction to women's lingerie *and* to Courtney Love,' he would later deadpan. (Four years later, in St Louis, Love and Silverchair again crossed paths. Only this time, she was topless. As she passed Johns, Love stopped and asked, 'Are you doing heroin?' When he said no, she replied, 'Good, because that's so '95.')

Other international acts at the 1995 Big Day Out paid Silverchair more respect. Brit rockers The Cult gifted them penknives and called them up onstage in Perth during the final date of the festival, declaring them 'Australia's finest'. Silverchair responded by donning wigs and dancing onstage, badly, as The Cult riffed on. At one gig, Johns sported an Offspring T-shirt, clearly unfazed by the fact that this was the band who'd outranked them on the recent Hottest 100.

But sometimes it was all a bit much for the fifteen-year-olds of Silverchair. Johns summed up the mixed emotions he felt about their success when he introduced the mosh-inducing 'Tomorrow' at the Sydney Big Day Out: 'This one is called "Cat's Scrotum",' he mumbled. Gillies and Joannou weren't sure if he was joking. All the acclaim and chaos were a lot for anyone to take in, let alone a sometimes moody teenager.

Another American in the Big Day Out melee was David Massey, the vice president of A&R with Epic Records, a subsidiary of Sony. Massey had an option to release Silverchair's music in North America. He was smitten by the band and promptly agreed to release what would be their first album, *Frogstomp*. And Massey didn't agree with Courtney Love. 'He's fifteen years old, he's got blond hair, but he's nothing like Kurt [Cobain],' Massey said of Johns. 'He's a bright, young surfer kid. They have their own identity. What impressed me most about them live was how well they actually played, how much presence they had on stage and how developed their sound is for their age. The audience response was pretty rapturous, and it made me realise there wasn't the tiniest issue of novelty.'

Well, maybe not, but any A&R guy worth his corporate credit card could spot the obvious appeal of the band— they were young, a little wild, had some great songs, and their ages gave journalists a handy angle. Silverchair had something for everyone, and in Daniel Johns they had a reluctant rock star in the making.

The immediate knock-on was huge; within three days of their Big Day Out spot, the follow-up to 'Tomorrow', the grinding 'Pure Massacre', debuted at number two on the Oz charts. A shot taken at the recent, crazy Vulcan Hotel gig was used on the single's cover, while the chaos at a show at Sydney's Phoenician Club, captured by director Robert Hambling, was used for the original 'Pure Massacre' video.

Their afternoon set in Sydney also went down in Big Day Out history. In 2014, website Tone Deaf cited it as one of the '12 Big Day Out Moments We'll Never Forget', ranking it alongside the antics of Iggy Pop and Courtney Love. Silverchair were the only Oz band on the list.

———◄◦►———

While Big Day Out madness was happening all around them, the band were keen to prove they weren't a two-hit wonder. During December 1994 and January 1995, the trio spent nine days with South African–born, Australian-based producer Kevin 'Caveman' Shirley in Sydney, recording *Frogstomp*, their debut album.

Shirley had worked the desk for some well-regarded Australian bands; he'd engineered the Baby Animals' 1991 debut album, which reached number one in Australia and sold 300,000 copies, but he was an unknown quantity as a producer. Watson was keen to have Shirley work on the album, in part on the strength of some demos he'd produced for The Poor, while O'Donnell liked Shirley's work with Sydney power-riffers The Dubrovniks. Although many at Sony thought Shirley a risky choice, it turned out to be another smart move by the two Johns.

Yet Shirley, an unapologetically commercially minded producer, wasn't sure he was the man for the job. 'I wasn't really that interested in working with them,' he said. 'They had such a cool thing going with Phil [McKellar] and Nick [Launay]; I thought they had a winning formula.' Shirley reluctantly agreed to spend a weekend with the band and record two songs, 'Pure Massacre' and 'Leave Me Out', as 'an experiment'. Pleasantly surprised by the results, he signed on for the album, for a fee of $20,000 and 'points' in the finished product. Before the band set up base at Festival Studios, Shirley spent a fortnight with them in Newcastle, working through each song that would make the album. 'I think I spent more time in pre-production than the studio,' he recalled.

Shirley was widely known as a 'rock dog'. A gradually emptying bottle of Jack Daniel's sat on the desk throughout every session he worked on. It was a sight that didn't rest well with Silverchair's parents, still the band's surrogate managers, who came into the studio each afternoon to check on their boys' progress. The Silver-parents said little, but Julie Johns did take Shirley aside after hearing how he'd double-tracked her son's voice during 'Israel's Son'.

'Is it really necessary to have that distortion?' she asked. 'He has such a beautiful voice.'

Shirley smiled, said little and got back to work.

Nor did the two Johns intrude greatly on the album-in-progress.

'They were involved,' Shirley said, 'but knew we were going in the right direction. I don't recall them ever saying, "This song isn't right".'

Any resistance Shirley originally had to working with Silverchair faded quickly.

'I lived and breathed that record,' he told me. 'I had an incredible feeling about it.' Throughout the LP, Johns played a vintage 1955 Les Paul, a loaner from Shirley, who didn't feel that Johns's current guitar had the requisite grunt. It proved to be a good call. Two years later, David Bottrill, who'd produce Silverchair's *Diorama*, was recording with the band Tool, and he asked guitarist Adam Jones what type of sounds he was after. Without another word, Jones whipped out a copy of *Frogstomp*. 'Make me sound like *that*,' he demanded.

Johns, Joannou and Gillies were still suburban kids at heart, and sometimes the studio bored them. When that happened, Shirley would send them outside to play cricket, or lock them in a room with a porn video featuring Ron 'The Hedgehog' Jeremy, which kept them titillated for hours. Shirley saw his role as 'rebel schoolteacher'. Sometimes, while Shirley worked away, Johns and the others would be crashing about in the studio corridor, riding on trolleys, bashing into walls. Then Shirley would yell, 'Right, we need you now', and they'd get back to work. One Festival Studios staffer recalls the band vividly. 'They made so much fucking noise.'

If Shirley had any hassles with recording *Frogstomp*, it was re-creating the 'feel' that Phil McKellar had captured so well on 'Tomorrow', the album's key track. The finished version of the song, the catalyst for Silverchair's supernova rise, was actually the result of painstaking editing on the part of Shirley and his crew. Like a sonic jigsaw, the song was seamlessly stitched together and then digitally sped up. It worked perfectly.

After four days in Festival Studios in Pyrmont recording the basic instrumental tracks, five more days were devoted mainly to Johns's vocals. Capturing his world-weary vocals—so unsettling from a teenager, and such a major part of the band's sound—was the most difficult part of the recording. On the first day, due to studio inexperience and a lack of proper vocal training, Johns ran out of voice. Literally. Then he caught a cold, which meant he had to return a fortnight later to finish five tracks. Gillies and Joannou slyly decorated his vocal booth with *Playboy* and *Penthouse* centrefolds, the perfect motivational tools.

The album was wrapped for the bargain price of around $40,000, a relatively low-budget affair, especially in light of how well the record would fare commercially. Johns titled the album *Frogstomp*, naming it in honour of an obscure Floyd Newman song he spotted on a Stax-Volt singles compilation among Watson's record collection.

The LP was released in Australia on 27 March 1995, debuting at number one in the album charts and staying in the top spot for three weeks. It was a trailblazer, the first debut album by an Australian act to chart at number one in its first week. By 10 April, as the band geared up for a Perth event known as Bunny Fest, a festival they headlined over You Am I and Tumbleweed, *Frogstomp* had been certified platinum (70,000 copies sold). By May it had sold more than 100,000 copies, principally on the strength of Triple J airplay and live shows. The two Johns did their best to uphold their low-key, street-cred strategy; in fact, it was only at the end of the year, under pressure from Sony executives, that Watson and O'Donnell agreed to a week's worth of television advertising—and only then if they could produce what amounted to an 'anti ad'. Almost in spite of itself, *Frogstomp* became the highest-selling Oz album of the year.

For a trio of teenagers still finding their true voice, *Frogstomp* was a rock-solid, if undeniably derivative, album. More than anything else, it was a record of its time, propelled by what would be recognised as the signature sound of early Silverchair, Johns's full-throated roar and serrated riffs, and the powerhouse engine room of Gillies and Joannou. They worked from the definitive grunge template as perfected by Soundgarden, Nirvana and Pearl Jam: quiet verses followed by loud choruses and a sound as thick as sludge. But Johns's old-beyond-his-years wail and the melodies that broke through the sonic murk were distinctive. *Frogstomp* proved that Silverchair were far more than a slavish imitator.

'The alarming thing is that the guys sound as mature as they do,' Shirley said in 1996. 'You can definitely hear the influences. But they weren't embarrassed about showing those influences.'

Johns, who still insisted that he drew most of his lyrical ideas from watching television, whipped up a batch of songs dominated by death and violence. 'Faultline' was written about the Newcastle earthquake of December 1989, which killed thirteen people. 'I just saw on the news that a guy's brother was killed, so I wrote lyrics about it three years later when I remembered it in a dream,' Johns explained. Simple.

The sombre, surprisingly restrained 'Suicidal Dream'— which Johns wrote alone—was the album's most disturbing track. Johns calmly sang his lyric 'I fantasise about my death/I'll kill myself from holding my breath' as if it were just another pop song. But Johns was insistent that it was in no way autobiographical. This would become a common misconception about his early work.

'It's about teenage suicide and the ideas people have. I don't try and write lyrics about me.'

Johns's lyrics for 'Tomorrow', famously, were inspired by 'this rich dude' he saw on a documentary. 'I was thinking about what a cock he was. It's just a song about any rich dickhead.' Johns wasn't ready for any sort of self-evaluation; at least not yet, although one US critic would soon write that Johns's disturbing lyrics 'could keep his high school guidance counsellor busy all semester'.

Frogstomp connected with more record-buying teenagers than the band or their label could ever have imagined. And despite attracting such condescending tags as 'Nirvana in Pyjamas', 'Silverhighchair' and 'Not Soundgarden, Kindergarten'—and a parody, a song called 'Frogstamp', the work of Aussie act Silverpram—most critics treated the album with respect. Writing in *The Sydney Morning Herald*, sometimes arch journalist Shane Danielsen called it 'an impressive debut', noting the band's 'ability to pile layers of punishing noise atop a tune worth humming'. Australian *Rolling Stone* gushed that 'Silverchair make a noise like they're here to stay . . . this is eminently moshable stuff, guaranteed to cause carnage in lounge rooms across the country'.

Silverchair had grabbed hold of the grunge movement with all six hands, even down to the fine detail of wearing the right T-shirts in public, supporting local heroes You Am I and Ammonia, and US bands Ministry, Helmet and The Offspring. Some wore influences on their sleeve; Silverchair wore theirs on their skinny, hairless chests.

Not surprisingly, the band were big winners in the annual Australian *Rolling Stone* Readers' Poll awards, published in April 1995, claiming Artist of the Year, Best New Band, Best Hard Rock Band and Brightest Hope gongs. 'Tomorrow' picked up Best Single, while the obligatory haters also ensured they 'won' Hype of the Year. But Johns and the others were getting used to critics.

'Hype sucks!' Gillies told a reporter at the time. 'We just want to be an alternative band,' Johns insisted. 'We don't want to be big at all. As soon as we get big heads, we're stopping.'

Even at fifteen, Johns and the others were developing thick skins. Yet being the frontman of the band, the focal point, meant an even heavier load for Johns to bear—he'd already had just about enough of people saying, 'Oooh, you just want to be Nirvana,' essentially because he was blond and they were a three-piece band who rocked hard. 'People give us shit,' Johns said. 'It's good in some ways. It stops you from getting a big head if you know, like, millions and millions of people hate you. And if people hate you, it makes you want to keep going, 'cause you want to prove them wrong.'

Take that, nay-sayers.

Johns readily admitted the influence of Pearl Jam on their runaway hit of a single 'Tomorrow', but began to play down the long-term impact of the multi-platinum grungers.

He was already moving on. 'That was early,' Johns threw in. 'That was on the first EP. At that time, we were very strongly influenced by Pearl Jam. That's all we ever listened to. And then we started listening to Soundgarden and Helmet and stopped listening to Pearl Jam.' A defensive tone crept into his diatribe: 'Because we were just starting out, we didn't know'.

On 12 April, 'Israel's Son', the third single from *Frogstomp*, was released. But it was a limited release; the single was only available commercially for three weeks, another Watson and O'Donnell move to control the exposure of the band, in the face of an alternative-rock-hungry public that couldn't get enough of them. And still the song bruised the Top 10, peaking at number eleven. The pair were now acting as caretaker managers for the band, along with the boys' parents, in particular Julie Johns. But what Silverchair really needed was a full-time manager.

Watson had never hidden his interest in managing the band and, in August 1995, he decided he was ready to look after Silverchair, quitting his A&R position with Sony. Despite a few expressions of interest, there was no other logical contender for the job, and the deal was sealed over a few lunches with the trio's parents. According to Watson, 'It was just a question of when I was going to jump ship'. Johns, in particular, seemed to relish making references to 'our manager', speaking as if Watson was some kind of inanimate object. But they were tight. The band trusted him. Frankly, when it came to the business of music, 'we didn't give a shit,' according to drummer Gillies.

Around the time that Watson took over management of the band, murmurs of Silverchair interest emerged in the USA. They already had the support of Epic Records, but needed US radio to get on board the Silverchair bandwagon.

◄o►

The Big Backyard was a government-subsidised initiative that produced half-hour-long, radio-ready programs of new Australian music on CD. It was distributed via embassies and diplomatic posts to more than 750 radio stations in more than 100 countries. Watson bought the Big Backyard mailing list and fired off a Murmur mail-out. It included a letter from the program suggesting stations check out this new Australian music, with Silverchair featuring prominently, of course.

Back in March 1995, a Perth-based fan had mailed a copy of 'Tomorrow' to a relative who worked at Detroit radio station 89X, which, on 27 March, became the first US radio station to playlist the song. Brian Philips, the chief programmer for Atlanta's 99X station, was in Australia on holiday just as 'Tomorrow' fever started to spread. He grabbed a copy of the song everyone was talking about and playlisted it on his return to Atlanta. Within a week, it was one of the top five songs requested by listeners. Chicago's Q101 also added 'Tomorrow' to its playlist; soon Seattle's KNDD did the same, as did Milwaukee's WLUM. The momentum was building.

The band had played three fly-by European dates, in Frankfurt, London and Amsterdam, between 29 March and

3 April. While in London, Watson fielded some more great chart news for the band, which he was very keen to share with Johns, Gillies and Joannou. When he walked into their hotel room, he was shooshed; they were engrossed in a pay-per-view movie, a novelty for kids raised on Australia's paltry three commercial television channels.

'Tell us when it's over,' they insisted, nodding at the screen.

Pay television and London were all good and well, but it was the USA where serious interest was developing in the band, and as Watson and O'Donnell knew, that was where the real money was to be made. It was the rock-and-roll pot of gold. Even The Beatles hadn't felt they were true super-stars until they made it in the USA—only then were they, in their own words, 'the toppermost of the poppermost'.

Epic had planned to run with 'Israel's Son' as Silver-chair's first US single and have the band tour to coincide with *Frogstomp*'s release late in the year. Now they had to change their plans and lead with 'Tomorrow'—and get the band over ASAP for at least a few dates. By 6 June, when the single was officially released to US radio, Epic's David Massey knew he had a monster on his hands. As he told American *Rolling Stone*, this wasn't record-company spin at work. 'Tomorrow' had been 'getting an amazing response from the public,' he said. 'It comes from the public as opposed to industry hype.'

As for Johns and the band, they had more pressing matters at hand: a homecoming gig at the Cambridge Hotel in Newcastle on 7 June. Right now, this meant as much to

THE BOOK OF DANIEL

them, perhaps more, than 'breaking' the USA. A sign at the door of the venue warned: Enter the Mosh Pit At Your Own Risk. The room was packed tight, and both band and audience threw themselves into their work, with Johns, Gillies and Joannou creating an unholy racket on stage. The trio rated the success of a gig by the action in the mosh pit; if bodies were flying, as they were tonight, they were definitely 'going off'. Johns registered this from the stage but barely said a word throughout the set; instead, he kept his eyes tightly shut and roared out his lyrics about death and despair and some 'fat boy' waiting for tomorrow, his long hair covering his face like a mask. He might have still copped the odd 'faggot' comment out on the street— Newcastle could be a tough town—but tonight Johns was the king of Newie. The gig officially went off.

On 21 June, the band—who'd arranged leave from school—played their first American date, in Atlanta, narrowly avoiding a visa hassle in Sydney that almost prevented them leaving the country. They made a press stopover in Los Angeles but didn't play shows there. Instead, they opted to do gigs in the cities where radio response to 'Tomorrow' was strongest: Atlanta, Chicago (on 23 June) and Detroit (24 June), at the 'birthday bash' for station 89X. It was a smart move: make a few splashes and let the ripples spread from there. And by playing radio-sponsored shows, the band were establishing some goodwill. It was an unspoken rule that, by playing a free radio show, a band in return often received good treatment from that station's programmers. Rock-and-roll quid pro quo.

Despite the local radio interest, no one could have envisaged the response at the Atlanta show at the Roxy. The venue housed 1500 punters at a squeeze. Mid-afternoon, a shocked Watson put in a call to O'Donnell back in Sydney: 'You're not going to believe this,' he reported, 'but we're at sound-check and there's a queue of 150 people going around the corner.' By six o'clock, two hours before the doors were due to open, a line of 3000 hopefuls snaked a kilometre down the street.

The mayhem continued throughout the short tour. At Silverchair's Chicago gig two days later, while the crowd moshed themselves senseless, a female voice shrieked from the balcony, 'Oh my God, they're so cute I can't believe it.' The *Chicago Tribune*'s Greg Kot reviewed the show, describing how the band overcame a wobbly start to 'put some wallop behind the insidious melodies of "Tomorrow", "Real [sic] Massacre" and "Israel's Son"'.

'There was no denying the savvy sense of dynamics, muscular melodies and tight ensemble playing,' he wrote. 'All of which suggested that Silverchair has the potential to match the impact of some of its influences, if not make Mom and Dad sell off their old Zeppelin albums.'

The band were brought back down to earth when Johns broke a microphone stand during their set, and the venue's owner insisted they pay for the damage.

When Johns spoke with Kot for their first American *Rolling Stone* story, which ran in late August, he was genuinely overawed by their swift rise. 'We didn't expect to sell heaps of records and go overseas,' he said, brushing his hair out of his eyes. Gillies also downplayed their success, insisting they only formed a band 'so we don't have to do an apprenticeship for a real job'.

Watson and O'Donnell had suspected the band would draw a strong response, but this was out of control, way beyond their wildest managerial dreams. By the time of the Chicago show, *Frogstomp*, which had been released less than a week before, had sold 5000 copies, 2000 in Atlanta alone, where it debuted at number eleven—even before it was fully stocked in stores. The following week, sales doubled. As 99X programmer Philips stated: 'It is not in my experience for a band to launch itself into the stratosphere this quickly. This is a very special thing.' Current hit records from Bush (*Sixteen Stone*), Green Day (*Dookie*), Neil Young and Pearl Jam (*Mirror Ball*) and The Offspring (*Smash*) were all in real danger of being frogstomped.

Watson and O'Donnell insisted, just as they did in Australia, that the band would only accommodate the 'right' type of media, even to the extent of turning down *Time* magazine's request for an interview. (Heaven knows how *that* went down with the record company.) The group's first US radio interview, with Sean Demory from WNNX, Atlanta, was a useful reminder that these rising stars were still kids. Most bands would have talked up whatever product they had to sell, but Silverchair were more interested in discussing the merits of roller-coasters, especially those at LA amusement park Magic Mountain.

'That is the best place in the whole world!' Johns gushed. Gillies let it be known that he and Johns rode the Viper four times and not once did he let go of the safety bar. 'No way did I put my hands in the air.'

Their exchange also touched on everything from seeing hardcore favourites Helmet at Brisbane's Livid Festival (Gillies: 'And that was very legendary') to in-flight meals— Johns was still very much a meat-eater, talking up a steak he had eaten while flying first class on Qantas—as well as arcade games, the meaning of the word 'bogus' and the lack of American beaches. ('Everywhere we've been,' Johns sighed, 'we've been about two million miles from the beach.') It was all good-natured chaos; Gillies called Johns 'an idiot' when he tried to confuse the DJ as to who played what in the band. When asked how long the band had been together, Johns replied: 'It's probably been like about six years, but we deduct time for sleeping,' which wasn't a bad line for a teenager.

As their verbal sparring match continued, the DJ went to play a Silverchair track.

'You don't have to play something off that CD!' Gillies and Johns shouted in unison. Instead, they requested a song from Helmet, very much their band of the hour. The interview ended with Johns and Gillies arguing about the merits of playing a Helmet song at their next gig.

'Please, Daniel,' Gillies implored, 'I want to do it.'

'No, Ben!' Johns insisted, digging in.

After a show in Detroit, the band returned to Europe, playing the Roskilde Festival, Denmark's answer to Lolla-palooza and the Big Day Out, on 30 June. There were more European festival dates in France (where they were almost wiped out by a speeding truck in the middle of the night), Switzerland and England, before returning home in mid-July, just as *Frogstomp* brushed the US Top 100 for the first time—two weeks later it was in the Top 50, then continued to fast-track its way to the Top 20, where it lodged in late August. It was officially a hit.

Back in Australia, Silverchair toasted *Frogstomp*'s success with another hometown show on 12 August, this time at the larger, 3500-capacity Newcastle Workers Club, an event christened the Llama Ball. A fave animal of the band, they would name their fan club the Llama Appreciation Society; Johns even titled his publishing company Big Fat Llama Music. *Frogstomp*'s liner notes made it clear that 'no llamas were harmed in the making of this album' and encouraged fans to 'support the liberation of the llama nation'. Producer Kevin Shirley was convinced they were going to name the album 'llama something', given the three's current obsession with the strange spitting beast.

'What is it about llamas?', a reporter asked Johns.

'They're the best animal in the world,' Johns insisted. 'They just look real dumb. They look stupid and act stupid. We like them.'

These llama-lovers were homecoming heroes.

4

I got stitches and everything . . .
It was so funny. It was heaps good fun.
Everything went wrong.
—Daniel Johns

EPIC WANTED A BIGGER-BUDGET video for 'Tomorrow',
instead of Robert Hambling's cheap-as-chips clip, so they
hired director Mark Pellington, later to become the director
of Hollywood flicks such as *The Mothman Prophecies*.
MTV soon had the sometimes-gruesome clip, with its pig-
faced man and lashings of blood, in their prized 'Buzz Bin'.
Given the amount of on-screen time that Johns was given,
those new to Silverchair would be hard-pressed to say who
else was in the band: Joannou and Gillies only occasionally entered the frame. It was no secret whom the band's
US label considered the star of Silverchair, judging by
this video.

Silverchair's timing couldn't have been better—all
the big rock acts were currently MIA. Nirvana was toast

when Kurt Cobain killed himself in 1994; grunge giants Pearl Jam were off the road, immersed in a legal battle with Ticketmaster over concert prices, while both Smashing Pumpkins and Soundgarden had retreated to the studio. American rock lovers wanted something loud and energetic and youthful, and they wanted it now.

Silverchair were just the band—and Epic fully understood this. '"Tomorrow" is a stone-cold smash,' Massey said at the time. 'It's a really American sound, it fits in perfectly.' Even parents loved Silverchair, as New York writer Geoff Stead noted: 'Silverchair's image has received the stamp of approval from the moms and dads of America. They believe the young Australian band is not tainted by the drugs and sex scandals which surround many groups.'

'I'm not a fan of their music,' said Glen Bernard, a parent of four Silverchair fans, 'but my kids love them, and it's good, clean fun.' As good and clean as grunge rock went, of course.

Timing, business-wise, also helped Silverchair's American invasion. Epic currently didn't have an in-house A&R rep, which meant they weren't signing many new US acts. Sony was forced to turn to international signings such as Oasis, Deep Forest, Des'ree and Silverchair to keep shifting product—and they were all big sellers in 1995. By 7 August, *Frogstomp* had been certified gold in North America, having sold half a million copies. And it just kept selling. In the format-crazy world of US radio, it was a far-reaching success, ranking highly in everything from the New Artist and the Mainstream Rock lists to the

Top Heatseekers chart, as well as the all-important *Billboard* Top 200.

Proving what a listener- and public-driven success this was, *Frogstomp* was certified platinum on 11 September 1995, well before most reviews of the album appeared. When it was reviewed, American *Rolling Stone* wrote that the band 'exude a rugged confidence and an otherworldly grasp of noise rock that belies their tender ages'. *Request* magazine's Jim Testa noted that '[*Frogstomp*] may not be the most original album of the year, but it's certainly one of the most accomplished, displaying . . . an impeccable grasp of the nihilism and frustrations shared by most young Americans.' Not a bad rap for three Aussie brats still in high school, kids still so young, as *Newsweek* pointed out, that the 'three of them combined are younger than Mick Jagger'.

Silverchair's first full-scale North American tour started with a sold-out show at Toronto's Opera House on 31 August, followed by another full house at Chicago's 1100-capacity Metro on 2 September, and subsequent sold-out dates in Boston, Washington DC, Atlanta, Los Angeles (at the legendary Whisky A Go-Go), San Francisco and Seattle, before ending with a free show on Santa Monica Pier on 17 September.

The American press, while unable to resist references to their age, clearly enjoyed talking with these straight-shooting Aussie kids; they displayed little of the bullshit and bluster of many successful rock acts. A writer from *BAM* magazine asked Gillies about groupies: how were the band faring? 'I don't really take any notice [of girls],' Gillies insisted, which flew in the face of a comment Johns had made, referring to him as 'Stud'. Gillies added that, anyway, it was hard to see where the female action was from his position up the back of the stage. 'I've got a shit view. I can't see jack.' And what about their parents, their on-the-road chaperones: did they cramp their style? 'Usually we don't see them,' Gillies replied. 'The only time we see them is when they say goodnight.' Then it was back to talk of Helmet and Magic Mountain.

By the time they reached Santa Monica, *Frogstomp* had sold more than two million copies in the USA alone and had hit a peak of number nine on the *Billboard* chart—outselling even Michael Jackson's *HIStory*. 'Tomorrow', meanwhile, was in the middle of a 26-week residency in *Billboard*'s influential Modern Rock chart. No Australian band since INXS had steamrolled the American charts in that way—and it took INXS several years on the road, living rough and sleeping in the tour van, to make even the slightest impact. Silverchair broke overnight. Despite their prevailing 'don't give a shit' attitude, the boys were fully aware of their good fortune. As Joannou told me in 2003, 'Watto [Watson] made it very clear how lucky we were that we weren't stuck in a van, trudging around, playing gigs to three people'.

But still the band carried on like teenagers. The three were especially fond of cutting each other down, particularly if one Silver-head started to swell—they hadn't lost their senses of humour. Johns referred to it as 'ripping each other off, burning, making fun' of anyone, especially if an ego got out of control. Behaving like a rock-star wanker had no place in their Silver-world.

'They seem oblivious to the Silvermania that is sweeping the US,' wrote *Rolling Stone*'s Mel Toltz, who caught up with the band during this American tour. 'Odd remarks and crude comments appear from nowhere and are volleyed back and forth across the room over an imaginary net.' In downtime, they played Sega or watched pay-per-view movies, some on repeat. Yet when asked what his favourite film was, Johns turned into a mumbly, diffident teen. 'Oh, I don't like movies much.'

While in Detroit, when a gaggle of teenage girls and young rock dudes gathered outside their bus, Gillies dropped his trousers and mooned them through the tour bus window.

'All right, Gillies! Way to go,' a suddenly animated Johns shrieked as the drummer's bum hit the cold glass. 'The big brown eye!'

After a New York show at Roseland, the backstage area became a war zone as they staged a food fight with their Chinese takeaway. Life on the road with Silverchair was something like a three-way version of *Bill & Ted's Excellent Adventure*.

In the midst of the madness, on 7 September, Johns and the band took part in the MTV Music Awards in New York. They were to perform 'Pure Massacre' and 'Tomorrow' while perched on a makeshift stage atop Radio City Music Hall's entrance marquee—between songs they were told they'd need to crawl back inside through a large window.

The three seemed, at least on the surface, more bemused than excited by the company of America's A-list of rock stars (including the ubiquitous Courtney Love) and movers and shakers such as Sony chief Tommy Mottola—married to Mariah Carey at the time—who introduced himself to the band in their dressing room. The trio only truly livened up when human livewire Taylor Hawkins, drumming for Alanis Morissette but soon to become a Foo Fighter, introduced himself and wished them luck. Rather than walk the red carpet with the other stars, the band walked around it—it was their way of staying one step removed from the glitterati. It was also because they actually feared getting in trouble if they trod on the red carpet. They had no idea about protocol. The VIP life took a bit of getting used to.

Johns looked every inch the teen grunge wonderboy as they played 'Tomorrow' atop Radio City in the late afternoon, his lank hair hanging in his face, his shirt a muddy brown, growling like a wounded bear. Drummer/tourist Gillies sported an I Love NY T-shirt as he beat the daylights out of his kit, his long hair flying in all directions. Joannou was a young man in black, his long shorts (short longs, more likely) halfway down his shins as he pounded away on his bass. Johns's face was a permanent scowl, as befit the song, but the sheer kick of playing in such rare air—perched above mid-town New York, onlookers and fans and the odd superstar staring up at him and the band—must have been the biggest thrill of his short career. Johns had watched the famous rooftop scene from The Beatles movie *Let It Be* loads of times; he'd also seen footage of U2 playing atop a building in downtown LA, singing 'Where the Streets Have No Name', so he knew the significance of an event like this. As he looked down on the gathering below, it dawned on Johns just how big the band now were. He'd come a long way from Jewells Tavern. They all had. And quickly.

On 10 September, the band supported the Ramones in front of a 20,000-strong crowd in Atlanta, at a show entitled The Big Day Out. (Station programmer Philips had obviously returned from Australia with more than a Silverchair CD.) Few big names outwardly impressed Silverchair, but this was a show that stuck with them for some time. 'They were legends; they were hell men,' Johns declared of the original New York punks. He later said it felt like he was 'outside his body' on the night: he was that thrilled to be sharing a bill with the Ramones, who would split soon after.

Silverchair were at the centre of a major buzz, and the album kept selling; *Frogstomp* spent a remarkable 48 weeks in the *Billboard* album chart. And the big names kept gravitating towards the band. Nirvana bassist Krist Novoselic fronted at their 15 September show at Seattle, and Johns spent some time with Novoselic and his wife, who were sitting at the side of the stage.

'He kept telling us about his toothache,' Johns reported. 'It was so funny.'

But the American tour ended on a bloody note for Johns. During the band's free final show on Santa Monica Pier, they experienced technical problems that slowed down their set and upset the crowd. Someone in the surly mob hurled a bottle onstage, which hit Johns on the left side of his head, opening a gaping wound. He kept playing, finishing the show with blood streaming down his face, looking more like one of the Newcastle rugby league Johnses than the softly spoken frontman of Silverchair. As soon as the gig ended, he was carted off to hospital. Johns still managed to laugh about it later on. 'I got stitches and everything and came back, and our sound guy was complaining about the PA and shit. It was so funny. It was heaps good fun. Everything went wrong.'

It seemed that to Daniel, at least for the moment, everything was 'so funny' and 'heaps fun'—a grunge great with a toothache, a trip to the ER to get stitched up, whatever. The pace of his life was incredibly fast, and he was soaking it up. It was *sick*.

◄◦►

If Santa Monica was a bust, Silverchair's return to Australia was a dazzling high—even better than Magic Mountain's roller-coasters. The annual ARIAs were held on Monday, 2 October, at Sydney's Darling Harbour. The whisper was that the 'old guard' of Farnsey, Barnesy and co. were about to be dethroned by three surf-loving punks from Newcastle. Janet Jackson may have been the guest of honour, and mainstream pop star Tina Arena won four gongs, but it proved to be Silverchair's night of nights.

The band cleaned up, winning awards for Best New Talent, Best Debut Single, Best Australian Single and Highest Selling Single ('Tomorrow'), as well as Best Debut

Album for *Frogstomp*. Typically, rather than come off like a bunch of poseurs and accept the awards themselves, the band sent along Josh Shirley, the son of *Frogstomp*'s producer, to collect their first two pointy statuettes. The plan was for Josh to collect every award, but, jet-lagged after an overnight flight from New York, he fell asleep at the winner's table and left his father to collect the rest of the silverware. No one, apart from 'Chair insiders, had any idea who this kid was.

But the band weren't just being whimsical. Josh Shirley was the only person, apart from Johns, Gillies and Joannou, to actually play on *Frogstomp*. You could hear him flailing about on the drums just before the start of the album's final track, 'Findaway'. The connection was meant to be explained by presenter Meatloaf, but the big guy didn't quite make it to that part of his cue card. The press, who the next day tore a few layers off the band for being smug, were actually missing out on a great story. 'It got a bit lost in translation,' producer Shirley accepted.

It didn't really matter to Silverchair. They hooked up with You Am I's Tim Rogers to close the night with a fast and furious cover of Radio Birdman's 'New Race', with Johns on lead vocals, and tore the roof off the place. Rogers was a big hero to the Silver-trio; Johns had even sported a You Am I T-shirt on an American television broadcast. Their excitement to be playing with him showed. As the song staggered to its close, drenched in feedback and sweat, Gillies leapt down from his kit, breathed deeply and then threw himself head-first into his bass drum. The night was done, just like Gillies' kit. Johns's guitar got a fair working over, too.

'We only practised for about an hour and thought, "Yeah, that's all right",' Johns said afterwards. 'Shit, it was funny.'

The new guard had entered the building, even if they didn't bother stepping onstage to collect their trophies. The lines between mainstream and so-called 'alternative' acts were blurring, with Silverchair leading the way. Multi-syllabled acts such as Regurgitator, Powderfinger and Spiderbait would soon be riding Silverchair's coat-tails right to the top of the pop charts.

Just as satisfying was the band's success at the 1995 Australian Performing Rights Association (APRA) Song-writer Awards, held on 12 December, when Johns and Gillies shared the Songwriter of the Year award. APRAs are greatly prized because they're judged by music-making peers. Silverchair didn't just have industry and audience approval; their fellow musos thought they were pretty cool, too.

The rest of Silverchair's 1995 was spent in constant motion. And there was more mayhem. During a 27 October gig at the Palace in St Kilda, Johns stage-dived into the crowd. Joannou and Gillies kept playing, all the while keeping a wary eye on their frontman. When Johns hadn't surfaced after a minute, they started to panic. As Joannou told me, 'Daniel stage-dived, and then people started to grab his shirt and stuff and he went, *"Whoom!"*, straight to the bottom'. Plucked out of the sweaty mass by security guards, Johns made it back to the stage, his clothes ripped.

But when his eyes started rolling back in his head, the show was over. Joannou and Gillies exchanged a look, both thinking, 'Fuck, he's dead!' Thankfully, there was an off-duty police car parked outside; Johns was raced to hospital, where he was held for observation. But still the tour went on—within two days, Silverchair were playing another (this time incident-free) gig at the same venue. Johns was fast getting used to emergency rooms.

Silverchair's next North American jaunt—hastily arranged after an injury to Chili Pepper Chad Smith forced the cancellation of a shared tour—started on 25 November, with a full house at the 1400-seat Southern Ohio Museum in San Diego. Dates continued through to 18 December, when the band shared the bill at LA's Universal Amphi-theater with Radiohead, Oasis and British Nirvana clones Bush. They put in a *Saturday Night Live* appearance on 9 December—Johns wearing an Ammonia T-shirt, a reminder that Silverchair weren't the only band on Murmur—and four days later played legendary New Jersey club The Stone Pony, the starting point for Bruce Spring-steen and his E Street Band.

While on the East Coast, they cut an unintention-ally funny segment for MTV's *Alternative Nation*. It was stone-cold proof that working from an autocue was not Silverchair's forte, as they laboriously worked their way through back announcements, radio promos and plugs, plugs and even more plugs. A frustrated Johns finally strayed from the teleprompter. 'The next video would be an ideal time to go to the toilet, get a cup of coffee, or something like that,' he figured, 'seeing as though it's our new video.' Later on, he failed to keep a straight face as he introduced Joan Osborne as 'Ozzy Osbourne's sister'. 'It's a pleasure being here,' Johns said as the segment finally ended. 'We're *so* happy.'

Silverchair closed 1995 with an outdoor New Year's Eve show in Perth. By then, *Frogstomp* was rapidly heading towards global sales of three million. The band had cleaned up at the ARIAs. Their estimated gross earnings for the year were A$6.4 million. They'd rocked Europe, Australia and the USA, coast to coast. You want an excellent adventure? It had been the biggest year of these kids' lives.

———◄○►———

All of three days separated the band's New Year's Eve show and their opening date of 1996, where they put in a rapturously received set at the inaugural Homebake, an Australians-only rock-fest held in Byron Bay on the New South Wales north coast. The crowd's response to Silverchair was manic, despite the teeming rain and horrendous conditions; they were forced to play a shortened set for fear of being electrocuted. Away from the main stage, punters frolicked in the sludge and coated each other with mud like grunge-loving hippos. The event was quickly renamed Mudbake.

In a hospitality tent backstage, Johns spoke with Jabba, the fast-talking host from Channel [v]. When asked about the bloody incident at Santa Monica, Johns shrugged it off with a smart-arsey teen retort. 'Yeah,' he replied in a sing-songy voice, 'I got a big cut on my head.'

'Did you track down who threw the bottle?'

'Yeah, and I beat the shit out of him. Hammered him.' Then, after a beat: 'Just joking'.

Daniel Johns was a (llama) lover, not a fighter.

But in January, the band learned—just as Johns had in Santa Monica—that success had a really strange way of biting you on the arse, typically when the outlook was ridiculously bright. It all started with a *Daily Telegraph* headline, which shouted: 'Silverchair shocked. Violence appals us, band says.' Another headline yelled: 'A script for murder'.

On 11 August 1995, in Washington State, sixteen-year-old Brian Bassett and his friend, Nicholaus McDonald, had shot Bassett's parents and drowned his five-year-old brother. When caught, they told police they were playing 'Israel's Son' at the time. Their trial opened on 18 January; both were being tried as adults. McDonald's lawyer, Tom Copland, claimed that his client and Bassett had been driven to kill by the Silverchair song and insisted that the track be admissible evidence. He stated that the song was 'almost a script' for the murders. There was even talk of subpoenaing Daniel Johns, who wrote the song. The funny truth of a very unfunny situation was this: when writing 'Israel's Son', Johns had no real intention other than trying to 'sound like Black Sabbath'. He was so thrilled with the song, in fact, that he played it to his dad, a Sabbath expert, who gave the thumbs up. As for some sinister lyrical message, that didn't even enter Johns's head.

Naturally, manager Watson sprang to the band's defence, making an official statement that read, in part: 'Silverchair do not, have not, and never would condone violence of any sort. Silverchair absolutely rejects any allegation that their song is in any way responsible for the action of the alleged murderers. It is a matter of public record that the song in question is inspired by a television documentary about wartime atrocities. The song seeks to criticise violence and war by portraying them in all their horror.' *Frogstomp* producer Kevin Shirley was shaken to his core, crying 'for hours' when told of the murders. 'It freaked me out completely,' he said.

Responding to lawyer Copland's argument, deputy prosecutor Jerry Fuller asked: 'What does this prove? Does this prove that Bassett hated his parents? Does it prove he had motive to kill his parents? No. All it proves is it was a song that he played.' The next day, Judge Mark McCauley ruled that 'Israel's Son' couldn't be played during opening statements and reserved judgment on whether the song could be played at all during the trial.

But the damage was done: suddenly a very green bunch of kids from Newcastle were receiving the same treatment as big names like AC/DC, who in 1985 had been linked— very tenuously, as it proved—to the Night Stalker murderer, Richard Ramirez. The so-called proof? An AC/DC cap that he'd left at one crime scene, and his love of the *Highway to Hell* album. British metal outfit Judas Priest had been sued in an American court by two families who blamed their 1978 album *Stained Class* for the suicides of their sons.

That case was also dismissed, but the stigma was pervasive. O'Donnell, Watson and the Silver-parents had every reason to close ranks just a little more around their charges.

Manager Watson considered this a pivotal moment for Johns, one that triggered his increased wariness of the limelight and would soon turn him into a virtual recluse. A *Daily Telegraph* article from October 1995, headlined 'How a $6m boy gets to school' that showed Johns, in school uniform, riding his pushbike, only exacerbated the problem. (Johns's estimated worth was calculated using the number of records sold at that time—300,000—multiplied by the $20 price tag of a CD. Hardly an ATO-approved method.)

'I'm not saying the media caused the problems which happened later,' said Watson, 'but there is not a doubt in my mind that they were one of several contributing factors.' O'Donnell agreed: 'I think the "Israel's Son" thing hit him really hard'.

But it wasn't as though Johns could go into hiding, at least not yet. The next move for Silverchair was their biggest yet: a US stadium tour with the Red Hot Chili Peppers, rescheduled from the previous November. The two bands connected well; Silverchair got on famously with drummer Chad Smith, the most sociable Chili Pepper, whom Joannou described as 'quite a dude'. The shows were huge, including a 9 February stop at New York's Madison Square Garden, the biggest indoor gig in the city that never sleeps, attended by 20,000.

'Playing the Garden was a dream come true for us,' said Johns. 'We used to watch Led Zeppelin's video *The Song*

Remains the Same [which was filmed at Madison Square Garden] two times a day, and to play there was mind-blowing.'

The band were now receiving a very different kind of attention from women. They'd moved on from simply being 'cute' and had become subjects of genuine female desire. During a warm-up show in Los Angeles on 4 February, a tiny scarlet-coloured bikini bottom fluttered through the air, landing at the feet of a bewildered Johns. He didn't know what to say—or how to respond. (Joannou and Gillies had girlfriends in Oz, while Johns remained single.) On the final night of the tour, 16 February, at Long Island's Nassau Coliseum, the band tried to stay focused while two topless strippers, hired by the Chili Peppers, pranced onto the stage and delivered a sexy bump and grind. On one side of the stage were some Chili Peppers, sniggering like naughty schoolboys; on the other were the Silver-parents, arms crossed, stony faced, unimpressed.

'The Red Hot Chili Peppers thought we'd be little arse-holes,' Joannou told *The Sydney Morning Herald* after the tour, on the basis of having not paid their dues. '[But] after they got to know us, it was cool.'

Clearly inspired, the trio organised a strip-o-gram for manager Watson's next birthday.

The fun ended pretty swiftly, because the band were having more trouble with 'Israel's Son'. Epic, their US label, had asked them to reshoot the video. Johns claimed that the label felt it was too violent, but he disagreed. 'I thought, "That is a good clip for us,"' Johns told MTV in February 1996. 'Then someone had to go and have a whinge about it

[and] now we've got to change it all because of [a] stupid thing.' According to Joannou, the one image that bothered Sony was 'a noose hanging off a beam of wood'.

'And a dog in a cage,' Johns added. 'They said it was too violent. We're like, *"Yeah, he's bad"*.'

Curiously, the reworked video, especially its use of lighting and colour, reeked of Nirvana's 'Smells Like Teen Spirit'. In it, Johns wore what one fan described as a 'grandpa sweater'—the very type Kurt Cobain once favoured. In an even more perverse twist, Johns wore a shirt with the number 27 on it—the age Cobain was when he died (ditto Janis Joplin, Jim Morrison, Jimi Hendrix and many other famous rock casualties). It was becoming even more clear how Epic was positioning the group for American youth: Nirvana reborn. Johns, in particular, was learning a big lesson about the role mythology and hype played in selling rock-and-roll records. The label's move didn't pay off: 'Israel's Son' failed to chart with any of the impact of *Frogstomp*'s other two singles, 'Tomorrow'—which clung to the *Billboard* charts for seven months—and 'Pure Massacre', which charted for three months.

Silverchair played—and filled—sizeable venues when they returned to the USA in February, including the 4500-capacity Odeum Sports & Expo Centre in Villa Park, Illinois, the 3500-seat International Ballroom in Atlanta and the Electric Factory in Philadelphia, which held 3000 punters. Naturally, their concert grosses increased—the Illinois show turned over US$74,500; more than US$44,000 was gener-ated at their Philadelphia gig. Commercially speaking, it was the best of times for a band who'd never had to endure the hardships of the sticky-carpet circuit.

By the time the band reached Europe on 20 February for a run of shows in England, France, Germany and the Netherlands, they were already looking ahead to their next album. They were done with the Seattle sound. Grunge was dead. It was time to move on.

'In a couple of months, after the European tour, we'll start with recordings for a new album,' Johns reported. 'You'll hear jazz, funk and rap. We already have a lot of new songs.'

The trio returned to Australia after a 6 March show in Cologne. Again, they cleaned up in the Australian *Rolling Stone* Readers' Poll, winning Best Band, Best Single, for 'Tomorrow' (a repeat of 1995), Best Male Singer, Best Hard Rock Band, Best Album Cover and Brightest Hope for 1996. And Johns was voted Best New Talent in *Guitar World*'s Readers' Poll, rolling Foo Fighter Dave Grohl and Korn. Johns's solo on 'Tomorrow' beat out contenders Eddie Van Halen and Dave Navarro. As the magazine stated, 'We suspected the teenaged phenoms of Silverchair were popular, but we didn't know they were immensely popular'. Johns, typically, played down the award. 'I don't really rate that as a solo. Basically, we really don't think that solos are worth doing for our music.' Guitar solos were just more rock-star wankery.

The band had one more show to close the globetrotting *Frogstomp* tour: a 9 April set on the final day of the Royal Easter Show in Sydney, kids' day at the Show. It made perfect sense that the prime entertainment for the day was three guys who could just as easily have been part of the crowd, shopping for showbags and riding the ghost train.

Twenty thousand fans turned up for the show. Backstage, among the music-business insiders, hot gossip was that the band would collect A$5 million for the publishing rights to *Frogstomp* and their next album. Onstage, the band ripped through a 75-minute set, Gillies performing the ritualistic trashing of his drum kit at the close of 'Israel's Son'. As fireworks lit up the sky, 100 punters were treated for cuts, scratches and bruises.

Afterwards, Johns fielded a few fan questions, courtesy of Wally Meanie from the ABC show *Recovery*. One punter asked about 'the teenage suicide in America', referring to the 'Israel's Son' demonisation. Johns snapped, straying way off the major-label-approved script. 'I think it's shit. It was just a lawyer making an excuse for a dude killing some people. We think the lawyer is a fucking idiot.'

And what about all this money they'd been making: how did it feel to be the $6 million band?

'We don't get as much as the press made out. That's a load of shit,' said Johns, the master of the pithy response.

What about all this equipment trashing they'd been doing lately: wasn't that a bit much?

'We just put a few dents in it,' said Johns, a smile returning to his face. 'We give the instruments character.'

Almost 100 gigs and several million sales of *Frogstomp* down the line, Silverchair were the kings of the world, teenage millionaires. Johns readily admitted that '*Frogstomp* changed what I thought my life was going to be'—until now he'd been convinced they were all set for a working-class existence like their parents.

So, now, what next? Just as importantly, could it last?

5

I was just like, 'Fuck this,
I'm just gonna sit in my room'.
—Daniel Johns

RATHER THAN MAKE MUSIC, the band's first priority in early 1996 was to get back to some kind of normal life. As Ben Gillies told Australian *Rolling Stone*, in the wake of *Frogstomp*'s runaway success, the trio needed to 'chill, and shit—go to school and hang out with our mates'. Swiftly, these three regular Newcastle dudes had become international rock stars, but their buddies back home were all too ready to remind them where they came from.

Johns insisted that, 'Our friends are cool, because we don't change at all. We don't think we're any better than anyone else. Our friends treat us the same. We're just the same people [who] go to our mate's house and hang out and play pool and fall asleep on the lounge.' The truth was slightly different—barely a day went past when the band didn't encounter a voice shouting from a passing car, 'Silverchair suck! Silverchair are wankers!' The songs Johns was about to write for their second album would express the discontent he was starting to feel.

Johns, Gillies and Joannou had two years of high school to complete, and it was a bit of a struggle to keep up academically. 'We do a lot of catch-up work when we get back,' Joannou commented, 'and we do have tutors.' Johns possibly struggled the most, mainly because he now didn't envisage any career beyond music. 'I want to do music for the rest of my life,' he insisted, 'and how well I go in maths isn't going to help at all.'

Despite Johns's resistance, the trio's parents ensured their education wasn't neglected. As Newcastle High principal McNair recalled, 'The families' wishes were for school to be a separate life from their rock star [life]'. The band and their parents struck up a workable arrangement with McNair: the trio received special credits in music, after organising to have a music program added to the school curriculum (which the band funded). One of their HSC requirements was a finished piece of work, so they simply handed in a CD. Easy.

Yet in the wake of all the *Frogstomp* madness, life was becoming just that bit harder for Daniel Johns, who was still only sixteen. Runaways would often turn up at the front door of his parents' house, seeking him out, as if Johns had some magic wisdom (or a bed) to share. Reporters and photographers frequently cruised past Chez Johns, hoping for a sighting of him, the so-called '$6 million boy'—it became a ritual, of sorts, for snappers from the *Newcastle Herald* to take up residency outside the house. At first, he'd been caught up in the whirlwind that was 'Tomorrow', a mad rush of gigs and recordings and overseas travel and excitement. But now Johns was starting to feel the pressure of getting ready to make a new record, one that the music biz 'machine'—Sony, management, the public—hoped would match the success of the first, while also dealing with these other unfamiliar intrusions on his life. *And finish school.* It wasn't hugely surprising that Johns sank into the first of several serious episodes of depression. Rather than write new songs for their second album, which was the plan, he holed up for a month, avoiding the world outside.

'I didn't want to go out and have someone go, "That's the guy from Silverchair," and fuck everyone else's fun up for the night,' Johns said, 'so I was just like, "Fuck this, I'm just gonna sit in my room".' It was a haven he would retreat to many times over the next few years. John O'Donnell, for one, noted how heavily it weighed on him. 'He wasn't the guy he used to be, hanging out with his friends. The tabloids started wanting pictures of him, people knew where he lived. We'd been telling the parents to get silent numbers, but they said no, it wasn't something people did.'

It was just as difficult for Gillies; his family didn't want to change their home phone number because of their business, so in between business messages they'd be fielding calls from Silverchair fans and haters. But because of his more extroverted nature, Gillies seemed to handle the pressure better than Johns.

The constant presence of the press took away one of the few simple joys Johns had in his life—hanging out at Merewether Beach. The situation really got out of hand when Johns tried to kick back there during a school holiday break. 'There were like 50 people around us screaming,' he said, 'and then people turned up with cameras and [the] paparazzi were there, and from that point, the beach wasn't such a tranquil and resting activity for me.' Johns duly gave up surfing, something he'd been doing even before he heard his first Sabbath riff.

John Watson was so concerned for Johns, in fact, that he had him stay at his Sydney home for a time. Johns's parents agreed that it was a solid idea. 'I was really worried about Daniel,' said Watson. 'He was wrestling with the fact that he had become "famous" and that life can be really strange sometimes.'

Johns eventually wrote most of *Freak Show*'s lyrics during those difficult first few months of 1996. 'I saw so much out there,' he noted, when asked about life on the road, 'so many weird things, that it really affected how I saw the world and myself. Some [*Freak Show* lyrics] were actually changed because they were too personal. But they're a lot more real this time around.' No more writing about 'fat rich dicks' or scenes he only witnessed on the six o'clock news.

In early May, producer Nick Launay—the man who'd edited the original version of 'Tomorrow'—headed up to Merewether to meet the band and listen to their new songs, with a view to producing their next record. He arrived at the Gillies home lugging a hefty snare drum, a gift for Gillies, which had been used by grunge stars Soundgarden. Three wild-haired kids rolled up on their skateboards.

'You Nick?' they asked.

'Yeah.'

'Cool,' the band replied as one, and got back to skating. Launay shook his head; he knew they were young, but these dudes were just kids.

During rehearsals, Launay found it a struggle to hold the band's interest for more than a few songs at a time. The three teens seemed keener to have him in the front seat while L-plater Gillies screamed around Newcastle at mad speeds in his new ride. By 17 May, the band finally began rehearsing new songs for their second album, which they previewed at a Newcastle University show six days later.

Johns grew particularly tight with Launay; the producer even stayed at the Johns family home during album pre-production. Johns thought Launay was 'rad'.

'He's really open-minded. Anything we suggested, a lot of producers would have said, "Nah, you're seventeen, you don't know shit," but he'd listen to us.'

Then there was Launay's unique look, which Johns admired. 'If you saw him,' Johns said, 'he's like a praying mantis with glasses. He's like a mad scientist.'

'I related to Daniel very well,' said Launay. 'We're both arty, skinny types; we're not blokey types.'

Launay also witnessed from close range how blokey a city Newcastle could be, and how Johns sometimes seemed a little lost in his own hometown. Johns and Gillies had recently told *Juice* magazine that 'Newcastle's the centre of a lot of fucking wankers', which didn't win them much love from the city's many rough nuts. The number of drive-by insults mounted.

———◄o►———

Recording for Silverchair's second album was set to begin on 30 May at Sydney's Festival Studios, where *Frogstomp* had been recorded. Of the songs short-listed for the second album, several, including 'No Association', 'Freak', 'Slave', 'Pop Song for Us Rejects', 'Learn to Hate' and 'Nobody Came' had been aired live in shows promoting *Frogstomp*. Brand-new songs included 'Abuse Me', 'The Closing', 'Petrol & Chlorine' and 'Punk Song #1', which was renamed 'Lie to Me' during the *Freak Show* sessions. Johns wrote seven of the songs by himself; of the others, Gillies either co-wrote with Johns or contributed his own tunes, 'Learn to Hate' and 'The Closing'.

'We wanted to make the songs more extreme and different,' Johns explained as recording progressed, 'so that means we've made the fast songs harder and the slow songs softer. We also experimented with different styles and instruments.' Johns seemed unfazed by the pressure of following up break-out hits such as 'Tomorrow' and 'Pure Massacre'. 'If people don't think [*Freak Show*] is as good as the first one, or people think it's better, it doesn't really bother us. We don't feel any pressure. We don't really have a plan. We're just going to keep releasing music.'

Johns name-checked hardcore American bands such as Helmet, Tool and Quicksand as big influences. His Seattle heroes—Nirvana, Soundgarden and Pearl Jam—were relegated to the waste bin of 1995. And *Freak Show* would deliver a few new musical twists, such as strings, Eastern influences and pop melodies. It was a stepping stone to a brave new rock-and-roll world for Daniel Johns, who might have been struggling with the wider world, but was growing increasingly confident as a musician and composer.

Recording of *Freak Show* ran until early July. On 6 June, Silverchair took a break and previewed some new tunes at the re-launch of Foxtel's cable music channel, Red. In the crowd was be-hatted rock guru Ian 'Molly' Meldrum, who flew in from Bangkok to check out the band. The faithful looked on in awe at their idols, but the gig could have gone better—the venue's power shut down during Silverchair's set when the combined needs of PA, lights and catering equipment kicked in. Silverchair retired to their trailer, taking solace in a rider fit for three kings.

The attitude of Johns and the others had now changed in the studio. Rather than rattling around the hallways creating havoc, they'd be the first people to clock on in the morning, raring to go. Launay would arrive at ten o'clock to set up and find that the three had already been at the studio for an hour. 'It was like going in with a wild animal,' Launay said, 'trying to hold them back so we had enough time to put tape on the tape machine and push the red button.' Their trolley rides in the corridors of Festival were kept to a minimum. And Ron Jeremy was nowhere to be seen.

Johns, courtesy of Launay, came to see the potential of the studio; *Freak Show* was a real awakening for him. While recording the song 'Abuse Me', Launay showed him what could be done with backward recording techniques.

'Bloody hell,' Johns said, lost in the music, 'it sounds like I'm singing in Arab[ic].' He was highly impressed with the man and his work. 'Nick's done some seriously weird shit.'

When it was time to record the song 'Petrol & Chlorine', Johns had a bombshell for Launay.

'I don't think there should be drums on the song.'

Gillies was equally surprised. No drums?

Johns explained a little more—he didn't feel that traditional rock drums would work on the song.

'But no hippie shit,' Johns told Launay. 'I reckon it should sound like one of those docos on SBS.'

Having thought it through overnight, the next day Launay brought in some CDs of Indian music to play to Daniel.

'That's it—exactly,' Johns said. It was a tabla he'd been hearing in his head.

In his search for musicians, Launay put in a call to the Indian consulate and came up with the name Pandit Suman, who taught traditional Indian dance in the Sydney suburb of Bankstown. When Launay met with him, he noticed a picture of sitar player Ravi Shankar on the wall of his studio—Suman had played with the Indian legend. It must have been a sign, because Johns had recently been listening to The Beatles' 'Within You, Without You', a song that introduced much of the Western world to the sitar. Shankar had been George Harrison's musical mentor and a big influence on 'Within You'. What were the chances?

Johns was nearby as Suman and his troupe set to work in the Festival studio. This was another eye-opener for the teenager: Indian musicians used completely different measures to Western players; they didn't count in fours. Johns, for a moment, thought they couldn't count at all, and wondered what he'd gotten into. But eventually the experiment came together particularly well, and became a standout of the finished album.

On 18 July, Johns, Gillies, O'Donnell and Watson flew to New York to begin mixing *Freak Show* at the Soundtrack studio with the highly rated Andy Wallace, who'd worked with Rage Against the Machine, Faith No More and Silverchair favourites Helmet and Sepultura. Wallace also produced Jeff Buckley's timeless *Grace*.

Johns's more serious approach in the studio extended into the mixing. 'We didn't want any interruptions from anyone,' said Johns. 'There were really no visitors in the studio apart from our manager.' Their parents stayed at home.

The mixing was interrupted for a three-month stretch when Wallace was tied up with Nirvana's posthumous live album, *From the Muddy Banks of the Wishkah*. This wasn't good. 'Waiting three months for the mix to happen was really painful for everyone,' recalled Launay, who for the first time in his career wasn't mixing an album he'd produced.

Johns was then the victim of another dumb distraction when he was accused of stalking by a Sydney prostitute,

Paula Gai Knightly. She alleged Johns had begun following her in March, calling out to her, 'I love you, Paula'.
By July, Johns, according to Knightly, had begun warning
her: 'I'm a natural-born killer. I'm gonna kill you tonight
and I'm gonna enjoy it.' Johns had an apprehended
violence order (AVO) taken out against him on 24 July,
and the formal application was set down for hearing. But
before the matter could proceed, police withdrew the AVO
when they learned Johns was working on the album mix in
New York at the time of the alleged stalking. Humiliated,
Knightly drifted back to New Zealand soon after, but the
damage was done: she'd contributed to Johns's increased
wariness of those who wanted a piece of him. Could he
really trust anyone?

The band undertook an Australian tour from 26 September to 7 October—during school holidays, like most of the
touring for *Frogstomp*—with American alt-rockers Everclear
supporting. As the tour drew to a close, Johns and band put
in a set at Brisbane's annual Livid Festival on 5 October
that *Rolling Stone* magazine described as 'pure rock and
roll'. Helped out on stage by Everclear, Silverchair waged
war on a cover of Black Sabbath's 'Paranoid', which closed
their set. Then Johns and Joannou mooned the crowd, as all
superstar teenagers should.

During Livid downtime, Joannou and Johns, decked out
in a Screaming Trees T-shirt, shared a couch with Wally
Meanie, who was covering the event for *Recovery*. Despite
his recent AVO hassle, Johns was in an upbeat mood, admitting that they'd swiped their mooning move from another

Oz great, Angus Young. 'It's an AC/DC trick,' he laughed, pushing his hair out of his eyes.

So, Johns was asked, is it some kind of statement?

'Yes,' he replied, feigning seriousness. 'It's saying, look, here are our asses.'

On a more serious note, Johns had started aligning himself with various worthy causes. Silverchair's Sydney show on 7 October had been a fund-raiser for the Surfrider Foundation—they'd contributed a song to *MOM (Music for Our Mother Ocean)*, a fund- and awareness-raising album compiled by Surfrider. The band's association with the foundation stretched back to 1994, when they'd played a benefit show for the hefty fee of one surfboard and wetsuit apiece.

Johns's guitar was decked out with stickers pledging his various allegiances: he was now saving whales, not just llamas. His guitar became his very own billboard. Though uncomfortable with being a teen role model, Johns was finding a way of using his position to make a statement. Alt-rock heroes such as Pearl Jam's Eddie Vedder and Rage Against the Machine's Zack de la Rocha were loudly, proudly political, supporting mainly left-leaning agendas, and Johns, too, was finding his own causes to believe in.

Johns was especially big on animal liberation, and a natural extension of this was becoming a vegetarian—later a vegan—a choice that his parents would also embrace over time. 'It's not any form of fascism or anything,' Johns told MTV. 'It started pretty much with animal-related issues. It was just a guilt thing. I'm the kind of person, as soon as I get something in my head, I feel guilty about it, so I did it to get peace of mind. Once I was a vegetarian, I started to doubt whether I should be consuming any animal products at all, so I did the whole [vegan] thing.' No more Qantas steaks for Johns.

———◄○►———

All Silverchair's globetrotting in 1994 and 1995 had stuck to the established marketplaces of Europe and the USA, and there were two quick shows in Tokyo and Osaka in April 1996. But manager Watson was surprised to get a call inviting the band to tour South America in November 1996; they hadn't sold many records there, although they did a lively trade in bootlegs. It was a sweet deal, too: three well-paid dates over a week, in Buenos Aires, Rio de Janeiro and São Paulo, the latter two as part of the Close-Up Planet Festival (Close-Up was a brand of toothpaste).

The band travelled light: the entourage was Watson; promo manager Susan Robertson; Peter Ward, who looked after the band's front-of-house sound; and production manager Bailey Holloway, along with the Silver-mums. Gig number one was the Buenos Aires Festival Alternativo on 23 November, playing on the main stage between Love and Rockets and expat Australian Nick Cave and his Bad Seeds. The sold-out event was held at the 25,000-capacity Estadio Arquitecto Ricardo Etcheverry. Silverchair kept some unusual company, sharing a hotel with former US president George Bush Snr and the Reverend Moon, plus a gaggle of his followers.

By the time team Silverchair reached Rio de Janeiro for the 29 November show at the Praça da Apoteose, word had spread as to where they were staying. A small but dedicated posse of Silverchair-lovers chased them down: one female fan even got into an amorous grapple with Johns by the hotel pool, before Watson shooed her off. Clearly South America loved Silverchair, especially their blond and blue-eyed frontman.

But the differences between Johns and the others was starting to show. There were their changing physiques—both Gillies and Joannou had gained some mid-teen heft, yet Johns was thin, almost gaunt. Their personalities were changing, too; during one South American show, Johns's guitar was giving him trouble and Gillies jumped into action, crooning 'Twinkle Twinkle Little Star'. He also led the crowd in an impromptu 'Fuck you! Fuck you!' chant. Gillies was becoming more gregarious, a man of the people, whereas Johns was shifting in the opposite direction, becoming insular, more withdrawn, wary of anyone he didn't know. *What did they want from him?*

'He just loves talking to people and meeting people, [whereas] I just hate meeting people,' Johns said of Gillies. 'I'm not very social, and I'm really shy when I don't know people. I hate it. It's just weird. Especially when you know that they're not there to be friends with you. They're just there because you're in a band.'

Johns's caution soon turned into something closer to paranoia. 'You always think they're watching to see what you're going to do wrong or something,' he told a reporter covering the trip.

None of this stopped the band from playing some of the most ferocious sets of their short lives; perhaps it contributed to it. At Rio's Sambadrome, before a crowd of 18,000, they tore into *Frogstomp*'s 'Madman', sending the crowd into overdrive. Andrew Humphreys, writing for Australian *Rolling Stone*, captured the madness of the moment.

'The crowd goes fucking nuts,' he reported. 'Girls in the front row are screaming hysterically as the mosh begins. Johns charges across the stage, feet shuffling, body shaking like an evangelical preacher possessed by the spirit of Jesus. From the side of the stage, someone says, "Fuck! They sound like Black Sabbath." Silverchair drive the point home, launching into a cover of "Paranoid". The gig, as they say, went off.'

As the band moved between Rio and São Paulo, the number of (mainly female) fans lurking in hotels and airports increased. It was obvious: Silverchair were now stars in South America. Yet they could still be very naive. When Joannou spotted Nick Cave stumbling back into his hotel one morning, physically supporting violinist Warren Ellis, he was confused.

'He's just getting home? But it's ten in the morning!'

The 1996 tour left its mark—record sales for the band in Brazil, especially, skyrocketed. *Frogstomp* went on to sell 30,000 copies; *Freak Show* 38,000. No formal count of bootlegs exists, but it's fair to say you could double, maybe even triple, those official sales numbers. Yet even though the tour was a raging success, the signs were there that the band—especially Johns—were becoming wary of the hangers-on and fair-weather fans they were meeting on the road. This just wasn't as much fun as it had been at the time of 'Tomorrow'.

———◄○►———

Three days after the São Paulo show, the band played a secret gig for American fan-club members at the Troubadour in Los Angeles, billing themselves as the George Costanza Trio. Freed from the restraints of being 'that kid from Silverchair', Johns really let himself go, telling fans that they should 'feel free to take your clothes off any time'. Judging by the shrieks of the audience, it seemed like a distinct possibility. At the end of their set, during the now-nightly ritual of equipment trashing, Johns ditched his guitar and dropped to the stinky stage floor, strangling the microphone while shrieking, 'Fuck you' in an ungodly wail; he rolled around the stage as though he'd been body slammed. It was a great piece of rock-and-roll theatre—and a nightmare for their road crew, who had to reassemble the pieces for a gig in Seattle two days later.

There was also a video shoot in Los Angeles for 'Freak' sandwiched in between these gigs, directed by Devo's Gerald Casale. Johns was all for working with Casale: he was a huge fan of art-pop oddballs Devo, best known for such left-of-the-dial hits as 'Whip It' and 'Freedom of Choice' and for wearing flowerpots on their heads. Johns liked the clip that Casale had just directed for the Foo Fighters' break-out single, 'I'll Stick Around': the band played while what Casale described as a mutant 'Foo ball'—allegedly the visual representation of Courtney Love—attacked the band. Although Johns probably didn't realise it, he and Casale shared similar backgrounds: Casale was from Akron, Ohio, a steel-town not unlike Newcastle.

Casale revisited the idea of the 'flying amoeba' in the 'Freak' clip, as various white-coat-clad scientists examined some weird lifeform under a microscope, while the band, playing inside an egg-shaped site, thrashed themselves raw and sweated like athletes. The change in Johns was more evident now than ever before—he stared down the camera, spitting out his lyrics with pure venom; he looked like he was on fire. Johns, to Casale, was 'a very smart, depressed kid seething with contained anger'. Court jester Gillies, meanwhile, turned up for the first day of the shoot wearing a very convincing pair of false buck teeth that completely threw the crew, who began devising ways to hide him from the camera.

'Freak' was probably the first time that Johns tapped into something deeply personal as a songwriter, the resentment he felt towards those who considered him not 'normal' (whatever that was). All those Newcastle locals who slammed Johns and the band might well have been in his thoughts. 'Body and soul,' Johns boasted, 'I'm a freak—of nature.' It was a pretty damned big 'fuck you'.

And how did director Casale respond to a song that roared into life with the rhyming couplet: 'No more maybes/ Your baby's got rabies'?

'Those are good lines for a fifteen-year-old,' he said, 'who came of age post-AIDS epidemic.'

But Casale wasn't impressed by the final version of the video. 'I was happy with my cut; the label was happy, [but] the Aussie manager had it re-edited with 20 per cent more close-ups of Daniel. Anyway, he butchered the narrative and made the viewer sick of looking at Daniel.'

Hardly surprisingly, Watson had a different take. 'I wanted more band footage,' he said. 'Every single change that was made to the "Freak" video was supported and encouraged by the band and the label, otherwise it obviously couldn't and wouldn't have been requested. The changes made the clip more compelling in the eyes of everyone except, apparently, the director.'

Soon after the video was shot, acting on a pitch from car maker Mitsubishi, Johns, Gillies and Joannou joined LA guitar hero Dave Navarro to test drive a 4WD on the beach of Malibu. The plan was for Navarro to write up the results for *Bikini* magazine. All progressed smoothly, until Gillies, bored with doing laps of the beach car park, steered the 4WD onto the sand, scattering volleyballers and sunbathers as he picked up speed.

Joannou took a turn at the wheel, and Johns drove the 4WD back to the car park. It was then that they heard the police sirens.

A very large African-American cop emerged from his cruiser, walking fast, clearly agitated.

'Where's your licence, boy?'

Johns opted to play dumb. 'Officer, we drive on the beach in Australia all the time. I'm sorry.'

It didn't fly. Johns was thrown into the back of the cruiser, the cop yelling at him, 'You're going to Juvenile Hall, boy!'

After some fast-talking from the band's American publicist, Johns was released and the charges were dropped. His release, though, was held up while he signed autographs for the police chief's daughter, a massive Silverchair fan. (A poster made from a photo of the incident hangs in the Silverchair office in Sydney.)

Back in Sydney, a week before Christmas, the band shot another video, this time for the dark rock ballad 'Abuse Me'. It was directed by Nick Egan, who'd worked with Bon Jovi, Alanis Morissette and Oasis. Like 'Freak', this was a performance video with a twist: the band played while various circus oddities—a dude strapped into the 'wheel of death', an illustrated man covered head to toe in tatts— drove home the album's freak-show theme. Egan's camera zeroed in on Johns, now a brooding presence on both stage and screen. ('That singer is fucking beautiful,' wrote one YouTube viewer of the clip.) When 'Abuse Me' was released as a single in April 1997, it included a remix of 'Freak' by dance producer Paul Mac, marking the beginning of a long and fruitful collaboration for Johns.

'Freak' was added to Australian radio at midday on New Year's Eve—the band then had ten days of R&R before starting their next Australian tour, this time in Hobart. There was a new album to release, and the HSC to sit. While Gillies claimed they were having 'the best time of our lives', it wasn't so clear that Johns shared his enthusiasm. They'd spend the next twelve months bouncing between school and the endless rock-and-roll highway.

6

There's a lot of good people in the industry
and there's a lot of dicks. So, you've just
gotta live with the dicks and get on with the
people that are all right.

—Daniel Johns

FREAK SHOW WAS FINALLY RELEASED in the first
week of February, a long seven months after recording
had finished. It was a transitional record for the band. As
expected, they paid plenty of lip service to the mosh-pit
marauders who loved nothing better than 'goin' off to the
'Chair'. Songs such as the sludgy opener, 'Slave', and 'The
Door'—which packed a riff so thunderstruck that fellow
mooner Angus Young would have approved—were cut from
the *Frogstomp* template. These were fast, loud rock songs to
be played at maximum volume and high speed. Gillies and
Joannou, especially, loved playing them live. But Johns was
growing a little tired of pure noise thrills.

The proof was 'Cemetery', the album's centrepiece.
Jane Scarpantoni, who'd played on albums as diverse as

R.E.M.'s *Green* and Sarah McLachlan's *Fumbling Towards Ecstasy*, was hired to compose strings, and it proved a savvy choice. Her sombre yet elegant arrangements stretched Johns vocally; his voice ebbed and flowed, much like Scarpantoni's strings. All up, it made for the most adventurous music the band had created, more about atmosphere than sheer volume. And this was in spite of Johns's doubts about whether the tune fitted on the album, 'because it didn't really seem like a band kind of song'.

There was quite the backstory.

While writing demos for the album, Johns had given Watson a cassette that included sonic sketches of two new songs, 'Abuse Me' and 'Pop Song for Us Rejects'. There was nothing on the second side of the tape apart from a slow, sombre, untitled acoustic ballad. Johns kept asking Watson to return the tape; he didn't want him to hear what was a rough outline of 'Cemetery'. Too late. After one listen, Watson believed that the song belonged on the album, so he cornered producer Launay, insisting that he should also give it a listen. He also told Launay that Johns wasn't aware that he had heard it.

'Okay,' Launay replied, 'so I don't know the song exists but I have to ask him to play it for me? Cool.'

Their ploy worked; Launay convinced Johns that, by adding drums and strings, 'Cemetery' would fit well on *Freak Show*, and the song was added.

Strings also left their mark on 'Pop Song for Us Rejects', via understated violins from Ian Cooper and Amanda Brown, formerly of The Go-Betweens. For possibly the first time on a

Silverchair song, the guitars were crisp and acoustic rather than distorted and electric, while the song's very hummable melody proved that the 'pop' in the title wasn't ironic. 'Petrol & Chlorine', the track completed with a little help from the Indian consulate, was a handy reminder of how much Led Zeppelin the trio had absorbed during their musical youth: Jimmy Page and Robert Plant loved nothing better than to drench their blues-based raunch in exotic Eastern sounds. Clearly, Silverchair were listening and learning.

'It's Led Zeppelin only and exclusively,' Johns confirmed, when asked about the track's roots. 'We really like that they mixed different instruments with rock music, and we want to do that same kind of thing.'

There was also a lot going on in *Freak Show* thematically. Whereas Johns had dismissed *Frogstomp*'s lyrics as throwaway observations from the couch, the rhymes of a kid with little life experience, the same couldn't be said of *Freak Show*. There was enough fear and loathing here to rival Hunter S. Thompson. When Johns wasn't ranting about babies with rabies, he was bellyaching (during 'Slave') that the 'only book that I own is called *How to Lose*/Pick a chapter I know them all, just choose'. And 'Freak' came on like a taunt to those critics wanting to cut these tall poppies down after the madness of Silvermania. As *Rolling Stone*'s Andrew Humphreys wrote in February 1997, 'Silverchair have always been easy targets for the hipster crowd, a band that's somehow cool to hate, for no particular reason'. As John O'Donnell saw it, 'Daniel was definitely venting, [the album] was definitely about him reacting to fame'.

On *Freak Show*'s release, Johns took to introducing 'Cemetery' as a song 'about a male prostitute'—was that how he saw himself now? Or was it a stab at the notoriously ruthless music biz?

'There's a lot of good people in the industry,' Johns said during an interview, 'and there's a lot of dicks. So, you've just gotta live with the dicks and get on with the people that are all right.'

Johns would later admit, worryingly, that he was entering into another dark period in his life 'where I hated myself, and, you know, would have quite happily ended it'. Whether he was referring to the band or himself was unclear. One of his many problems was that he was simply unsure that Silverchair deserved so much success so early on in their career; he was constantly reminded of the work that other bands put in and that sometimes they didn't even get a whiff of success.

'I felt like I wasn't worthy of what had come to me at a really early age,' he said in 2004.

In early reviews for the album, critics picked up on Johns's lyrical SOS. The message was clear: he was having trouble adjusting to life in the spotlight. 'It doesn't take much scrutiny,' *Rolling Stone*'s Michael Dwyer wrote of 'Freak', 'to reveal a metaphor for the dirty business which has already swallowed Silverchair up to their tender necks'. Writing in America's *Spin* magazine, Chuck Eddy echoed Dwyer's thoughts: 'If the whole world was gawking at my growing pains, I'd feel like a *Freak Show*, too'. Johns responded by piercing his eyebrows and slapping on some Max Factor, as if to say, 'I'll give you a freak show'.

The upside of *Freak Show* was that there were very obvious signposts—the lush 'Cemetery', the experimental 'Petrol & Chlorine'—that Johns was taking creative control of the band and pushing them away from the sludginess of grunge and alt-rock. Upon the album's release, Johns talked up the differences between *Frogstomp* and *Freak Show*. While admitting some songs were 'definitely heavier', he pointed to a more melodic direction, as well as highlighting the use of strings and sitar. 'It's got a bit more variety,' he said. 'It's more complex than the first album.'

In the same interview, Johns opened the door for bassist Joannou to co-write songs. Up until now, the bulk of Silverchair songs had emerged out of rehearsal room jams: Johns would lock into a riff, Gillies would work out a rhythm pattern and Joannou would kick it all along with some heavy bottom end. Then Johns would hide himself away to work on the lyrics. The majority of the songwriting credits were Johns's, or shared with Gillies. 'It's not like Chris isn't allowed to join in writing the songs,' said Johns. 'He just hasn't really come up with anything yet. Maybe on the third album—who knows?'

It didn't turn out that way. Just the opposite, in fact.

Offstage, Johns was moving away from his bandmates and friends. The amount of time they'd shared touring over the past two years meant they spent less non-Silverchair time in each other's company. Before the band broke, they were mates who'd go to school together and then hang out at Chez Gillies or go to the beach. They were tight, they were buddies. But now, when returning from a tour, they'd head in different directions: Johns went home with his dog, Sweep, and wrote more songs, while Gillies and Joannou would hook up with their respective Merewether crews and party hard. It was at this time, too, that Gillies and Joannou met their first serious girlfriends.

'Before, every day, we used to go everywhere together,' Johns said. 'But because we've been touring so much together, I just wanted to be by myself for a long time.'

At the same time that Johns was turning inwards, Silverchair were becoming very much his band, the outlet for his songs and his feelings.

So now that the album was done, how were they to capitalise on the band's two-million-plus *Frogstomp* sales in the USA? Manager John Watson was about to learn a lesson about dealing with the monolith that is the American music business, while Johns was set to experience a little more unwanted controversy of his own.

———◦———

Johns had announced, just before its release, that the album's title was *Freak Show*. As he explained, he likened life in a rock-and-roll band to 'the old freak shows in the '40s, just travelling around, doing your show and going to the next town and doing it again. We saw there was a similarity and thought it would be a good theme for the album.'

What Johns didn't anticipate was the controversy the album's artwork would stir up. The nine images that decorated *Freak Show*'s sleeve—a wolf man, a bearded lady and assorted circus sideshow weirdos—were from the Circus World Museum, located in sleepy Baraboo, Wisconsin. The band stumbled across them in a magazine and immediately agreed they were perfect for the album. But many felt it was in questionable taste to highlight the physical deformities of these 'sideshow freaks'. The backlash was so strong that their American label, Epic, had to issue a disclaimer insisting that the band 'are not in any way showing disrespect for the carnival performers of yesteryear. They simply think it's interesting that the human appetite for the bizarre seems to be timeless.' (No mention of possible music-biz inferences in the artwork, funnily enough.)

It's more likely that the band just thought the images were 'cool' or 'sick', but they had even bigger problems ahead. The American label opted for 'Abuse Me' as the album's first single, rather than their Australian number one, 'Freak'. It was felt that a mellower song would sit more comfortably on US radio. Interestingly, at the time two Aussie acts—Savage Garden and Merril Bainbridge—were scoring huge US chart success with mellow songs, namely 'I Want You' and 'Mouth'. Even Smashing Pumpkins had turned down the volume a notch with their latest single, 'Thirty-Three'. John Watson feared alienating the hardcore Silver-fans who loved 'Tomorrow'. But Sony had the last word.

Watson put in a call to the band. Were they okay with Epic's decision to lead with 'Abuse Me' and then release 'Freak', even though that hadn't been the case in Australia? How did they feel about that?

'Well,' Johns replied, 'it's just a question of doing what sucks the least, isn't it?'

His manager couldn't have put it better.

———◄○►———

If the band had lived the two previous years in top gear, 1997 was spent in overdrive. Their first date for the year was in Hobart on 10 January, and their final show was on 20 December in Perth. In between, they played 100 gigs, toured the USA and Europe three times, and completed four Australian jaunts, as well as playing shows in Canada and the Philippines. Just like The Beatles 30 years earlier, the Philippines show was a first—and a last—for the band, as out-of-control fans kicked down doors, inflicted A$10,000 worth of damage and drifted into the unpatrolled backstage area to meet their idols. It was chaos.

Silverchair had a lot to prove with their new record. By the second half of the 1990s, the bands at the vanguard of grunge and generation alt-rock—Pearl Jam, Nirvana, Soundgarden, Smashing Pumpkins—had either split, imploded or shifted styles. It was the year that 'rocktronica' (aka electronica)—a flashy fusion of rock attitude and dance beats—was declared the future of music, thanks mainly to career-making albums by The Prodigy (*The Fat of the Land*) and The Chemical Brothers (*Dig Your Own Hole*). Silverchair were out to show that they weren't 'one-zit wonders', as a wisecracking writer suggested.

First up, they launched their new record in style at the Circus Oz tent in Sydney's Moore Park, on 20 January. The venue was ideal: after all, the album was called *Freak Show*, and Johns had been comparing life on the road to a travelling circus. The stage was decorated with cut-outs of the muscle men and circus oddities from the album's cover that had caused such a fuss in the USA. In the crowd looking on was Snazz, the illustrated man from the 'Freak' single cover, who'd also appeared in the 'Abuse Me' video. More than a thousand people, including media from *Spin* magazine, MTV and elsewhere, squeezed onto the wooden benches around the tent's edge or were sardined into the mosh pit.

When the pre-show murmur died down, a shirtless MC appeared onstage and introduced the opening act, a fire-eating sword swallower. Once he'd done some freaking of his own, the lights went down and the band appeared on stage, as if out of nowhere, Johns wearing a T-shirt that proclaimed, 'Nobody knows I'm a lesbian' (subsequently auctioned for charity for more than $1000). The new album's first Oz single, 'Freak', turned up early in the eleven-song set, along with a mix of five more *Freak Show* tunes as well as *Frogstomp* standards 'Pure Massacre' and 'Tomorrow'. Then Gillies and Joannou disappeared in a puff of smoke, leaving a solo Johns to strum a sombre 'Cemetery'. The band proved to a tough local audience that they had the presence—and the tunes—to be a worthy headliner. Tall poppy syndrome be damned. The launch was a success.

While launching the album was the band's immediate priority, Watson and the Silver-parents were trying to keep the band's momentum rolling *and* ensure they didn't miss too much school. It was a tricky juggling act. Typically, teen stars would drop out of formal education and opt for full-time tutoring, but this wasn't quite the case for Silverchair. The band sometimes relied on a tutor named Jim Welch, but those close to the Silver-three knew that attending school as often as possible would keep them sane and grounded. They were about to enter their final year of high school, and were committed to sitting the HSC.

The subject of an on-the-road tutor came up when the band were interviewed on MTV's *120 Minutes*.

'He ditched us last night,' Johns smiled, as his eyes drifted towards Welch just off the set, 'and went to the opera.' Turned out their tutor had a taste for *Les Miserables*.

Yet again, Watson found himself turning down more requests for interviews and photo shoots than ever before; he rejected up to 90 per cent of requests during the *Freak Show* period. He also made sure that, while touring overseas, the band never performed more than five shows a week; at one point, he turned down a six-figure fee for a show at Wembley Stadium so the band could swing an extra two days at home. On another occasion, they spent $40,000 on airfares purely to get back to Newcastle for a welcome six-day break between gigs.

Still, there were highlights. The band were offered a prized guest spot on the hugely influential *Late Show* with David Letterman during early February.

'Our next guests,' Letterman announced in his laconic manner, 'are a trio from Australia whose debut album sold over two million copies—not bad for a bunch of schoolkids . . . Folks, please welcome Silverchair.'

Johns looked every bit the serious young artiste as they played their single 'Abuse Me'. He was so lost in the song that he rarely interacted with the others during the performance. Gillies took the event seriously enough to wear a shirt, not a common sight during their year of the Freak Show. Letterman had an unspoken rule of thumb—if he liked you, he'd stroll over after the song and shake hands, perhaps even ask the drummer about his kit. ('Are those your drums?' was his standard icebreaker.) Clearly, he rated the band highly because he walked onto the stage when the song ended. 'Thank you, son,' he said, shaking Johns's hand so hard you could almost hear him wince in pain.

At the band's 24 February show at the Palace in Los Angeles—a time when *Freak Show* had just gone gold in the USA, selling 500,000 copies—Ozzy Osbourne turned up with his daughter, Aimee. The band coped well with playing before one of their (and their parents') idols, dedicating their crashing cover of Black Sabbath's 'Paranoid' to the man who liked to call himself the 'plumber of darkness', referring to his pre-rock vocation. (Johns met Aimee afterwards, and they dated for a short time.) Sammy Hagar, occasional Van Halen vocalist, was another Silverchair convert, fronting at a show and asking to have his photo taken with the band. Even porn star Ron Jeremy showed up backstage, stirring up memories of the X-rated videos they'd watched repeatedly while making *Frogstomp*. Johns looked equally thrilled and disturbed at meeting the man dubbed 'The Hedgehog' as they posed for a snap. Fortunately, Jeremy's prodigious dong wasn't on display.

Newly pierced and eye-shaded, Johns wasn't the only one breaking in a new look. After their 30 March set at Melbourne's Offshore Festival, alongside Blink-182 and Tool, drummer Gillies complained to Johns that his unruly mane was getting in the way of his playing. Johns duly shaved Gillies' head, leaving him, in the words of David Gillies, 'as bald as a baby's bum—just like Yul Brynner.'

<hr />

Freak Show may have gone gold in the USA, but there wasn't quite the same frenzy that greeted 'Tomorrow' and *Frogstomp*. Still, Silverchair had reasonable pulling power, filling venues such as the 4500-seat Plaza of Nations in Vancouver, Chicago's 3400-seat Aragon Ballroom and the 6000-capacity Arrow Hall in Ontario. The latter show grossed a handy US$89,000, while the Aragon Ballroom set and a show in Worcester, Massachusetts, also grossed more than US$50,000 each. Later in the year they'd truly hit paydirt with a show in The Woodlands, Texas, which grossed a very useful US$185,808. A bunch of hopefuls going by the name of Matchbox Twenty opened that night.

Despite the work the band were putting in to promote *Freak Show*, and reviews that were, in the main, more positive than for their debut, the album wasn't a break-out success (and would only sell half of *Frogstomp*'s three million), which suggested that perhaps Epic had messed up the choice of first single. A rushed and undeniably dodgy video for 'Abuse Me' didn't help. *Freak Show* debuted on the *Billboard* album chart at number twelve, but it slipped away quickly. Of course, it would reach the top spot on debut in Australia, while in Canada it debuted at number two, in Germany at number twenty-eight, France at number twenty, the UK at number thirty-eight and New Zealand at number eight. But these were good, not great, figures, in regions where sales were measured in thousands, not millions. Still, such new(ish) Silverchair fan bases as France, the Netherlands, Germany and South America started buying their records in good numbers. The band were going global.

But the boys' excellent rock-and-roll adventure was starting to become, well, not so excellent. Nonstop global travel may have been a dream made real for these Novocastrians when 'Tomorrow' blew up, but they were now several big tours—and enough frequent-flyer miles to rival Richard Branson—down the line. The idea of racing around the corridors of five-star hotels in the middle of the night, banging on strangers' doors and running like hell, as they'd boasted of in the past, had lost its appeal. As Johns had made quite clear with *Freak Show*'s title and many of the songs' lyrics, he was having some trouble adjusting to the leeches and star collectors that frequent the music industry, and the personal cost—his first major bout of depression—was a clear sign that he mightn't have the resilience for this life.

The band were also losing patience with one of contemporary rock and roll's necessary evils: fencing inane questions from VJs and DJs, designed to generate the snappiest 'grab' for a short-attention-span marketplace. When promoting *Frogstomp*, Johns, Gillies and Joannou happily played bullshitters, talking up invented pasts and twisting answers to the same questions into any number of different responses. But now that they believed more strongly in their work, they were given few opportunities to speak with even a little intelligence—they were still those 'kids from Oztrailya'. Their conversation with *Modern Rock Live* typified the dumbing-down approach they found so frustrating.

> MRL: I actually read in an interview, I don't know if it was you, Daniel, or Chris, or Ben, I don't know who mentioned that the last record you did, after listening to it . . . you guys weren't particularly happy with it.
>
> Johns: Um, no, we're happy with it, it's just that we're more happy with the new album. The first album had three or four songs on it which we didn't particularly like but that we had to put on to make up an album's worth of songs. But we're as happy as you can be with the first album.

Equally vacuous were the obligatory caller questions. 'Does one person write the songs, or do you collaborate?' asked someone who obviously hadn't bothered to check the liner notes. 'I was wondering,' asked another, 'what are your views on musicians and their drug addictions and stuff? 'Cause you guys are real famous now and are you, like, into that stuff?'

In a discussion with *TV Hits*, Gillies was asked: 'Would you agree that your audience is still pretty young? Is that what you're into—screaming teenagers?' You could almost feel Gillies cringe. Next question: 'So it doesn't bother you that your audiences on the *Frogstomp* tour mainly consisted of teenage girls?' Then came the topper: 'Are you in search of a typical or original sound?' Another interviewer asked Johns: 'When you're on tour, do you get a lot of older women coming onto you?' Johns snapped back: 'We wish'. It was a frustrating time for a band that were doing their best to prove they weren't some disposable music-biz creation, one-hit wonders.

Johns found himself still playing down Seattle sound-alike accusations when he spoke with *The Orange County Register*. It was just *so* 1995. 'You can always hear a band's influences on the first album,' he said. 'It's that way with everyone. We're over it.' At least one album over it, as parts of *Freak Show* proved. 'If people can't take us seriously,' Johns told *The Denver Post*, 'they're never going to.' He got even feistier when speaking with the *Toronto Sun*. 'It's good to be able to say "fuck you" to everyone who said we weren't capable of producing a second album.'

———◁◦▷———

Australia still loved the band. In June, Silverchair set new sales records when the 4000 tickets for their Brisbane Festival Hall show sold out within a day, a first for an Australian act. Their concert at Darwin's MGM Grand Casino also set a new box-office record.

Yet in spite of the thumbs ups that *Freak Show* had been receiving at home, and the occasional high such as Letterman, the relentless mixture of touring, studying and being teen role models was causing the band some real trouble, especially Daniel. 'Johns is slim to the point of thin,' wrote *The Sydney Morning Herald*'s Bernard Zuel in April, 'his jeans and shirt hanging loosely from him.' Other writers noticed the changes in Johns. 'Daniel, almost 18 now, looks shy and vulnerable, his eyebrow pierced and wearing silver-glitter eye shadow, his fingernails painted with half-peeled-off nail polish.' Johns appeared 'dangerously emaciated', according to another.

Frustrated by the impositions his stardom was placing on his family, and feeling as though his life was out of his control, Johns was slipping into another period of depression, which manifested itself in his sunken features and rake-thin physique. It was almost as if he was trying to physically disappear. And Johns was well and truly over the glamour of globetrotting. 'I just enjoy being at home,' he said mid-tour. 'I just sit at home with my dog and watch telly. I don't know if sitting at home every day is normal, but that's what I do.'

'When we're bored and tired and not in a good mood and pissed off, that's when we write songs—that's how it turned out so dark,' Johns told the MTV audience. 'And it doesn't bother us if we're successful anymore. As soon as we don't like it and it annoys us and we can't write any more songs, we'll just stop. Go back to the beach.'

A writer who was on the road with them in LA noticed how swiftly Gillies and Joannou tired of pranks and hijinks—while Johns didn't even bother getting involved. 'Their devilish grins fall away, replaced with bored expressions similar to the one worn by Daniel Johns, who is staring out a window. There they sit, three antsy teen rockers in skate-rat duds, trapped in a fate about as fun as spending a Saturday night with the parents.'

———◄○►———

In Sydney on 2 June, the group spent a day in the now very familiar Festival Studios, this time with engineer Wayne Connolly, cutting the song 'Spawn'. The track was to be remixed by UK whiz-kid Vitro, for a soundtrack of unusual collaborations: Korn with the Dust Brothers; Slayer teaming up with Atari Teenage Riot; Filter joining forces with The Crystal Method, and so on. The *Spawn* album epitomised a moment when hard-rock acts were hoping to grab a little of rocktronica's cool. At the same session, Silverchair also thrashed out a cover of The Clash's 'London's Burning', which was destined for a Clash tribute disc featuring Bush, Rancid, The Mighty Mighty Bosstones and Moby. Johns and the band were starting to develop a taste for crossing over into unfamiliar musical territory—and being tapped for tributes showed that they rated highly as an international band.

The group made it back to Sydney for a surprise gig at Luna Park on 26 July. The audience was made up of 200 Triple J prize-winners, while the show was a benefit for the Reach Out appeal, which raised cash and awareness for youth suicide prevention. The live video for *Freak Show*'s final single, 'The Door', was taken from this secret show.

The Luna Park set was revealing. Fire starters such as 'Slave' and the obligatory 'Tomorrow' set the mosh pit alight, but Johns's peculiar behaviour was also leaving its mark. Between songs he tinkered with an instrumental version of 'Advance Australia Fair' and introduced 'Abuse Me' as 'a song about masturbation'. His blond hair covered his face throughout—that and his new thing for knitwear made the ever-present Kurt Cobain comparisons unavoidable. If he'd switched to playing guitar left-handed, you'd have sworn the Nirvana leader had risen from his grungy grave.

But Johns's peculiar attitude mattered little to the fans, as 'Cemetery', the third single from *Freak Show*, raced into the Australian charts at number five on 7 July. Each of *Freak Show*'s singles had blitzed the ARIA Top 10.

After two weeks of school, the next stop for the band was Europe.

When Silverchair played at the Bizarre Festival in Cologne, Germany, a television camera caught Foo Fighters Dave Grohl and Taylor Hawkins and Veruca Salt's Nina Gordon and Louise Post discussing the band.

'What do you think of Silverchair?' Grohl asked the others.

'They rock,' said Louise Post, without a moment's hesitation. 'Let me tell you something about Silverchair. That kid—that boy—he warmed up for one hour the other day when we played with him. Beautiful voice. Very impressive.'

Grohl agreed. 'That kid has a really good voice.'

While the praise was great, especially from someone as revered as Grohl, what the band needed was some downtime, even as they rolled through Germany, Sweden, the Netherlands and Austria during August and September, as well as playing a handful of Canadian and American dates. They were drained.

But the ARIAs were next. Johns, his hair matted into something approaching dreadlocks, a grimace transforming his pretty face into a scowl, his voice all sandpaper and broken glass, rocked the awards with a blistering version of *Freak Show*'s 'Freak'. When he screamed, 'If only I could be *as cool as all of you*', a few industry types could be seen squirming in their seats. Then he hurled his guitar into his amp and stormed off. By the time Silverchair were declared winners of the Channel [v] award for Best Australian band— which they'd win so often the award should have been re-named in their honour—Johns was long gone. Claiming an asthma attack, he was halfway back to Newcastle when the envelope was opened.

Apart from the Australian release of 'The Door' on 6 October—*Freak Show*'s fourth Top 10 single at home— much of October and early November were absorbed by studies; the band finally completed the HSC on 14 November. It was a burden the three were desperately keen to get out of the way, partly in the hope journalists might drop it as a point of discussion. School may have given them a much-needed break from the spotlight, but there were escalating hassles from envious classmates, who found the sight of a rock superstar riding his bike to school a bit hard to let slide without comment—or worse. Gangs of kids would hang around the school gates, waiting for Johns to emerge. Then the taunts would begin.

'I was always getting a hard time from people because I wasn't a football player and I wasn't out drinking beer and eating steak,' Johns said of the time. 'Later it started getting violent. I thought they were fucking morons.'

Johns described to *Juice* magazine how this hassling intensified. 'I was getting beaten up, constantly being called faggot, people throwing shit into our pool and hassling my family. That was really hard. I didn't want to inflict anything else upon my family.'

Finishing school was a massive relief, even though some scars remained. 'Psychologically it damaged me,' he admitted.

Johns, as he frequently and freely revealed, was fast becoming a loner. 'After spending so much time on the road over the last couple of years, and being surrounded by so many people all the time, it's good to be able to get away for even a few hours with just your dog,' he told *Hit Parader* magazine. 'You get time to think a little and get a hold on everything that's happened. You can always trust your dog.'

It was sad, in a way: Johns's best friend had long been Gillies, but now he preferred the company of his pooch.

———◄○►———

The band rounded out a mad year with their first major Australian tour, the Summer Freak Show. Strangely, while they'd covered much of the planet promoting their first two albums, they'd rarely toured Australia beyond the capital cities and larger regional centres; it was almost as if they were working in reverse. They were now set to play twenty shows over five weeks, commencing on 21 November and swinging through less-visited locales such as Mackay, Ballarat and Dubbo, where they played in a spider-laden aircraft hangar on the RAAF base. Magic Dirt opened these all-ages shows. Their lead singer, Adalita Srsen, would become Johns's occasional girlfriend, and, allegedly, the woman who freed him of his virginity during this tour. (When asked about his 'first shag', Johns described it as 'pretty uncomfortable—like everyone's [first], I think.')

The Summer Freak Show was the Australian rock event of 1997. Now chaperone-free—everyone in the band had turned eighteen—the trio started to cut loose. While their peers were in the midst of Schoolies' Week, the traditional drunken post-exams blast, the band were busy with their own version of this teen rite of passage. Sure, they had to work, but there was plenty of downtime and the shows were a (well-paid) riot. This was the end of the Freak Show road, which had begun back in Hobart in January. 'It was drinking galore, freedom, lots of fun,' said drummer Gillies. 'We let our hair down and had a good time.' Mind you, drinking only took place post-show. The band had a firm 'no booze before gigs' policy.

At the Melbourne Festival Hall show in mid-December, Johns was torn between darkly comic monologues about his lifetime loser status—'I was only a seconder at scouts; I mean, imagine that, I was even coming second in scouts, for Christ's sake'—and playing the full rock dude. He flicked plectrums into the crowd and stopped to examine a bra thrown from the mosh pit. 'How do you put these things on?' he asked. 'Don't know much about them.'

At the same gig, Johns also fell into a rant about critics who felt his dark emotions didn't ring true. 'The people who say stuff like that are just dumb old fucks who can't remember what it's like to be young,' he said with a snarl. 'Just because you're a teenager doesn't mean you don't have those emotions. Those people are just jaded, silly old cocks.'

Writing for online site *Addicted to Noise*, Andrew Tanner saw the changes in the late 1997 version of Daniel Johns. 'Johns, who only a year ago was the most diffident of frontmen, now prowls the stage with growing confidence, his long blond hair fashioned into a mane of spiky dreadlocks. He looks sort of like a younger, leaner Johnny Lydon.'

Each gig closed with a bang, when Johns, sans guitar, threw himself into the Paul Mac remix of 'Freak' (Mac even joined the band onstage at their Sydney University show on 8 December). Gillies—now sporting a mohawk—then stepped out from behind his kit and whaled on some tom-toms and a bass drum as 'Freak' built to its wild climax.

'We wanted to do something really different in our set,' Johns explained, 'that no one would expect. We've been toying with the idea of doing the "Freak" remix for a while now. It seems to be going down really well.'

That was an understatement. Crowds threw themselves into it with as much energy as the band, who, freed from their regular Silver-roles, went nuts.

The Freak Show campaign ended in Perth on 20 December, and Silverchair's hectic year was over. But instead of winding down, Daniel Johns was about to disappear into some of the darkest days of his life.

7

I couldn't leave my house without thinking
something terrible was going to happen.
I was really freaked.
—Daniel Johns

COMING OFF THE LONG AND WINDING ROAD that
was the Freak Show, Daniel Johns was mentally and physically drained and in dire need of serious downtime. Joannou
and Gillies were also feeling some pain, but they recov-
ered through travel: Joannou and his girlfriend headed
off to Thailand, Gillies and his partner travelled to North
Queensland and Byron Bay. When they returned, both
kicked back in Newie with their mates, surfing, hanging
out and doing a whole lot of nothing.

Unlike his bandmates, as Johns readily admitted, he
was no 'social butterfly'; he was more inclined to hole up
in Merewether with his dog and his guitar. 'I was pretty
lonely,' he said, when asked about life after *Freak Show*. In
some ways, he envied his bandmates. 'We'd just left school

and all our friends were going to university. Ben and Chris were going out with their girlfriends, doing their thing, and I was living in a house by myself, just writing.'

Johns was having real trouble adjusting to his new, post-HSC life. 'As soon as we ended school, it became a thousand times harder; we found out that school was an escape. I started to realise, "Fuck, this is my life, this is all I've got".'

By early 1998, Johns began to feel the pressure to generate new tunes for the band's third album. The demands of playing live, travelling and doing press were intrusive— they cramped his creativity. Whereas in the past, many of their songs had emerged from jams, Johns now wanted to write alone. He was taking over as the band's main songwriter, and his only chance to write was back home in Newcastle.

Johns had been planning to take creative control of the band for some time. Near the end of the *Freak Show* tour, he'd spoken with Gillies and Joannou. He told them that the only way he could continue as part of Silverchair was to write all the band's music. He had conceptual ideas for the band, ideas that couldn't come out of the type of jams that had produced their first two albums. Joannou and Gillies agreed; they wanted Silverchair to continue and accepted this was the best way to make that happen. Sure, it was a power play on Johns's part, but one that, over time, proved to be the smartest move they could possibly make, as their music matured greatly. At the same time, Silverchair from now on could be seen, with some justification, as 'The Daniel Johns Band'. Yet despite the freedom this arrangement gave him, Johns had some emotional baggage to confront. He still felt like a prisoner of Silverchair, albeit one who had been granted creative day release.

Johns's musical mood was changing. He wanted to make 'orchestral rock', mixing the standard guitar/bass/drums with strings and other exotic instrumentation. The positive response to the less rocky songs of *Freak Show*, such as 'Cemetery' and 'Abuse Me', had opened his ears to a whole new world of sound. Johns wanted to create music that didn't depend on volume and his full-throated roar to express what he was feeling. He believed that Silverchair needed a serious musical makeover. Grunge was dead.

But the past four years had taken their toll. First there was the massive hit of 'Tomorrow' and the band's rapid ascent in the USA. Then there was the pressure of hitting back after such a huge first-up hit, as well as the apprehended violence order, the 'Israel's Son' controversy, graduating from school, becoming a public figure and teen role model and the obligatory backlash—it was a lot to digest. It was easy to forget that he was all of eighteen when *Freak Show* ground to a halt in December 1997.

Johns felt he had lost control over his life; instead, it was in the hands of people in the music business. He began suffering panic attacks. And he continued to grow apart from his bandmates. 'When we started out,' Johns explained, 'at thirteen or fourteen, we were exactly the fucking same. But as we grew up and went through the same kind of experiences, it's interesting how it affected us and shaped our personalities. We went through the whole being-famous-and-going-through-adolescence thing together, and came out the other side complete opposites. I've no idea how it happened.'

'As our popularity grew, so did people's expectations,' Johns admitted. 'When you're a guy in a band, everyone thinks you should be happily swimming in girls. But it's just not that way unless you're a really confident person to start with. Every time the crowd got bigger, I felt more empty when I walked offstage. Towards the end of 1997, I gradually began to feel more and more alienated from people.'

Johns's parents convinced him to see a psychotherapist, to 'learn to associate with people', by his own definition. But he didn't take well to therapy; he'd walk into a session, sit down and say, 'Just give me the tablets, and I'm going.' He didn't fancy the idea of being picked apart by someone who didn't know him—he'd already had enough of that from the media. Johns ended the sessions after two months.

But there was one piece of advice he did take on board; he needed to gain some independence. He moved out of his family home after buying a two-bedroom house near Merewether Beach, with an uninterrupted view of the ocean. His decorating style was best described as extreme minimalism—the house's interior furnishings comprised a couch, a television, a bed and a stereo. That was pretty much it. Johns only stepped outside to walk his dog, Sweep, or hit the video store, renting 'anything to pass the time and help me get through another day'. (He quickly racked up a $1600 bill.) He listened to very little music; he had no interest in the charts or what his peers were doing. He'd rather watch a movie. Johns's always-supportive parents looked after his groceries and any other needs, keeping a watchful eye on their oldest child.

But for someone seeking some privacy, Johns could have chosen a better location: his new digs were near a public car park, often filled with hopeful Silverchair-watchers or Friday-night yobbos. He was reluctant to leave his house, for fear of being hounded by paparazzi or beaten up by hoons.

'My view of reality became distorted,' Johns revealed. 'I began to feel really anxious and paranoid. I couldn't leave my house without thinking something terrible was going to happen. I was really freaked by phones. When mine rang, I'd have to leave the room to get away from it.' Johns was disappearing deeper and deeper into a funk of alienation and depression. And then he stopped eating.

Johns figured that the only part of his life he could take charge of was his food intake. It was his way of controlling 'the chaos I was feeling inside'. He started to test himself, trying to discover how little he could eat and still get by. Johns saw it as a bizarre personal challenge. Eventually he was down to nothing more than a few pieces of fruit a day, maybe some soup; whatever it took to stop him from blacking out.

'The only way I can describe it,' Johns said afterwards, 'is to say that it felt comforting to be in control of some-thing, like I hadn't totally lost it. The problem is, you think you're gaining control over something, but in reality, you're losing control over the functioning of your body. Within a few months it got to the point where I was eating just so I wouldn't collapse.

'At the time, my parents and my brother and sister were the only people I trusted and could see without feeling anxious. Of course, they were all worried sick about me, but I couldn't really see how bad it was.'

Johns was so lost, in fact, that he was convinced that 'every chef in the world wanted to poison me' and that even a harmless apple contained hidden razor blades. He'd look in the mirror and see the startling physical changes he was undergoing, but then he'd shrug and figure that somehow his clothes had grown bigger since he last wore them.

In the midst of this madness, Johns found himself unable to shake a cold; hardly a surprise, given his diet. He saw his family doctor, who gave it to him straight: forget the cold—if he didn't start eating, he was going to die. He'd seriously damaged his immune system. Being a vegan— and suffering paranoid delusions that his food had been poisoned—exacerbated Johns's decline. His weight had slipped to less than 50 kilos. He was little more than skin and bones. His eyes were dark-ringed and hollow; his hair wild.

Johns's doctor explained that he was already displaying the physical signs of those with advanced eating disorders: receding gums, exposed teeth, protruding bones and sunken cheeks.

That consultation proved to be a turning point.

The doctor prescribed Aropax, an antidepressant designed to mollify his anxious state of mind, and Johns moved back in with his parents. (The move might have been coming anyway: his neighbours had complained about Sweep's barking and Johns's fondness for playing loud music late into the night.)

What Johns didn't realise was that the antidepressant he'd been prescribed, while probably necessary, was another method of blocking out the rest of the world—not unlike locking himself away in a beachside house or giving up food. Johns began sinking into what he would call an 'antidepressant haze', a mental fog in which he'd be lost for the next three years. As much as his bandmates wanted to support him, Johns had shut out the world. They felt frustrated by his inertia.

Gillies sometimes checked in with Johns, but found these get-togethers frustrating. 'I was friends with the guy, but when all he wants to do is sit around all the time and do nothing, after a while you go, "Fuck, this is boring, let's go and do something". But if you did go out, someone would say something [to Johns]. It was frustrating seeing a friend go through it. We'd achieved so much, and we could have done anything we wanted—and then that happened to him. You care about the guy, but there's nothing you can do. All you could say was, well, I hope he works it out.'

Manager Watson was also relegated to outsider status. 'He made it pretty clear that he didn't want people to contact him. He wanted to be on his own,' Watson recalled. Nonetheless, Watson was getting updates from Johns's family and felt very concerned. 'We had a lot of pretty intense conversations.'

Johns later explained that he felt his condition was 'too personal' to share with family and friends. 'When I was really bad with the eating disorder, I thought that I might die and I think everyone that knew me thought I might die if I kept going.' But Johns insists he wasn't suicidal.

Johns may have been slipping away from his family, his bandmates and the world in general, but he did start writing. Initially, he wasn't writing songs, as such—there was too much pressure to do that—so instead he wrote poems, more than 100 in all, scribbled on scraps of paper, all capturing his strange state of mind.

Poetry provided the perfect emotional outlet for Johns. What better way to confront his problems than to write them down? During the early part of 1998, he took all the poems he'd written, cut them up, and made a collage of the words that made the most sense to him. He read them back, liked what he'd written, and began transforming the pick into song lyrics. It was another step into the unknown.

'I didn't ever want to get too poetic with lyrics in the past, because lyrically I've been very influenced by old-school punk bands like Minor Threat and Black Flag,' Johns explained. '[But] I wanted to really focus on what I was feeling at the time. I really wanted people to focus on the lyrics and what I'm trying to say in the songs and then focus on the music, rather than the other way around.'

As *Rolling Stone* magazine would go on to note, Johns's new lyrics—derived from these poems—were 'full of sickness, needs, obsessions, uncertainties and pain'. Rather than slag off 'rich dicks', as he did during the days of *Frogstomp*, rant how 'baby's got rabies' or stick it to the phoneys in the music industry, Johns now had some deeply personal, real-life pain to document. Not surprisingly, this would make for some of the most powerful songs of his career. Johns had finally found his own voice.

The lyrics of what would become 'Ana's Song (Open Fire)' typified Johns's highly personal approach. It was by far the most autobiographical lyric Johns had written, actually composed when his eating disorder was at its worst. 'It was the first time I exposed my eating disorder to anyone,' he said. Johns singled out the line, 'In my head, the flesh seems thicker' as representative of what he was going through while anorexic. 'I'm sure the reason some people get eating disorders has to do with a distorted body image, but often it has nothing to do with looking a certain way,' he explained. 'It's about gaining control over a part of your life. It's about an obsession, whether it's an eating disorder or whether it's a distorted image of one's self.'

———◄○►———

The band convened on 22 February to record a song (sort of) titled 'Untitled' with producer Nick Launay for the *Godzilla* soundtrack. It was an old tune that had first been recorded for *Freak Show*, but hadn't made the cut. It had then been considerably reworked for *Godzilla*. The session was the first time that Johns, Gillies and Joannou had been in the same room since 20 December of the previous year.

Johns wasn't quite ready to debut any new material to his bandmates—not yet, anyway.

The band were testing themselves during this one-off: were they comfortable together in the studio? Was Johns okay? Reassuringly, making music still felt right, and the session, though brief, went well. The next four months were consumed with Johns's slow recovery and the gradual development of songs for their third album. Launay was locked in to begin pre-production in June, so Johns had a lot of finetuning to do; he needed music to accompany his scraps of poetry. This he did in isolation.

In early June, Launay spent a week at Casa del Johns, where Johns played him his new material. Then it was time to get ready for the studio.

With the exception of the one-off 'Untitled' session, Johns had barely spoken with his bandmates all year. Emotions were raw. Drummer Gillies felt rejected by his close friend, who'd shut him out during his breakdown, while Johns, despite the confidence he was showing as a songwriter, was worried that Gillies would reject the new, deeply personal music that he was writing. He just wasn't sure that this music was right for Silverchair—perhaps he should keep these songs for a solo album? Launay assumed the role of mediator, and spoke on Johns's behalf, explaining the situation.

'Daniel is your best friend in the world,' Launay told Gillies, '[but] he doesn't believe you'll like his new songs . . . he's scared you'll reject them.'

Gillies said that wasn't the case.

'I don't want to do a rock record, anyway,' Gillies explained. And he wanted his friend back.

It was then that Launay suggested they spend a day together in a rehearsal room—rather than the Gillies' garage—and see what came of it. On the designated day, Johns walked in, sat on a chair and, without making any eye contact, simply said, 'Okay, I've got this song' and began to play.

'I was really nervous,' Johns said. 'I thought they'd go, "What the fuck is that?"'

But Gillies liked what he heard.

'I reckon that's heaps good—what if I put a beat to it?'

The old firm was back in business; within minutes the three mates were teasing and taking the piss out of each other, just like the early days. At one point, Launay turned to Joannou and said, 'Will you look at these two? They should give each other a hug.'

'It was really emotional,' said Launay, 'on-the-point-of-crying sort of stuff.'

Over the next week, they realised they had a full album's worth of material—half of it rock-based, the other half more experimental.

Later, Johns explained to *Rock Sound* magazine that some of the more restrained passages in his new songs did throw his bandmates, just a little, but added, 'They could see that these ideas were going round in my head and that there was no other option. Ben and Chris are enormously alike—they have the same interests and the same view of the world, whereas I'm different. But I respect them, you know? They're my friends. Our temperaments are at odds with each other, but that's okay. We complement each other, which is the essence of Silverchair.'

Gillies had written one song, entitled 'Trash', which didn't make the album, turning up later as a B-side. Joannou had also tried to write music, but, as he admitted, 'it really sucked'. With the exception of 'Spawn Again', co-written by Johns and Gillies, the songs on the *Neon Ballroom* album would be all Johns compositions. Johns was now the sole songwriter, a change that Gillies may have come to accept, but one that didn't sit so well with his mother. She was hoping some of her son's tunes would make the final cut, as they had on the first two albums, thereby generating song-writing royalties and keeping things more even within the band, creatively speaking. That's not how it panned out.

'Emotion Sickness', which was to become *Neon Ball-room*'s mood-swinging, richly evocative opening track—and Johns's favourite cut on the album, the 'essence' of the LP in his view—was a vivid snapshot of his fragile state of mind. 'It's about depression or anxiety or anything like that,' Johns said. 'It's about trying to escape it without resorting to an antidepressant or some kind of pill.'

What 'Emotion Sickness' really needed was a great piano player. And Johns's connection with David Helfgott, the subject of the Oscar-winning biopic *Shine*, was one of the high points of the album's creation. That connec-tion began with Larry Muhoberac, an arranger who'd been hired to work on 'Emotion Sickness'. When Johns met with Muhoberac, the composer asked him how he imagined the piece would sound. Johns was untrained and had no knowledge of formal composition, so he proceeded to articulate how the song played out in his head, all the while wearing a green beanie that made him look like some sort of alien.

'It goes, you know, kind of—*Bling! Bling! Bling!*' Johns said, as he ran around the studio, his arms flailing in all directions.

Producer Launay watched all this unfold. 'The stuff he was coming out with was brilliant.'

Then it was suggested that Helfgott would be the right person to execute the 'manic' piano parts that Johns was describing to Muhoberac. The band agreed to meet Helfgott at Watson's house; at one stage, he excused himself so he could slip upstairs and brush his teeth—with Watson's toothbrush. Throughout the meeting, Helfgott kept putting his arm around Gillies and muttering, 'Very different, very different.' The drummer didn't know quite what to make of the highly emotional piano man; he'd never met anyone like him before. None of the guys had.

Helfgott, who'd undergone shock therapy to treat a diagnosis of schizoaffective disorder, was a red-hot ball of energy from the moment he entered the studio on 19 August. As he didn't possess an 'inner voice', Helfgott felt it important to utter every thought that entered his head.

'Ah, Ben, the timekeeper, very strong, he's the man with the beats,' Helfgott said upon catching up with Gillies. Then it was Launay's turn: 'The decision maker! Where would we be without the decision maker?' All of his proclamations were teamed with a bone-crushing embrace: Helfgott was a hugger. And a kisser, too, when the mood took him.

Then he turned his attention to Johns. Helfgott's eyes widened when they sat down together. 'You're an angel! You've been sent to sing to us like an angel!'

At one stage, Helfgott reached across and quite innocently grasped the singer's penis. 'He didn't know that he was doing it,' Johns said, a little shocked. 'He just has to be intimate.' This sort of stuff didn't happen in Newie.

Working with Helfgott presented unique challenges. Whenever he attempted a take of the song, after being counted in, Helfgott would loudly exclaim: 'And here we go!' When he ended the take, he'd then announce: 'There she goes! It's a good one.' All of his chatter had to be erased from the recordings, which ran for some three hours.

He also refused to sit still at the piano, unless someone was sitting alongside him, hugging him as he played. All the while Helfgott was exclaiming, 'Very exciting! Like this bit!' As this was happening, he needed Muhoberac nearby in order to advise him what came next. It was chaotic.

'The end result,' as Launay recounted, 'was this crazy thing of . . . David sitting on a bench at the piano with Larry hugging him with one arm and pointing with the other, saying, "Okay, David, now we're going to play this part".'

Johns clearly fell under the spell of the indefatigable and highly personable Helfgott. 'David was great,' Johns said after the session. 'David played his piano part like a classical composition. Then he started improvising around what he felt, which was exactly what I was looking for. Only a pianist as inspired as he is could have managed what he did.'

When asked about their connection, when we exchanged emails in 2006, Helfgott said this: 'I felt a strong bond with him [Johns]. He was extremely kind and sharing; it was a great experience for me.'

This wasn't the only lively day inside the Festival studio. The New South Wales Public School Singers choir was tapped to sing on 'Anthem for the Year 2000'. Conducted by George Tobay, the young voices gave the song an eerily similar mood to Pink Floyd's 'Another Brick in the Wall'.

'Anthem for the Year 2000' was a riff-crunching rock beast that would become *Neon Ballroom*'s lead single. But whereas 'Ana's Song' and 'Emotion Sickness' were deeply felt lyrics about the trauma Johns was going through, 'Anthem' came from somewhere else entirely. A dream, in fact.

As Johns explained to *Guitar* magazine, he'd had a dream where the band were playing at a huge stadium but their gear wasn't working: everything was broken. It was every musician's worst nightmare. But then something amazing happened. 'Thousands of people had their hands in the air, clapping,' Johns said, 'And I started singing, "We are the youth, we'll take your fascism away" over the handclaps, in order to compensate for the lack of instruments.'

As soon as he awoke, Johns reached for his guitar and a notepad. 'I did it from start to finish in, like, five minutes. It was the quickest song I'd ever written, and the first verse starts with drums and vocals—just like the dream, only with the handclaps.' Johns had spawned a near-perfect rock monster: the song was huge. 'Stadium rock without the wank,' he explained.

'Anthem for the Year 2000' also tapped into Johns's growing social awareness. He even drew links between its theme and the worrying outbreak of One Nation and Hanson-ism that were creeping into Australian politics and society at the end of the millennium. Politics was beginning to piss him off.

'I think the government treats us like shit,' Johns said. 'They think the youth is a bunch of people who are wasting their lives on drugs and loud music. The song draws a parallel between politicians and how they view youth and how they put certain restrictions on them. It draws a parallel between that and the record industry and taking away from young stars and using young people—and taking their innocence.'

On closer inspection, maybe 'Anthem' wasn't strictly a political rant—it tapped into some of the problems that had been troubling Johns since the time of *Freak Show*: was he a true artist or a rat in a cage?

'Satin Sheets' was his comment on class. It was about 'the corporate world looking down on people', according to Johns. 'If I walk into a restaurant or something,' said Johns, 'there's this whole yuppie mentality of people who think I shouldn't be there because I don't brush my hair.' But Johns had the last laugh. 'I've probably got more money than them.'

'Miss You Love' and 'Black Tangled Heart' were other poems-cum-songs written by Johns during band downtime. But they reflected a different problem that he was experiencing: his inability to form a lasting relationship. While he'd had girlfriends, everything seemed to fade after a month or so. 'I think I've got some kind of phobia. I'm scared of getting too attached to someone. Just when someone gets close to my heart, that's when I cut them off.'

Except for his faithful pooch Sweep, of course. He was a stayer.

———◇———

More guests made cameos as the *Neon Ballroom* sessions continued into the first week of September. Johns's friend Paul Mac played on 'Anthem', 'Spawn Again' and 'Satin Sheets'. Mac had a habit of hitting the keys so hard that a piano tuner was needed after every session, hence a liner note saying that he 'attacked' the piano. Midnight Oil's Jim Moginie added what the band fondly dubbed 'keyboards Mogenius' to 'Anthem', 'Ana's Song' and 'Miss You Love', three key *Neon Ballroom* tracks. Sydney musical journeyman Chris Abrahams played piano on 'Black Tangled Heart'. Jane Scarpantoni, whose string arrangement on *Freak Show*'s 'Cemetery' was a standout, added various arrangements to *Neon Ballroom*, along with eight other violinists and cellists. And in a classic case of cronyism, Johns's long-time companion Sweep howled during the album's closer, 'Steam Will Rise'.

Johns particularly loved working with Scarpantoni. Whereas 'Cemetery' had been written as a ballad and only had strings added as an afterthought, Johns was now writing with strings specifically in mind. As arranged by Scarpantoni, naturally.

'She was classically trained,' he said, 'but [has] a rock mind. She understands my language; I describe things more as scenery or pictures, and she latched on and got the right kind of mood.' Not that Johns completely understood her language. During the sessions, she mentioned the classical term 'legato' to Johns (translated in layman's terms as 'smoothly'). He replied, 'Yeah, right, more "legato",' looking a little lost. But you sensed that Johns was storing the information away, as his musical vocabulary grew. The studio was no longer somewhere to bash out songs and then rattle around the corridors on trolleys or watch porn. Johns now saw it as a place where he could give some life to the musical pictures in his head. The studio was serious creative business.

'When I first started,' Johns reasoned, 'it was more about playing live, and everything was about energy. Everything was about being really loud. [But] the thing that keeps me doing it is just creating music and exploring different elements of musical and lyrical angles.' Yet in spite of Johns and the band's musical progress, the *Neon Ballroom* sessions were still the most taxing of their recording life. Johns was recovering from his eating disorder, and Gillies and Joannou could sense the discomfort that permeated every session. Gillies described the feeling this way:

'[It was as though] this elastic band of tension was pulled tight around us.'

'It was everything—Daniel wasn't well, we were having to do another record, thinking whether this is what we really wanted to do. We were also thinking that if our lead singer's not well and doesn't really want to do it, well, then, shit, I don't want to do it.' Launay's studio perfectionism—he'd often ask for twenty or more takes of individual parts—didn't make the situation any easier.

'Ana's Song' was the last track recorded, and it took some hard talking by Johns to convince everyone else that the song belonged on the album. Johns hadn't played it to Watson until late in the sessions, when they were doing string overdubs at Sydney's Paradise Studios. Watson recognised that it was the ideal second single, but after a few listens to the song, he also knew that its anorexia theme was a big controversy just waiting to happen. Watson put in a call to John O'Donnell and told him to drop everything and get down to the studio. The Murmur boss agreed it was a great song but also thought there was no way it could go on the album. Ex-journo O'Donnell could already picture the headlines it would generate.

The two Johns spoke with Daniel.

'You just don't understand the scrutiny this will bring,' Watson told him. 'You're just coming out of a dark place, and this might take you straight back there.'

On the flipside, Watson, by his own admission, also understood that the song summed up the whole album—and it was this that made Johns dig in.

'I want to make an emotionally true record,' Johns said, 'and in order to do that, it has to stay. I don't want to censor myself at all.'

'Ana's Song' was in.

After almost two months of recording—a far cry from the rushed sessions for *Frogstomp* and the stop-start creation of *Freak Show*—*Neon Ballroom* seemed just about ready to throw open its doors. But Johns and Launay discovered one final hitch. After what they thought was a final week in the studio, they detected a strange, muffled quality to Johns's vocals. During playback, it sounded as if a sheet had been laid across the speakers. His vocals would have to be re-recorded.

A genuinely pissed-off Johns took a fortnight's break to regain his physical and emotional strength. He admitted that 'there was a lot of smashing things because of the frustration' during those two weeks off. But he and Launay eventually reconvened, and the album was finally done by early October 1998.

'All the struggles were worth it,' said Johns, as he left for LA, where the album would be mixed. 'We've made an album that combines lots of different sounds and instruments that you don't usually hear together. We wanted to carve our own little piece of turf, blending futuristic noises with more classic influences.' Then he added, in a telling kiss-off to grunge, 'We're fed up with all the usual comparisons that people keep making about our music. I wanted to make guitar [rock] pretty much a non-issue. I wanted us to make an album that was different from everything else that's out right now.'

—◁○▷—

Neon Ballroom hit Australian stores on 8 March 1999. Releasing their albums during the first quarter of the year would become a trend that would continue through the band's career. And as statements of musical independence go, *Neon Ballroom* was a success. Though not shy of Silverchair's trademark force-10 riffs, it broke the band out of the grunge ghetto that had characterised *Frogstomp* and *Freak Show*. The opener, 'Emotion Sickness', set the tone for the entire album. The LP began with a tense, terse mini symphony enhanced by Helfgott's frantic piano playing; this was no 'Tomorrow', that was for sure. Johns's voice drifted for much of the song, floating, until he suddenly burst into life, screaming, 'Everything is clearly dying.' It was powerful stuff, as if he'd just awoken from a tormented sleep.

There'd been some in-house resistance to opening the album with 'Emotion Sickness'—if *Neon Ballroom* had begun with 'Anthem for the Year 2000' (already a number three hit in Australia), for instance, it would have been seen as an entirely different record. But Johns went with his instinct.

'We were warned not to do it, because it would alienate and confuse people, and turn them off the album,' Johns said. 'But . . . as soon as someone said that to me, I said, "Yeah, I'm definitely going to do it". It shows the ambition behind the record and sums up what I was trying to do.' The contrariness of the decision must have appealed to Johns, too, because their upcoming live shows would also open with 'Emotion Sickness'. Seven minutes of heaving psychodrama was hardly a party starter.

'Ana's Song (Open Fire)', the album's third track, made it equally clear that this was a new Silverchair, as Johns worked his way through his recent troubles as if he were on the analyst's couch. Gillies' powerhouse drumming and Joannou's solid bottom-end left their mark, although it was Johns's searing honesty that elevated this track, as it did the bulk of *Neon Ballroom*. Johns's personal anguish was underscored on several tracks by Scarpantoni's classical leanings, especially on the lush 'Paint Pastel Princess', the turgid 'Black Tangled Heart', and 'Miss You Love', a gentle, waltz-like ballad with a dark underbelly. If there was one track on *Neon Ballroom* that summed up Johns's tortured soul, this was it: an anti–love song that combined a gorgeous melody and a perversely glum lyric.

'I wanted to write a song that people could dedicate to their lover on the radio or dance to,' said Johns. But this was a slow song with a twist. 'It's actually about not having love and not being able to find love, and being lonely.'

But the band still had a mosh pit to satisfy if they were to continue selling records (another case of needing to do 'what sucks the least'). Tracks such as 'Spawn Again' and 'Dearest Helpless' were throwbacks to the simpler times of their first two albums. Although neither was a standout—'Spawn Again' was actually pretty dreadful—both packed a kick like a mule, and were bound to send bodies flying live. But you couldn't help but think Johns was merely paying lip service to the fans who had snapped up *Freak Show* and *Frogstomp*. These songs were for them, not for him. They didn't fill any holes in his soul.

So how much musical experimentation could Johns get away with before his audience started looking elsewhere? If anything, *Ballroom* adequately managed to fulfil Johns's need to scratch his creative itch without alienating the faithful. For every lush, cinematic mood piece there was a raw, bleeding rocker. As each-way bets go, the album was a winner. But with the benefit of hindsight, perhaps Johns was selling himself just a little short. Should he have pushed himself further?

Local critic Barry Divola, writing in *Who* magazine, sensed this, describing *Neon Ballroom* as 'an experiment that didn't quite have the *cojones* to back up the vision'. But most critics embraced *Neon Ballroom*'s broader vision. *Massive* magazine, for one, took a *vive la différence* approach: '*Neon Ballroom* is different, Silverchair is experimenting and the results are awesome'. Craig Mathieson, a close follower of the band, wrote a four-star review for Australian *Rolling Stone*: 'It's an ambitious, varied record, one brimming with intelligent ideas—some not always realised—but worthy nonetheless'. Ken Advent in the *Cleveland Free Times* wrote that 'Silverchair is making a concerted effort to stretch the band's musical boundaries . . . when Silverchair is on top of their game, there are flashes of a visionary band like Pink Floyd filtered through the heavy guitars'.

Johns's development as a writer was the focus of a lot of attention. *Electric Music Online* stated that 'the biggest credit has to go to Daniel Johns. His songwriting skills have improved out of sight—no longer is he simply copying his peers and influences, [he's] writing songs with their own structure and sound.' New Zealand's music mag *Rip It Up* echoed this sentiment. 'All the time you know Daniel Johns's songwriting skill has progressed beyond playing three chords and shouting very loudly.'

———◄○►———

Silverchair's attention now turned to their upcoming tour. In order to re-create the lush sounds of much of their new album, they spent two weeks at home, in late November 1998, auditioning keyboardists. (They'd toyed with, and then dropped, the idea of bringing in a second guitarist.) The band settled on Sam Holloway, late of moody Melbourne band Cordrazine. Not only was Holloway classically trained, but he also looked good on stage and was a bit of a lad, which sat well with Joannou and Gillies: they had a new playmate. Johns, meanwhile, found a glittery shirt that shone like the night sky, which he felt was perfect for live shows. It wasn't something Kurt Cobain would have worn, which was yet another reason to go with it.

The debut public appearance of the newly four-piece Silverchair was on 21 January, at a surprise hometown gig. Billing themselves as the Australian Silverchair Show, they shocked locals at Newcastle's Cambridge Hotel when they opened for an AC/DC tribute act, airing new songs and early standards. It was the perfect way to dust off the cobwebs. It was also the chance for Johns to try out another new outfit: tonight, it was a red shirt and loose-fitting tie, matched with long grey shorts (or short grey longs, it was hard to tell). It was as though he'd raided a broker's wardrobe for the night. The band played so well they were called back for an encore, not often the case for a support act. Headliners ACCA/DACCA were left to cool their heels backstage.

The next day, the revitalised band were in Sydney, filming the 'Anthem for the Year 2000' clip with American director Gavin Bowden, who'd shot videos for MTV faves the Red Hot Chili Peppers, Live and Rage Against the Machine. In line with their new 'keep it different' policy, the band had sent out invitations via their fan club and chairpage website, letting it be known that a mob was required. On the second day of shooting, 1200 believers turned up in Sydney's Martin Place—the band had expected 300—transforming it into a seething mass of Silver-madness. 'Anthem' blared repeatedly through an outdoor PA during the shoot, as the army of extras staged their scripted riot, tagging posters with spray cans and generally running amok, all the while being sprayed with power hoses. Johns and the band, meanwhile, rocked the hell out of the song on an industrial *Metropolis*-inspired set—shades of Queen's 'Radio Ga Ga'. Johns was all business; he glared at Bowden's camera as if it was trying to suck out his soul.

Another feature was a cameo from Australian television actor Maggie Kirkpatrick, 'The Freak' from long-running

'70s prison soapie *Prisoner*. In the clip, Kirkpatrick played a figure that resembled Pauline Hanson, a metaphor for the song's 'authority sucks' message. It turned out that Kirkpatrick had links to the band: she was a fellow Novocastrian, and her niece and nephew were Silver-schoolmates.

'My first reaction was, "Why me?",' she told the *Sunday Herald Sun*. 'I later found out that the boys were from Newcastle, and being an old Newcastle girl myself, I was more than prepared to help them out.'

Not that Silverchair had much time to swap hometown stories. By the time the water cannons had been shut down and order restored to Martin Place, Johns and the band were on a plane to Melbourne, en route to a headlining spot at the Peaches & Cream Festival. Ahead of them lay another heavy year's worth of travelling, playing—and messing with their audience's heads.

8

Can I get a hallelujah?
Can I get a halle-fucking-lujah?
—Daniel Johns

AN ANXIOUS JOHNS was sitting in Sydney airport, along-side Gillies and Joannou, looking out at a threatening sky.

'Oh shit, we're all going to die really, really dramatically.'

Those were the first words he uttered when the band convened to begin the Australian leg of their 1999 world tour, promoting *Neon Ballroom*. It was hardly the most optimistic of beginnings. It was 2 March, and the trio were en route to Brisbane and then much of the Western world. The grind, nearly 100 gigs in total, had begun.

When they arrived (safely, as it turned out) at Brisbane, prior to their 3 March show at the Tivoli Cabaret, Gillies, Joannou and new boy Holloway hit the pool, as a rainstorm burst through the oppressive Queensland humidity. Johns, meanwhile, was holed up in the hotel with a journalist, talking about himself, a situation that would be repeated throughout this year of touring. If he wasn't on stage purging, he was locked away with a reporter, doing a different sort of purging.

Rolling Stone music editor Elissa Blake was travelling with the group, writing a cover story for the magazine's May 1999 issue. But what she thought would be a typical band-on-tour feature quickly changed into something radically different and far weightier. Johns needed to spill. He felt it was important—almost a community service, in fact—to let *Rolling Stone*'s readers know exactly what he'd been through prior to the recording of *Neon Ballroom*.

Almost nonchalantly, he turned to Blake:

Johns: A lot of people have been very worried about me.
Rolling Stone: Do you want to talk about it?
Johns: Yeah, I do.
RS: What was going on while you were writing this album?
Johns: I was dealing with a lot of psychological things. I cut myself off from everyone that I knew for about six months.
RS: Was it depression?
Johns: It was associated with depression. I started getting really bad anxiety trouble. I ended up getting medication because every time I left the house I'd be really badly shaking and sweaty.

Johns proceeded to detail his season in hell: the isolation, the panic attacks, his eating disorder, his fear that in the midst of his breakdown he might actually die. He even showed his medications to Blake—nine sheets of coloured pills, including two different varieties of sleeping pills. 'I'm just trying them out,' he said. Johns seemed unconcerned; it was as if he was talking about his favourite sweets.

Johns had also spoken openly to a newspaper staffer two days earlier, and the local media jumped on the story. 'Eating Disorder Rocks Teen Star' was *The Courier-Mail* headline that manager Watson read over his bacon and eggs. He was livid. Once again, his band were front-page news for all the wrong reasons. Watson was especially angry that he'd been deceived into arranging a photo of a gaunt Johns, thinking it would run with a live review of that night's show.

But Johns had willingly chosen to share his problem with his audience. The way he saw it, among his many fans there may have been someone who could benefit from knowing that even Daniel Johns suffered typical (albeit extreme) teen problems. Once Watson had calmed down, he began to accept what his youthful charge was trying to do by being so frank with journalists. 'I have a great deal of concern for Daniel as a human being,' he told *Rolling Stone*'s Blake, explaining that Johns 'wanted to help other people and now we just have to do our best to help him'.

When Blake's story was published, Australian *Rolling Stone* was flooded with responses. Many were written by teenagers with similar eating disorders. They were relieved; they didn't feel alone anymore. Some even sent poems to Johns via the mag. The volume of mail was so overwhelming that Blake forwarded many to John Watson, who then relayed them to Johns. It was the strongest response to a story that the magazine had ever had. The issue, of course, all but jumped off the shelves.

There was also a lot happening within the band. Things had begun changing onstage: Johns suddenly exploded when he plugged in and played the band's new material. The sparkly top he'd found in a Newtown op shop was standard stage-wear now; the old cargo pants and band T-shirts were gone. Johns was now the centre of attention, slashing at his guitar and windmilling his arms like a young, blond, even-scrawnier Pete Townshend. The band chaperones were gone, school was out, and Daniel Johns had morphed into an electrifying, seriously watchable rock star. But Johns also knew there was a big difference between 'person' and 'persona'.

As one writer observed, 'Daniel from Silverchair puts Daniel Johns in the public eye, where he feels uneasy. But Daniel from Silverchair also sells the albums, which satisfies Daniel Johns's self-belief in his songwriting and quietly fierce ambition.' It was a complicated relationship.

Johns started offering some curious onstage rants, dating back to the tour's first show at Cobram, in Victoria.

'Right,' he yelled, 'put your hand up if you had a stage in your life where you felt alienated from the rest of the world. Okay, yoga is for you. It stretches the mind, and everything is about spirituality. Spirituality or drugs. You're gonna take your pick, right? Or Jesus, but Jesus at times can be very stressful. Because you don't know whether to read the Old or New Testament. Two different stories; it fucks me up.'

You could hear a collective sigh of relief when Johns screamed, 'Are you ready to rock and roll?' and crashed into 'Pure Massacre'. He was emanating a weird vibe.

What most crowds didn't know was how hard it was for Johns to get on stage at all. While he might have been busting some of the most outrageous moves of his life—playing, as one reviewer described, 'as if the power chords had taken over his body'—Johns was in the midst of a new problem, a serious prescription-drug dependency. He needed pills to help him play, pills to help him come down from the show, pills to help him sleep. It was rough.

Johns didn't look wasted as much as he did disorientated, which might have explained another rant, this time during a gig at Melbourne Park: 'Is this live on the radio?' he asked the band, as he spat on the stage. 'It is? Then radio listeners can go to the toilet because we're going to conduct an experiment. Okay, here's the deal, Melbourne—' he was clearly getting into the idea buzzing about his head— 'I swear to God no one we've been to has been able to do this, so if you can, you're the reigning premiers of the world. Are you ready? Okay. Everyone upstairs stand, stand tall, stand proud. Everyone on the floor sit. Get down low, go, go, go.' Then, after a beat, as half the crowd rose to their feet and the other half searched for somewhere to plant their backsides, Johns the comedian kicked in. 'There's a fire in the building, a fire! Fuck.' Then, after another pause: 'That looks good. Stay there.' Daniel asked for a camera, took a snap and then got back to work.

'Can I get a hallelujah? Can I get a halle-fucking-lujah?'

Joannou, Gillies and Holloway were becoming tight; as the tour progressed, they were often found together at the back of the bus bellowing 'Sweet Home Alabama', or scoping out local hot spots. But Johns would be a million miles away, staring out of the window as the road flashed by. Gillies and Joannou agreed that there were many tense moments on the *Neon Ballroom* tour, as there were during its recording. 'You could just feel this tension in the air.'

Johns's bipolar onstage persona didn't help. In London, he referred to himself as 'a lesbian wanker'. In New York, before a crowd that included *Neon Ballroom* collaborator Jane Scarpantoni and American *Rolling Stone*'s David Fricke, Johns fell into a rap about his wish to become Posh Spice. Why? 'Because I'm a bitch, and I'm gonna be married to a famous soccer player.' At a key LA showcase, with startled Epic A&R staff looking on, he gave an impromptu Bible reading. Johns also slipped a 'motherfucker' into the lyrics of 'Freak', as if that song needed an extra up-yours. Johns suspected that these crowds just wanted to hear 'Tomorrow', which he now played solo, in a truncated, acoustic version—it was another 'fuck you' to the fans.

Johns seemed to be messing around with the concept of rock-star behaviour. He was coming on like a cross between a rock-and-roll madman and an awkward stand-up comic. He was trying to have fun, but not everyone bought into the joke, like a bewildered crowd in Bologna, Italy.

'Who here is ready for some rock-and-roll action?' Johns asked, only to receive a muffled response. 'That's fucked.

If you're not ready, we're not ready, and until you are ready, you as one, we will not continue.' He then screamed: 'ARE YOU READY TO ROCK AND ROLL? CAN I GET A HALLE-FUCKING-LUJAH!'

Finally, the crowd stirred a little. But Johns wasn't finished. 'Who here likes spaghetti bolognese?' he asked. When the crowd didn't react at all, he shrugged. 'Wasn't the reaction I was after, but that's cool because I think it sucks.'

Johns had also begun to frequently talk to himself between songs. Almost like a tennis player, he was urging himself on ('I can do it'), or mouthing obscenities. 'I hate you, I fucking hate you,' he yelled at himself in Minneapolis, before telling the crowd, 'Okay, listen. We spent several fucking hours signing hundreds of CD covers, and it was all for you. They're fifteen bucks—over there.'

Chinese whispers began circulating that Johns was taking something stronger than antidepressants, although he'd not owned up to anything heavier than pot and booze.

Punters couldn't help but notice how lost the frontman seemed, among them a German fan, writing on Chairpage about Silverchair's Dusseldorf show on 4 April. 'There was almost no contact between the band members,' she wrote, yet when she saw them in 1996, 'They were three funny young guys who just had fun playing music.' Johns said plenty to the crowds each night—not all of it logical—but shared little onstage with Gillies, Joannou and Holloway. He was in his own private universe.

Two nights after the Dusseldorf show, back in the UK, Johns actually stopped the band midway through 'Pure

Massacre' when a stage-diver was kicked by a security guard. 'Hey, what the fuck do you think you're doing, man?' Johns yelled, as the band crashed to a halt. 'You don't go kicking people like that.'

There was a similar incident in Vienna in mid-April, when a stage invader was dragged away by bouncers in the midst of 'Anthem for the Year 2000'. 'Fuck the security! Fuck the security!' Johns screamed. Now it seemed as though both audiences and security were getting under Johns's skin. And the tour still had eight months to run.

———◄○►———

The notices for the tour were as mixed as Johns's attempts at being funny. Reviewing their 4 March Sydney show, Jon Casimir from *The Sydney Morning Herald* was unimpressed. 'What was meant to be a triumphant [gig] was largely a forgettable evening.' Shrewdly, Casimir also observed this: 'Johns increasingly appears to be fronting another band . . . There is a distance between the band members . . . Johns seems self-conscious, as if age and experience have leached some of the raw joy from the job of performing.'

The band were in Chicago on 15 March when *Neon Ballroom* debuted at number one on the Australian album chart, repeating the runaway success of *Frogstomp* and *Freak Show*. It went on to sell 204,000 copies at home. The album made its debut on the US charts a week later, at number fifty. It was certified gold (sales of 500,000) by the first week of April and would spend 30 weeks on the *Billboard*

Top 200 chart. In Canada, the album entered the charts at number five, while the album's European chart debuts were the best of the band's career: number twenty-nine in the UK, number thirteen in Germany, and number twenty-three in France.

Over time in the USA, *Neon Ballroom* achieved roughly the same sales as *Freak Show*—633,000 to *Freak Show*'s 620,000—but not a notch on *Frogstomp*'s two-million-plus. Yet sales of Silverchair's third album increased elsewhere. It sold 101,000 copies in Germany, 116,000 in Brazil and 25,000 copies in Sweden. On 10 May, when 'Ana's Song (Open Fire)' debuted at number fourteen on the Australian singles chart, it became the band's eleventh consecutive Australian Top 40 single. Silverchair had become the most successful Australian chart performer of the 1990s, even outshining Savage Garden.

The returns for the band's North American live shows were consistent, even though they were playing smaller venues than in 1997. During a run of dates in March, they filled the 1500-capacity Roxy Theater in Atlanta, and the 1400-capacity Vic in Chicago. In Canada, with fellow Australians Grinspoon along for the ride, they packed the 2500-capacity club The Warehouse in Toronto and the 1200-capacity Le Spectrum de Montreal. In another case of choosing a support act who'd soon blow up—Matchbox Twenty had exploded since Silverchair's last US tour—rock plodders Nickelback opened up at their next date, at Vancouver's Croatian Cultural Centre on 26 March. Not all of their shows were so successful: only 800 punters fronted in Columbus, Ohio, while the

Daniel Johns at the Big Day Out, Auckland, 1995. 'We were pretty happy,' Johns said after winning the *nomad* competition that kickstarted Silverchair's career.

Johns on stage in 1995 at the Big Day Out on the Gold Coast. 'So, this young guy . . . looks like my dead husband, Kurt,' slurred Courtney Love from a nearby stage. 'How lame.'

Johns with Silverchair bandmates Ben Gillies (centre) and Chris Joannou (right), in 1994, just before they signed a record deal. 'People basically leave us alone, but some call us long-haired louts,' Daniel said about life in Newcastle.

Johns, Gillies and Joannou (right to left) in London, 1995. When Johns was nine, he formed a rap duo with Gillies called the Silly Men—the pair had history.

With Tim Rogers, You Am I's front man (second from left), at the 1995 ARIA awards. 'Shit, it was funny,' Johns said of their ferocious jam on the night of Radio Birdman's 'New Race'.

Playing Sydney's Luna Park, a secret show for radio station Triple J's competition winners. That station was the first to play 'Tomorrow' on a regular basis.

The band in a lighthearted mood around the time of the *Freak Show* album.

At Luna Park in 1997. Johns sank into a deep depression after Silverchair's initial success. 'I just sit at home with my dog and watch telly. I don't know if sitting at home every day is normal, but that's what I do.'

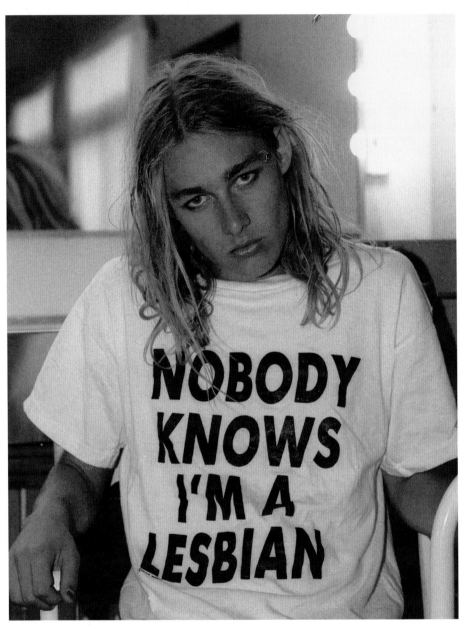

Johns backstage at the preview of the *Freak Show* album, Moore Park, Sydney, in February, 1997. He was never averse to a good wind-up; he once referred to himself as a 'lesbian wanker' and also fantasised about becoming Posh Spice.

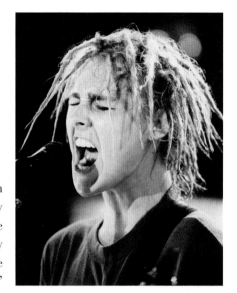

On stage at Sydney's Hordern Pavilion in December 1997. 'When you're a guy in a band, everyone thinks you should be happily swimming in girls, [but] every time the crowd got bigger, I felt more empty when I walked offstage.'

Johns (centre) with Joannou (left) and Gillies. Johns quickly grew to understand the business of show. Many of his decisions were based upon 'what sucks the least'.

Johns in Newcastle in 1999. By now he could see that he and his bandmates were growing apart—he'd become withdrawn and wary of outsiders. 'It's interesting how [our experiences] affected us and shaped our personalities.'

Playing the final show of their Neon Ballroom tour at Sydney's Homebake festival in December 1999. Many thought it might be the band's last-ever performance.

On stage during the Diorama tour in Melbourne in 2002. Before recording *Diorama*, Johns bravely erased all the new songs he'd prepared. 'They just sounded too much like the last album.'

Silverchair playing live in Brisbane in August 2007, while promoting the *Young Modern* album, their swan song.

On the set of the video for 'Straight Lines', filmed at Sydney's Homebush railway station. It was a number-one hit in February 2007.

The Silver-trio in happier times in Surry Hills, 2007, while working on the *Young Modern* LP.

Johns striking a pose during the band's third and final Big Day Out, January 2008. 'Sydney,' he told the crowd before playing 'Straight Lines', 'sing it like you're on *Australian Idol*.'

Performing at the Groovin' the Moo festival in Maitland, May 2010, their final tour. 'It's good to be home,' Johns told the crowd.

Conducting a ritual guitar sacrifice at the same event. Johns would hang up his guitar for several years after the band's last show in Darwin, just two weeks later.

At the premiere of 'Atlas', a piece commissioned by Qantas, at the Sydney Opera House, 2012. The finished work divided his fans—where were the guitars?

Johns at the Australasian Performing Right Association awards (APRAs) in March 2015, where he first played 'Preach'.

With Midnight Oil's Peter Garrett, something of a role model for Johns, at the 2015 APRAs.

Johns and other award winners at the 2015 APRAs.

Performing at the 2015 APRAs at Carriageworks in Sydney. It's hard to believe it's the same Daniel Johns who once wore flannel and big shorts and wailed about 'Tomorrow'.

2460-seat Boathouse in Norfolk, Virginia, wasn't even half full when Silverchair plugged in on 2 June.

And still Silverchair kept touring—and Johns continued behaving in occasionally comical, sometimes bizarre ways. It seemed as though he had moved beyond his audience, who still bayed for older songs such as 'Tomorrow' and 'Pure Massacre'. On other occasions, he was quite clearly playing up his role as frontman: why not give the crowd some razzle-dazzle to go with the rock? In Tampa, Florida, on 2 May, Johns dusted off his rock-and-roll evangelist persona. 'Can I get a hallelujah?' he asked the crowd. 'Let's hear it for Jesus!' he yelled. 'Let's hear it for Satan! Let's hear it for sex, drugs and fucking rock and roll!'

His bandmates were growing uncomfortable with Johns's strange turns. Joannou felt that Johns was challenging himself by digging a metaphorical hole on stage and then seeing if he could pull himself out. But it wasn't always something the bass man enjoyed watching, especially when Johns turned abusive: 'Sometimes you thought, "This is good, he's becoming his own person". Other times you thought, "Oh boy, where is he heading tonight?" There was definitely a case of, "Just three more months, just three more months".'

Gillies, meanwhile, maintained his 'man of the people' role, signing autographs and chatting with fans at shows long after Johns had left the building. And he didn't mind the attention, either. A writer I spoke with, who'd spent some time on the road with the band, recalled watching Gillies actively pursuing a 'tattooed rock chick', a roadie for LA punks Bad Religion: women were never far from the drummer's mind.

Another sign of Johns's increasingly unpredictable behaviour was his tendency to lecture his audience. If he wasn't grumbling about their lack of response, he was drilling them about animal rights. In Boston on 30 May, he posed the question: 'Do any of you believe in shooting ducks?' When many replied in the affirmative, Johns shot back: 'Anyone who answered "yes" is a fuckwit'. Despite the Animal Liberation tattoo on his ankle, not many in the crowd knew Johns was an advocate; at least not until this particular spray.

In St Louis, Johns again turned on the crowd: 'You guys are too quiet!' he yelled. 'I've tried but you aren't saying anything. We're going to play now, so you shut the fuck up and we will play. Just sit there like you are and rock out like you fucking should!' During 'Freak', he gave the crowd the finger, and changed the already tweaked lyrics to: 'Body and soul/Suck my dick'. Happy he was not.

In Atlanta three nights later, a protest group by the name of Be Level-Headed picketed the Hard Rock Fest '99, where Silverchair were playing. They cited 'Suicidal Dream' and 'Israel's Son' as 'particularly offensive'. Acting on a request from organisers, the band dropped both songs from their performance. Nonetheless, Johns, dripping sarcasm, stopped the show mid-set to give Be Level-Headed a fair serve: 'That's what we do with our music, we promote violence, according to the church. The church is always right. So, we promote violence, sorry. Can I get a halle-fucking-lujah?'

Johns then jammed 'Advance Australia Fair', which was completely lost on the American crowd.

Occasionally, Johns would slip up and hint at the source of his irritation. After playing a desultory 'Tomorrow' in Denver, he said: 'Thanks, that's our only hit. That's when we were an Australian teenage grunge sensation. Now we're just a rock band, according to the press.'

Despite all this turmoil, the band still pulled the A-listers. In Vancouver on 14 July, Johns got into a shouting match with a surly punter while Hole's Courtney Love and Samantha Moloney looked on. In San Francisco, Limp Bizkit's Fred Durst stood at the side of the stage, mouthing most of Johns's lyrics like the star-struck fan he clearly was.

If Johns wasn't getting into verbal spars with punters, he was inviting them up on stage. He tried this out in Dallas in early June during 'Anthem for the Year 2000'; by tour's end it became a regular feature of a night out with Wacky Daniel. Johns would assemble a choir onstage, and then encourage them to chant 'We are the youth' at the top of their lungs. The lucky ones stood on a specially prepared choir stand, wearing T-shirts printed by the band. It was anything-goes chaos.

But despite the many faces of Daniel Johns—Rock God, crowd-baiter, blasphemer, hit-and-miss stand-up comic, evangelist, choir master—he remained at a distance from both bandmates and crowd. While Gillies, and sometimes Joannou and Holloway, were signing autographs and posing for snaps with fans after their shows, Johns would either be holed up on the bus or hiding out in his hotel room. People bothered him.

Back in Australia during July, Johns encouraged another onstage invasion during 'Anthem'. But when one female fan tried to get too close to Johns, he freaked out. 'Let go of me now,' he said. 'I've dealt with psychos enough this week.' Johns wasn't blowing smoke—a few days earlier, on 26 July, he'd been cleared of an allegation of harassment filed by Jodie Ann Marie Barnes, another Silverchair obsessive, who had a long history of mental illness. Her application was dismissed, but not before a Newcastle newspaper ran a photo of Johns with the headline: 'He's Got a Gun!' Johns snapped back: 'I hope that the media covers the truth of this matter as prominently as they covered the lies'.

Next up was another lap of Europe, supporting old buddies the Red Hot Chili Peppers, and a final fling in the USA, before an album-closing circuit of Australia, in late November and early December. The sometimes bizarre, physically and emotionally draining *Neon Ballroom* tour ended in Sydney's Domain on 11 December, when the band headlined the annual Homebake festival. With Triple J having gone nationwide, and television shows such as *Recovery* spreading the word about homegrown music, it was a good time for local bands—many of whom, such as Grinspoon, Powderfinger and Jebediah, were inspired by Silverchair's success.

Silverchair had made it known that the Sydney Homebake show would be their last for at least twelve months. They were exhausted after the past five years, and needed a break from music, the road and from each other.

'I'm dreaming about seeing friends and not being tied to a schedule,' Johns said prior to the show. 'Stuff that doesn't involve promoting the band or being Mr Silverchair.' Just before going on, he was in a more upbeat mood, laughing with a Channel [v] reporter about 'Smooth', the hit for Rob Thomas and Santana. 'It's got that Latino groove,' Johns said, smiling, 'which the kids are loving lately.'

And what can the crowd tonight expect?

'Just pyrotechnics,' Johns said with a reasonably straight face. 'Guns. Explosions. Cannons. Anything that makes a loud noise and shoots something hard . . . it's what the kids want.'

Backstage, a rumour was doing the rounds that this was it, the band were breaking up. Side of stage, Natalie Imbruglia looked on, alongside her sister, Laura. The doe-eyed pop star (and former *Neighbours* actress) had hooked up with Johns two months earlier at the ARIAs; their relationship blossomed as they locked into a serious conversation at an afterparty at the Gazebo Hotel. In fact, they were still talking the next morning in a Kings Cross bar.

Taking the stage at Homebake after Powderfinger, Jebediah, Eskimo Joe and Deadstar, the sight of Johns in his amazing technicolour rock suit—a purple, spangled, mirrored, custom-made rock suit, no less—sent the Domain crowd nuts. Johns was a true star, as conflicted as that role made him feel. The band understood the significance of the event, too, and had organised a bigger light show, more of a production. No guns or cannons, admittedly, but it was still a visual feast.

Liberated by the fact that this was the end of the tour—and thrilled to be back in front of an Australian crowd—the band shed the year's baggage like an old skin. They poured themselves into 'Israel's Son', where Gillies—introduced to the crowd by Johns as '154 kilograms of glory!'—took the lead, pounding his drum kit like it had done him wrong. Johns called for some 'hallelujahs', before the band unleashed 'Emotion Sickness', keyboardist Holloway doing a fair take on Helfgott's frenetic piano part. Before 'The Door', Johns went one further, demanding a final 'halle-fucking-lujah'. The crowd obliged.

By the time they reached 'Miss You Love', the Domain had been transformed (as reported in *Rolling Stone*) into 'stadium rock proper, from the single spotlight on Johns for the first verse to the background drench of red in the chorus and the rapturous crowd singalong'. Johns—as he'd done frequently during the *Neon Ballroom* shows, when not pissing people off—turned on the charm, riffing on Lou Bega's 'Mambo Number Five' and Christina Aguilera's 'Genie in a Bottle' (no 'Smooth', though), before tearing into 'Freak' and then 'Anthem for the Year 2000'.

'Louder!' Johns yelled to the Homebake masses, slowing down 'Anthem' until they joined in with all the gusto he demanded.

Finally, drained, the band ran offstage, with the thunderous roar of 20,000 fans ringing in their ears.

But the show wasn't over yet.

Johns returned to the stage a few minutes later. 'We're not supposed to do an encore, but we'll do it because we love you.'

They duly brought down the curtain on the night, the tour and the album—and, some thought, maybe even their career—with a roaring 'Spawn Again'.

As they drove back to Newcastle, Johns's bandmates were readying themselves for a whole lot of nothing, unsure if they'd ever tour or record again. Johns had no idea himself.

9

When I finished [the song] . . . it was like
I was on top of the world, looking down on
everything. It was better than any drug.

—Daniel Johns

AFTER THE *NEON BALLROOM* TOUR, Johns was determined to wean himself off the antidepressants that he had
come to rely on throughout 1998 and 1999. It was tough
therapy. Johns returned to the therapist's couch, an experience he found 'uncomfortable', but more rewarding than in
the past. He'd also 'kind of' broken up with Imbruglia (his
words), due to the difficulties of being based in different parts
of the planet. He didn't want to shift to the UK, where she lived.
He needed, again in his own words, 'to get my shit sorted out'.

'All of a sudden,' Johns said, as his antidepressant
dependency waned, 'I started appreciating the ups, which
I hadn't felt for such a long time.' The one drug he now took
was Valium and, even then, only when he needed to face a
group of people.

It was during this period of recovery—and a proposed one-year break from Silverchair—that Johns and his friend Paul Mac started to piece together a project that would become known as *I Can't Believe It's Not Rock*. This was an important relationship for Johns, the first time he'd stepped beyond the confines of his day band.

The Mac–Johns partnership was an unlikely liaison, at least on paper. Openly gay, Mac was best known as part of underground dance duo Itch-E and Scratch-E. He left his mark on the local industry when he publicly thanked Australia's ecstasy dealers while collecting a Best Dance Artist ARIA in 1995. (Johns, a teenager at the time, saw Mac's infamous ARIAs speech on the television and made a decision on the spot. 'I fucking *have* to meet this guy.') Mac was a funny, friendly dude, as warm as a headful of the 'love drug'. These were not the kind of traits you'd typically ascribe to the withdrawn Johns, who didn't trust too many people, yet he connected powerfully with Mac.

'I love the guy,' Johns told me, without hesitation. 'Music is our middle ground, but we have a really good friendship. There's something about when we play music together. It's great. He's really important to me.'

Their connection ran deeper than music, as Johns pointed out. While Johns was working his way out of his antidepressant, post–*Neon Ballroom* stupor, he'd spend days with only Sweep for company, rarely leaving the house. Occasionally he'd drive down to Mac's home studio in the Blue Mountains to jam and hang out. But there was one day when Johns simply couldn't face the trip: the idea of leaving his house and dealing with the drive freaked him out. Mac knew the solution. He jumped in his car, drove the three hours from his Blue Mountains home to Johns's spread in Newcastle, and played chauffeur for the day, shuttling Johns back and forth.

The other Silver-guys, meanwhile, spent their downtime enjoying the spoils of several years' hard slog. Joannou bought a good-sized property on the New South Wales Central Coast at Macmasters Beach for a little over A$1 million. It was the site of a former B&B, which now encompassed a main dwelling, a guesthouse and a studio. He became a regular face on the Sydney social circuit, often with his girlfriend, fellow muso Sarah McLeod of the band Superjesus. Gillies bought several small properties in and around Newcastle and briefly took a job at Sound World records in Hunter Street, Newcastle, stocking shelves and ringing up sales, sampling the so-called 'real' world. 'I don't know how I lasted six months,' he admitted. The 9-to-5 wasn't for Gillies.

Johns, meanwhile, had found a multimillion-dollar spread in Merewether's very own 'millionaire's row'. The spacious interior was decorated *à la minimalist*: here a stylish lampshade, there a Brett Whiteley print. A shining piano sat in his lounge room, on which Johns now wrote. Next to the piano was a huge entertainment centre. Some of Johns's own art—a handy outlet when he wasn't writing music—was framed and scattered around the lounge room. A telescope stood in an otherwise empty room. There was a home studio downstairs. The sun shimmered off a swimming pool on the deck. The only real rock-star trapping was a framed copy of Black Sabbath's *Paranoid* album, an eighteenth-birthday gift from former girlfriend Aimee Osbourne.

The view of the Pacific Ocean from Johns's deck was stunning, virtually uninterrupted. On some nights, the horns of the tankers about to enter Newcastle harbour were the only noise that cut through the silence. It could be a lonely, solitary place. Five minutes down the road, in what was once a typically modest Merewether house, Johns's parents lived in a now stylish two-storey suburban home.

Johns has no problem with Merewether's solitude. In fact, he was so comfortable that he rarely left during 2000 and 2001. His parents would phone, Johns would say he was okay: he was working; there was no need to worry.

Johns's days would fall into a familiar pattern: he'd drop Sweep at his parents' home and, while they'd walk his dog on the beach, Johns would return home, sit at his piano and write. But there was little of the darkness of early 1998, when he almost died. He was just lost in his work; he was obsessed. Some nights it was too much; there was music everywhere and Johns would wear earplugs to bed, because he 'could hear melodies in the cicadas outside' that stopped him from sleeping.

Johns had no qualms about his obsessive, hermit-like behaviour; it was almost expected of him. His family, too, were starting to accept his reclusiveness.

'They've seen me much worse,' Johns insisted.

Back at Silverchair HQ, there'd been some big changes. The band had split with their label, Sony—a crushed John

O'Donnell said 'it was like walking away from mates'—and signed directly with Atlantic in North America, the home of AC/DC and Led Zeppelin, pocketing a sweet six-figure advance. Manager Watson set up his own boutique label in October 2000—*Spinal Tap* fan Watson named his company Eleven. Over time it would become the label of choice for Missy Higgins and Paul Mac, and it would release all future Silverchair music in Australia.

The first Eleven release, in December 2000, was Daniel Johns and Paul Mac's experimental five-track *I Can't Believe It's Not Rock* EP. At first, the music they made together hadn't even been planned for release; it was just for fun, a chance for Johns to work with someone new. But he and Mac liked the results so much they decided to release it publicly, but not in the typical manner. It was a record so deliberately under-the-radar it was first sold only via the internet, with some proceeds going to charity. 'It's a different sort of project,' Johns said, 'so it makes sense to release it in a different sort of way.'

Johns and Mac premiered a few of the songs with a performance on the ABC television drama *Love Is a Four Letter Word*, an episode filmed not long after the EP's release. Mac played keyboards and Johns—decked out in porn-star shades and one of the most garish cardigans ever seen— sang and played guitar, grinning madly. It didn't seem to matter that they were miming; they were having a blast. The program's producer, Rosemary Blight, was thrilled. 'Daniel Johns was fantastic,' she gushed. 'He arrived with the brilliant Paul Mac, played great music, sent the crowd wild.'

Johns rounded off his big day out by smiling for photos, signing autographs and playing soccer with the series' star, Peter Fenton, former frontman for indie rock band Crow. But no one in the Sydney studio knew what a struggle it had been for Johns to actually get there. He'd hardly left his house for the past twelve months.

◄○►

Johns's slow return to the spotlight cranked up another gear when he agreed to play two big gigs, the Falls Festival and Rock in Rio III, thereby scotching rumours that Silverchair's Homebake finale was the end of the band. His bandmates were surprised when they got the call.

'I thought, "Holy fuck!"' Gillies said, when he was told Johns had okayed the dates. 'We'd just had this weird tour: things were a bit rocky—we weren't sure if we were going to stay together.'

The Falls Festival was held at Lorne, a coastal town a couple of hours' drive west of Melbourne. The festival stretched over two days, with the midnight New Year's Eve slot reserved for Silverchair, the headliner.

As was their way, Joannou and Gillies arrived earlier on the day of their gig, wandering through the crowd and checking out other bands on the bill, which included Sarah McLeod and Superjesus. But Johns arrived with barely enough time to change and prepare himself for the set. Wearing a knee-length, designer-made, sequinned coat, even more dazzling than the glittery outfit he sported during the *Neon Ballroom* tour, Johns led the band through a favourites-heavy set, including a slightly reworked 'Ana's Song' and 'Freak'. They also debuted two new songs, 'One Way Mule' and 'Hollywood'.

'It was great, we had a ball,' Joannou reported from backstage after the well-received set. By that time, Johns was well and truly out of there, but if he'd hung about, he would have definitely agreed.

As good as the experience was, the Falls Festival was purely a warm-up. Silverchair's spot at the Rock in Rio festival on 21 January 2001 was the first time they'd been in South America since the craziness of 1996. Rock in Rio was the largest rock-and-roll gathering in the world, a cross between the Big Day Out, Woodstock and the UK's mammoth Glastonbury Festival—and then amplified by eleven. Aware of the significance of the event, the band rented a space in Newcastle and put in weeks of solid rehearsals. Only then were they ready to rock. In Rio.

The vibe at Rio was overwhelmingly positive. Sure, the portaloos overflowed, and most of the 250,000-per-day crowd—the event stretched for seven days in the midst of a sizzling Brazilian summer—headbanged ankle-deep in the sea of mud created by the high-pressure water hoses used to spray the revellers. But this was an angst-free, good-natured rock-and-roll celebration. Patronised by Brazilian teenagers starved of live (Western) rock bands, it was a massive success, and raised around US$1.5 million for local charities. As for the crowd, they spray-painted their hair every colour of the rainbow and flaunted T-shirts that screamed 'Fuck me I'm famous'. Inflatable sharks bounced around the massive mosh pit like beach balls at a Flaming Lips show.

The stage itself was a monumental piece of engineering. Forty metres high and 90 metres wide, it was built from 200 tonnes of steel. Oasis's Noel Gallagher took in the stage setting, the massive crowd and the entire event, and shouted to a journalist: 'It's actually fucking genius. It's the most disgusting, brilliant, outrageous thing I've seen in my life.'

Silverchair were billed as the penultimate act on the event's final night, directly before the Red Hot Chili Peppers. On the band bus heading to the show, Joannou summed up everyone's feelings: 'It's beyond being nervous,' he said. 'I mean, even 100,000 people is incomprehensible. So, the prospect of over 250,000 just doesn't register.'

Band nerves were given another serious jangle when they arrived at the site and were told that they were due onstage in 45 minutes, not two hours as they'd expected. Someone had buggered up the scheduling. They each took a deep breath and started hurriedly scribbling a set list.

A chorus of screams rang around the stadium when Johns's image first appeared on the massive video screen at the rear of the stage; his spangly coat was dazzling. The ladies loved him. Johns responded by dropping into a sexy falsetto during a blazing 'Israel's Son'; by the end of that first song, he and the band were dripping sweat, sucking in lungfuls of oxygen. As the set progressed, they mixed up the moods, playing the mellower 'Ana's Song' and a majestic 'Miss You Love' alongside the fast and furious 'Pure Massacre' and 'Slave'.

They also aired new tracks 'Hollywood' and 'One Way Mule', as they'd done at the Falls Festival.

Johns was a man liberated. He playfully greeted the crowd in Portuguese—'that's Brazilian for thank you'—and gave a clearly unscripted speech about war and peace. 'You're here to Rock in Rio for peace in Rio and all the rest of the countries,' he stated with half a smile. 'Okay, you don't like certain places and they don't like you, but that's cool. It's all about peace. Well, sometimes it's about peace, sometimes you need to be violent . . .' Johns even made a curious aside about being a buddy of Ronaldo, the Brazilian soccer hero. 'He's our friend!' Who cared if he was making shit up?

A massive singalong erupted at the start of 'Anthem for the Year 2000'. It was so loud, in fact, that Johns stopped playing, clapping his hands above his head as 250,000 fans screamed his lyrics right back at him. A teary-eyed female fan held up a T-shirt declaring 'We are the youth'. A song that had come to Johns in a dream about rocking a massive stadium crowd was now coming to life before his make-up-stained 'panda' eyes. (The heat had taken its toll on him.) It was an incredible, once-in-a-lifetime sight.

'You guys have been the biggest and the best crowd ever in the whole entire world,' Johns said—and this time he meant every word. 'You rock. It's crazy.'

The band closed with a roaring take on 'Freak', Johns, seemingly possessed by the spirits of Tiny Tim *and* Ozzy Osbourne, switching between a squeaky falsetto and a zombie growl. Joannou, Holloway and Gillies eventually stumbled offstage as Johns drenched the audience in a spray of feedback—for his finale, Johns stood at stage front with his guitar balanced on his shoulders, behind his head. It was the perfect rock pose.

This time, post-gig, Johns did hang about. He and the others smiled for photos and scribbled autographs. Johns positively beamed. They even re-connected with *Frogstomp* producer Kevin Shirley, who mixed the band's live sound for the mammoth television broadcast of the event.

'That was great,' Shirley said of the band's set. 'It was an amazing gig; I thought they were fantastic.'

Johns finally headed back to the hotel, leaving Joannou, Gillies and various members of their management and crew to kick on at a local strip club. There they witnessed the truly bizarre sight of a transvestite doing his/her thing to Midnight Oil's 'Beds Are Burning'.

The next day, Johns's face was splashed all over the front page of the local newspaper, *O Globo*. Their set was described as the 'surprise highlight of the day'. It left everyone wondering whether it was Silverchair or the Red Hot Chili Peppers who'd closed Rock in Rio III. Gillies summed it up when he declared: 'Rock in Rio was undoubtedly the most amazing experience we've ever had as a band'. As for Johns, he was thankful that the lengthy flight home from Brazil gave him and his bandmates time to slowly return to earth. When he did, Johns recalled that he still had a new album to write.

◄○►

Diorama was a record with a false start. Johns felt dissatisfied with some of the music he'd been writing during 2000; the songs seemed too easy, too familiar, full of the crashing riffs and heavy feelings that had marked *Frogstomp* and *Freak Show*, and to a lesser extent *Neon Ballroom*. He needed to change things up, embrace the future.

Johns's frustration boiled over in February 2001, soon after returning from Rio. He spent two virtually sleepless weeks walking Merewether Beach and fretting about whether he'd ever move forward with his songwriting. Finally, Johns made a huge decision and erased the two hours' worth of material he'd recorded.

'They just sounded too much like the last album,' he told me, when I covered the making of the record for *Rolling Stone*. 'I knew it was a risk, but I [also] knew if I kept them they'd be a safety net.'

Not surprisingly, this was one hell of a liberating act. A new song called 'Across the Night' soon emerged. Johns had been working out the many pieces of the track in his head for weeks before it finally all came together during an all-night writing session, with the rain pelting down outside.

Song completed, Johns, with the ever-present Sweep, went and stood in the downpour, soaking himself in an effort to come down from this natural high. 'When I finished [the song],' he said, 'it must be the feeling people get when they do intense meditation. My body felt really long, my spine felt really elongated; it was like I was on top of the world, looking down on everything. It was better than any drug.'

Then he headed back inside, stood in the shower 'and pretended I was still in the rain'. He finally crashed at about 6.30 in the morning, mission accomplished.

Gradually, *Diorama*'s songs started to take shape: the elegant 'Luv Your Life', the hook-heavy 'The Greatest View', among others. Johns previewed the new tunes to a select group of people: his brother, Heath, manager Watson and Paul Mac. But not his bandmates. Not yet.

Paul Mac wasn't prepared for the shock he felt on hearing these new songs. After Johns played him a few different pieces, Mac was lost for words. He was amazed.

'Fuck,' he finally gasped, *'what is this?'*

'I didn't get it,' Mac laughed when I asked about his reaction. 'Because he's not [musically] trained, here's this incredibly complicated stuff.'

Mac's new role was to act as musical translator, helping Johns get down on paper the music he was hearing in his head.

With recording planned to begin in April 2001, Gillies and Joannou got a call from Johns to visit him at home; he wanted them to hear his new material. For Johns, there was some of the same trepidation he had felt unveiling the *Neon Ballroom* songs, when Nick Launay acted as mediator. But this time around he went it alone. The others settled in while Johns lit a joint—he'd been smoking a lot, finding it a useful writing aid—sat down at his grand piano and played the oddly titled 'Tuna in the Brine' to the Silver-pair.

Just like Mac, neither Joannou nor Gillies knew quite what to say. Finally, Gillies broke the ice. He was impressed but a little bewildered.

'How the fuck are we going to remember that?'

Johns started another song. 'This one sounds Beach Boys-y,' he told his bandmates.

'Some of those arrangements are pretty complex,' Joannou understated neatly after another lengthy pause. Still, they accepted what Johns was trying to do.

Not only did Johns have the thumbs up from Mac, but his bandmates were also on board with the new music he was writing—and the three also discovered a shared addiction to the hit new television series *Big Brother*, which became their one main distraction during this lively time. When not glued to the small screen, Johns kept writing these bold, cinematic songs, which were the next logical step from *Neon Ballroom* tracks such as 'Emotion Sickness' and 'Miss You Love'. But this time around there was a key difference—Johns wasn't digging into his heart of darkness for inspiration; instead, he was opening up to the world around him. He'd made a decision to write a hopeful, outward-looking album rather than another 40 minutes of self-flagellation; he was going to tap into his imagination, not his pain. It also helped that for the first time he was writing on piano and recording music on reliable home-recording gear (which Mac had helped install), rather than banging out demos on his guitar and recording them on cheap cassettes. Now he could experiment with vocal ideas and more complex arrangements before the band hit the studio proper. This was to have a major impact on *Diorama*.

But choosing a producer wasn't easy. The band needed someone different, someone who could grasp where Johns was heading. The nod went to Canadian-born, British-based David Bottrill, a bookish type with a shaved skull, glasses and a thoughtful nature. He'd produced albums by Tool, King Crimson, Peter Gabriel—even pop belter Toni Childs. Bottrill's work with Tool proved he could handle heavy sounds, but his production work with Gabriel was just as crucial, because Gabriel was a songwriter who shared Johns's widescreen ambition. Bottrill had been introduced to Silverchair by Tool's Adam Jones, who was mad for Johns's guitar sounds.

Before disappearing into the studio, the band spent some time at Mangrove Studios on the Central Coast during April, finetuning their home recordings with Phil McKellar, getting them ready for Bottrill. For the Sydney-based producer, it was a sort of homecoming; he'd remained on the Silverchair radar since producing the first version of 'Tomorrow' for *nomad*. Upon hearing these new songs, McKellar was floored. He thought that 'Tuna in the Brine', in particular, was a stone-cold classic.

'Hearing those demos,' he recalled, 'I knew something magic was going to happen. I really liked the immediacy of the demos; I had shivers up my spine. Daniel's such a talent.'

Johns, Watson and producer Bottrill had first met in LA; not long after that, Bottrill had an interesting meeting with reps from Atlantic, whose head of A&R, Kevin Williamson, was a big Daniel Johns advocate. He considered him 'a star'. He'd been listening to some of the demos, among them 'Tuna in the Brine', but when Williamson played that to other Atlantic staffers, there was a deafening silence in the room.

'How are we going to sell that?' someone asked.

It was a fair question.

'To be honest,' Williamson said, 'that . . . did make us all take a step back and go, "How are we going to get this on the radio?" But at the same time, I think Daniel knew he had to let it all out and then sit back and evaluate it.'

'There was no secret about Daniel's grand plans [for the album],' producer Bottrill said to me, 'but [Atlantic] felt he'd still write the big rock hit. But he simply didn't want to do that.'

Bottrill hooked up with Johns and the others in June 2001, in the band's comfort zone of Newcastle. It was a strangely familiar environment for Bottrill, who'd grown up in the very blue-collar town of Hamilton, Ontario. ('But it doesn't have a beach,' he laughed.) Bottrill was quickly introduced to the harder edge of Newcastle after the first day of rehearsals, when he and Gillies went for a drink in a nearby pub. They'd barely sipped their first beer when a fight erupted, the brawlers spilling over them and into the street. Gillies shrugged and kept drinking; Bottrill wondered what he'd gotten himself into.

Johns requested that the band not revisit what he called the 'night orientated' vibe of *Neon Ballroom*, so Bottrill would convene with the band at 10.30 a.m. each day for the next few weeks as they worked through the new songs. Silverchair were now working the morning shift, even though Johns admitted 'it was really weird' to play music so early in the day.

'I was trying to reverse things this time around,' he explained.

Once these rehearsals were wrapped—and after the band's first meeting with Atlantic's Kevin Williamson, who travelled to Newcastle and subtly suggested to Johns to 'at least give me a couple of songs we could get on radio'— formal sessions for *Diorama* began in July at Sydney's Studios 301. (The Whitlams and Midnight Oil were recording *Torch the Moon* and *Capricornia*, respectively, elsewhere in the complex.)

Erecting the Silverchair table-tennis table was one of the first priorities for the band, as they settled in. As always, videographer Robert Hambling recorded the making of the album. Engineer Anton Hagop was producer Bottrill's quietly spoken sidekick (he went on to win an ARIA for his work). Assistant engineer Matt 'Gizmo' Lovell, a Novocastrian who'd learned his trade at Sydney's Festival Studios alongside Kevin Shirley, helped out on the technical side, and then documented events for the band's website. As Lovell would tell me, he had various roles, not the least being 'vibe guy'. During more difficult moments, Lovell's amiable yet forthright nature helped alleviate any tension.

Basic tracks were recorded during July and August. Old faithfuls Paul Mac chimed in on piano and Jim Moginie added some keyboard squiggles to 'The Greatest View' and 'One Way Mule' (the latter the only song Johns saved from the tape he'd scrapped earlier in the year). Bassist Joannou and drummer Gillies spent a lot of time playing table tennis with Watson, but Daniel Johns rarely left the control room. He was absorbed in the making of this record.

'This was absolutely Daniel's album,' Bottrill said, 'and the band were happy about that. He really wanted to make this statement. Ben and Chris were curious as to how it would play out—they were happy to run with it. I'm not sure if they shared Daniel's vision, but there was no backroom bitching.'

Johns knew exactly which songs on the album were better suited to a big production: he could hear where the orchestra belonged. 'Tuna' was pivotal. Bottrill thought 'Tuna' was an 'epic'. 'My first reaction was, what a great piece to work on. [And] that is the album, right there.'

In late September 2001, the band (plus Bottrill, his two engineers and Johns's sidekick, Sweep) shifted camp to Mangrove Studios. Here they started to experiment with some of the songs, adding extra texture to the basic recordings. Johns's mood was up—the songs were coming together almost as he'd planned them in his head. The only interruption was a visit from a Channel [v] crew, who announced that the band had won their fifth consecutive Viewer's Choice award. Johns, Gillies and Joannou laughed their way through the interview, which was aired at October's ARIA awards. It wasn't lost on them that they'd won an award by doing very little. They were Australian music's Invisible Men.

'We know other bands deserved it,' Johns mugged to the camera, 'but we're the 'Chair!'

By early October, the band were back in Sydney's Studios 301, confronting the most challenging—and costly—stage of the recording: the orchestration for six of the album's tracks. Once again, Johns co-composed the arrangements for three of these ('The Greatest View', 'World Upon Your Shoulders' and 'My Favourite Thing') with Larry Muhoberac. Then came the real glittering prize: a fortnight with legendary American arranger/composer Van Dyke Parks, who penned arrangements for 'Across the Night', 'Tuna in the Brine' and 'Luv Your Life', writing parts for strings, woodwind, brass, harp and percussion.

The 60-something Parks was 24-carat rock-and-roll royalty. With his natural charm, distinctive Southern accent and thing for bow ties and braces, Parks was not your typical studio dude: Bottrill quickly tagged him 'the campest straight man I've ever met'. Parks had collaborated with Beach Boy Brian Wilson on his great lost album, *Smile*, and was often cited as the man who steered Wilson away from the more commercially orientated Beach Boys, freeing his music while Brian messed up his mind. With Wilson, Parks co-wrote the classic 'Heroes and Villains' (and the not-so-classic 'Vegetables'). Parks had also worked his sonic alchemist's trick on albums from The Byrds, Fiona Apple, Ry Cooder and U2. Typically, Parks downplayed his legacy, calling himself a 'whore' who made his living in the hustler's paradise that was Hollywood.

Avuncular and often downright hilarious, Parks was a studio master—and he quickly recognised a spark in Johns that he recalled from his own musical youth. They became very close friends.

'I see all the musical qualities in him I heard and saw in Brian Wilson,' he told me, during the only interview he

granted while working on *Diorama*. '[Daniel's] an unde-
feated romantic; an informed optimist. I know there's a
lot of dark meat on that bird, but lurking in there is the
voice of the human spirit. When I got the new material,
I was astounded by the musicality, the lyrics, brimming
with enthusiasm and a life force that guarantees this group
as a continuing major force in music.'

Mind you, Parks almost didn't make the trip at all. Watson
had put forward Parks's name as a possible collaborator, but
believed there was a slight problem. 'I think he's dead.' (Parks
found this so funny that he started signing off emails as 'the
recently deceased Van Dyke Parks'.) When they learned he
was still breathing, Johns and Watson put in a call to Parks.

'The first thing we heard was Van Dyke on the other end,
playing the piano,' Johns recalled. 'I thought we were on
hold before I realised. That was a good lesson: sometimes
it's best to give yourself up musically rather than saying
something.'

'I know a lot of talented guys, I've worked with them—
I've almost made a career out of surrounding myself with
talented people,' said Parks, during a rare moment of
downtime at Studios 301. 'This offer came out of the ether;
it was a blessing. When I looked into this work, immediately I wanted to weep. I thought the vocalist was in dead
earnest; I liked that person, I wanted to know who he was.
And this beat seeing David Crosby in a jacuzzi. This is
someone I wanted to know.'

Parks's children had been big fans of *Frogstomp*. 'It
was throbbing through the walls, especially when they

had guests. I got curious about it, but could never have imagined that I would be fortunate enough to work on a project of theirs.'

Johns and Parks conjured up some true musical magic in the two weeks they shared. The orchestrations were signature Van Dyke Parks: epic, sweeping and dramatic, full of rich sonic detail and golden melodies (possibly too much detail; a lot of what was recorded was trimmed during the album's final mix). The most ambitious songs of Daniel Johns's life had been transformed into the band's best recordings—and some of Parks's finest work.

10

He was just doing his job—
and his job fucked with my head.
—Daniel Johns

BY EARLY DECEMBER, Johns's mood wasn't so upbeat. He'd been in Los Angeles for a fortnight, mixing *Diorama* with Bottrill. Throughout the making of the album, the execs from Atlantic Records, while they liked what they were hearing, still hadn't heard that one key song they felt would get the band radio airplay. Atlantic's concerns boiled over while Johns was absorbed with finishing the mix of the album. They asked him to write a song 'to order', something that would fit on American rock radio. Nickelback's dire 'How You Remind Me' was currently all over the charts; couldn't he come up with something like that?

Johns wasn't the first rock musician to be confronted with this dilemma. When British band Radiohead delivered their 1997 album *OK Computer* to their US label Capitol, the execs there thought it was commercial suicide and lowered their sales forecast from two million to barely half a million. The band changed nothing; the LP became a classic and, over time, sold five million copies. On the flipside, when AC/DC's American label (also Atlantic) ordered them back into the studio to 'write a single' in 1978, they came up with the great 'Rock 'n' Roll Damnation', which became their first UK Top 40 hit—so sometimes the ploy worked. But writing a song on spec held no interest for Daniel Johns, especially when he'd almost finished work on Silverchair's most accomplished and detailed record.

'He'd made his statement,' figured Bottrill, 'and he had nothing left.'

When I met Johns in LA, briefly, he was quiet, sullen and clearly distracted by the demands of Atlantic. In the past, he'd been shielded by Watson from much of the business of music, but was now face to face with the commercial expectations of a major label. This was a new and uncomfortable situation for him, far worse than deciding 'What sucks the least?'.

'We just weren't right, we weren't compatible,' Johns said of his relationship with Atlantic's Kevin Williamson. 'He was just doing his job—and his job fucked with my head. He knew that Americans wouldn't buy that record, while I was eternally optimistic that if it's good enough they would.'

Eventually, a compromise was reached when Johns wrote a song called 'Ramble', but to record it necessitated an operation almost on a military scale. Johns, Bottrill and the crew had to fly from LA to Sydney and get together with Gillies and Joannou to cut the song. The band agreed that it was the most extreme act of record-company excess they'd ever witnessed. And Johns did not love the song.

According to Johns, 'Ramble' was a 'piece of shit. I hate it'. This by-the-numbers rocker ended up as a B-side for the 'Without You' single, even though Kevin Williamson thought it was 'a good song'.

Further complicating an already uncomfortable scene in LA was the increasing pain Johns was feeling in his knees. There were several contributing factors at work here: the stress brought on by both finishing the record and trying to pull a hit out of his skinny backside, and the fact that his diet, although improved, still wasn't quite what a nutritionist would recommend. In fact, David Bottrill could only ever recall seeing Johns eat fruit during the months they spent together.

'Don't just eat the fruit plate,' he advised Johns.

The producer also noticed that his star performer was developing some severe rashes.

Although Johns was well enough to walk away from the studio when the mix was eventually completed in early 2002, Bottrill could see that Johns's health was failing. 'He was getting tired more often—and a lot quicker.' One morning Johns awoke and his knees ached; he said it felt as though he'd somehow twisted them overnight.

There was one highlight during their stay in LA. Johns, Bottrill, engineer Lovell and Natalie Imbruglia, with whom Johns had re-connected, had a chance meeting with U2's Bono in a club, and he invited them back to his suite at the Chateau Marmont, LA's premier rock-and-roll hotel (the same hot spot where the Red Hot Chili Peppers had written some of their *Californication* album, and John Belushi had died of a massive drug overdose).

'What are you doing in town?' a bathrobe-clad Bono asked Johns, as other guests—Billy Corgan and Gwen Stefani among them—drifted about his suite.

A bit wary that they'd be seen as abusing his hospitality, the Silverchair crew reluctantly handed him a tape of the *Diorama* track 'Luv Your Life', which Bono then proceeded to play over and over again, to the increasing chagrin of his other guests. Bono loved the song so much that he later declared, 'Swim to Australia to hear it if you have to.' His statement, ironically, would prove to be very close to the truth.

———◦———

The first single to be released from *Diorama* was the defiant 'The Greatest View', a very clear statement from Johns about the new, positive state of both his mind and his music (if not his body). 'The Greatest View' was made available on www.chairpage.com before its official release and rapidly became the most downloaded song in Australian music history. Ten thousand copies of the single were quickly streamed. It was another smart move on Silverchair's part—what better way to re-connect with your music-starved fans than offering them a freebie?

Complete with a dazzling new ensemble—a sheer black shirt, flecked with gold, pin-striped trousers and a hefty tuft of chin hair—Johns looked the part when he and the band stepped out to play the 2002 Big Day Out. He wasn't messing about, either: during 'Israel's Son', he pulled out every move in the rock-and-roll book, mock-shagging his amp, wringing raw feedback out of his guitar, waving and gesturing to the sizeable crowd. But the truth was that his body was hurting; his knees had swollen up like balloons, his joints ached. It was hardly the ideal way to start a lengthy cycle of promoting and playing a new album. Mega doses of painkillers helped get him through each (thankfully short) 50-minute set of the Big Day Out tour.

While not as talkative on stage as in the past, Johns did manage one public address before playing 'Miss You Love'. 'This song's one to calm down to,' he told the masses at the Gold Coast Big Day Out. 'Take it easy. Chill out. Enjoy yourself. Have a drink. Kiss. Make out with whoever you feel like.'

As funny as it was, there was a strained look on his face; the guy was in serious pain. Johns spent a lot of the gig with his heavy-lidded eyes closed. He still had no real idea what was going wrong with his body. Offstage he could barely walk, as the pain began to affect his knees, ankles, back and neck. The six Big Day Out gigs proved to be the only shows he'd play in 2002.

Johns's latest drama didn't prevent 'The Greatest View' from galloping into the Australian singles chart, debuting at number one on 4 February, soon after the 'Chair's last

Big Day Out set. It was a great relief for the band, given they'd spent so much time out of the spotlight while Powderfinger had taken over as the country's favourite alt-rock band. But the Brisbane band's songs didn't have the same obsessiveness heard in Johns's best, while their frontman, Bernard Fanning, despite owning a great, soulful voice, had nothing on Johns in the enigma/charisma department. And he definitely could not rock a glittery suit like Johns; Fanning wouldn't even try.

'The Greatest View' summed up Johns's new positivity; he described it to me as a song written for his parents, who'd always watched over him, especially when he was deep in depression in the late 1990s. But when a song opens with the line 'You're the analyst', it wouldn't be a stretch to think some of his on-couch experiences also influenced the lyrics. In his first round of press for *Diorama*, Johns repeated the words 'light', 'energy' and 'positive' like a mantra, even as the pain in his knees—and everywhere else—increased.

'It's not a record that is born out of misery, it's a record that is born out of optimism,' producer Bottrill told *The Sun-Herald* in January 2002, describing Johns as 'much more into the positive aspects of life now. Misery is easier than joy, I think, but ultimately joy is more satisfying. It's rare that you get to the end of a project and you're not sick of each other, but this was more like a relationship that I didn't want to end. I miss them all.' Bottrill called *Diorama* 'one of the greatest realisations of an artist's visions that I've been involved with'. He also told me that almost every band he's since worked with have referred to *Diorama* as a 'classic'.

Johns readily admitted that the three *Diorama* songs featuring heavy guitar grunt—'One Way Mule', 'The Lever' and 'Too Much of Not Enough'—were included purely for the benefit of those long-term fans who'd stuck with them since 1994. To Johns they were afterthoughts, songs that didn't 'fill any holes in my soul'. But commercial suicide was not a step that would thrill the band's management or US record company, who'd dropped a lot of money on *Diorama*. Johns knew that his audience had to be coaxed along, step by step, into his new music. He accepted that there'd always be an element of compromise, even if the 'Ramble' exercise had felt like a waste of time, money and what little energy he had at the time.

'You can't deny [the element of compromise],' said Johns. 'It's always there when you've got people who've supported you and bought your albums and gone to your shows: you have to say, "Here's a song for you". It's for the loyal people. Hopefully the other songs will challenge them. It's hard for bands to make the transition and still be taken seriously. But we were fourteen, and our fans were fourteen; we have to change. They've grown with our music, hopefully.'

Even though Johns still had his dark days, he was pushing himself to generate a more positive, uplifting message with his songs. He was older, he was antidepressant-free, he was in love with Imbruglia, and he was coming closer to realising the music he was hearing in his head. If only his body didn't hurt so much.

In the commercial scheme of things, *Diorama* was always going to be a tough sell. There was no obvious hit single, not a lot of trademark rock crunch, and little of the mad energy that had marked the band's earlier work (and, as it transpired, virtually no touring to support the record). The response to *Diorama* took a fairly predictable course: the first reaction was surprise but, once the music sank in, few critics thought it less than praiseworthy (apart from the fickle British music press, who never rated the band, but that was to be expected).

American *Rolling Stone* gushed: 'Johns and company have become genuine artists on their own terms. Heavy orchestration, unpredictable melodic shifts and a whimsical pop sensibility give *Diorama* the sweeping feel of the work of Brian Wilson or Todd Rundgren'. The reputable *All Music Guide* seemed shocked that the band had made it through the 1990s and outlived grunge: 'Mostly this is a wonderful surprise from a band thought to have been finished in the late 1990s'.

Silverchair had finally shaken off their Nirvana-in-pyjamas legacy with an album that displayed Johns's rich songwriting gifts and sizeable imagination. The album raced to number one in Australia on 7 April, going platinum in two weeks flat. Silverchair became the first Australian band to have four albums debut at number one. Not even INXS or Midnight Oil had managed that.

<hr />

Diorama's overseas release and promotion became a drama to rank with any in Johns's life to date. The overseas release

date was originally planned for July, and shows scheduled for June in London and New York had sold out well
in advance. But the release was rescheduled to 27 August
2002 when Johns was given a formal diagnosis—chronic
reactive arthritis—for his condition and cancelled all live
appearances. By now he couldn't even walk, let alone hold
a guitar.

Johns learned that he was in the unfortunate position of
being among the 6 per cent of Caucasian males—usually
in their twenties—who, due to a certain type of blood
tissue, are predisposed to this condition. (Another sufferer
is Australian test cricketer Michael Slater.) Similar to the
over-all 'achiness' that you experience during a bout of
influenza, but way more debilitating, reactive arthritis is
the body's own response running amok to a bacterial infec-
tion. Generally, knee, ankle and toe joints become painfully
inflamed, but the condition can also affect other parts of the
body. Because Johns's immune system had been weakened
during his eating disorder, and due to his susceptible blood
tissue type and high stress levels, reactive arthritis hit him
hard and fast. All album promo was on hold while he began
a search for suitable treatment.

Despite favourable chart placings in Canada and
Germany (the album was released in Europe on 29 July),
Diorama limped into the US charts at number 91 and was
gone within a fortnight. And this was despite Atlantic's
innovative promotion plan—web chats, free downloads and
streaming of earlier live shows, all on the band's official
website—designed to work around Johns's illness. There

was even talk of a limited theatrical release for the *Across the Night* DVD and a 'virtual tour', hosted on the band's website. None of this generated anything resembling a reasonable return on Atlantic's hefty investment.

Johns didn't seem too concerned when we spoke at the time about the album's state of wellbeing (or otherwise). 'I'm told it's not [dead],' he said, 'but I'm pretty confident it is. Everything's been contradictory. It's the only record I've made in my career that I'm really proud of, and it's the only one that's failed in America. I think it's a good indication of where my head is and where the American public's head is.'

But, throughout much of 2002, Johns had little time to think about the downward turn in his band's commercial worth. He'd become a virtual cripple. After the Big Day Out dates and a few shows in New Zealand, Silverchair management had done everything they could to keep the band touring: they'd pushed back the start date for rehearsals to help Johns recover; when that proved to be futile, they rehearsed without him, trying out a substitute guitarist, Dave Leslie, which would at least free Johns to focus on singing. (One of Johns's early heroes, Helmet guitarist Page Hamilton, had also expressed interest in standing in.) Julian Hamilton, who'd been hired as the band's new keyboardist, recalled how odd that particular experiment was. 'Rehearsing 'Chair songs with another guitarist playing Dan's part was very strange, let me tell you.'

In mid-2002, with the planned *Diorama* world tour only days away, Johns was finally brought into the rehearsal room; it was the last chance to run through their proposed set as a full band. Everyone was shocked by his appearance.

'Dan looked terrible,' said Hamilton. 'He was thin and weak, he looked out of his mind on painkillers. It was heartbreaking. He had a big smile and was pleased to see us, and we were stoked to see him—but we all knew there was something really wrong with him being there. You could tell, as much as the guy wanted to play and get involved, he was just too sick.

'That's when it sunk in for most of us, I think: there would be no tour.'

Within a few days, Hamilton and the rest of the band and crew got the call they'd all been expecting: the tour was off. The mood in camp Silverchair had never been darker; not only did they realise that the new album was about to stiff overseas, but their star was also in dangerously bad health.

—◀◦▶—

Johns would spend much of the next year searching both Australia and the USA for the right type of therapy to quite literally get him back on his feet. Imbruglia was by his side for much of the journey; his mother, Julie, also helped with the search. There were times when the pain he was feeling was so intense that he couldn't share a couch with another person; any movement would hit him with what felt like several thousand volts. The only time he willingly moved was to use the bathroom—he even tried not to drink too much water so nature didn't call too often. He couldn't take a shower, because the water pressure was simply too overwhelming, while the idea of singing, which involved deep breathing, was incomprehensible. Eventually, he'd be hospitalised; the left side of his body pretty much paralysed. He needed a wheelchair to make even the shortest journeys.

Johns's trauma lasted the better part of eight months, and he was in pain every single day. He was forced to move back into his parents' home; his body just wasn't up to the challenge of climbing the stairs at his house. Shockingly, he made a suicide pact with his brother, Heath, who was in the midst of his own turmoil, unable to find a job and feeling hopeless.

'We had set a date,' Johns told a reporter from UK tabloid *The Telegraph*, 'and if things hadn't gotten better by then, we would agree to kill ourselves . . . It was about the lowest I have ever been. I hated being so helpless.'

This was a staggering admission from Johns, a telltale sign of just how grim his life had become. He couldn't make music; he could barely hold a pen to write; having anyone near caused him debilitating pain; his doctors couldn't even tell him how long the agony would continue—Johns was a wreck.

Fortunately, by the time the Johns brothers reached their agreed deadline, things were on the up for both siblings. Heath had found a job, while his older brother finally found solace via a holistic practitioner in LA, who started him on a six-month regime that involved taking some 80 homeopathic pills per day, along with physio, aerobics and intensive massage. Johns also used an oxygen tent. 'I hated it,' he admitted, 'but it worked.' He slowly moved out of the wheelchair and onto crutches; sometimes he walked with a cane—a fancy cane, it should be said. The guy had style.

'The cane's a better look than crutches,' he said, managing a rare laugh. 'The crutch is not as cool.'

When we spoke at length in 2002 about his ongoing physical therapy, the description of what he was undergoing was enough to bring tears to my eyes, let alone Johns's. His body was being stretched and strained in all sorts of painful yet therapeutic ways. Still, he was surprisingly upbeat.

'There's no one who can give you sure answers that it [reactive arthritis] won't happen again in five years, but the doctor in LA is confident that she can fix all of this,' Johns said. 'I'm not going to get too depressed about it, because I can manage it. It's not too bad. But six months ago, if someone had told me this is the way it's going to be for five years, I would have killed myself.' Judging by the pact he'd made with his brother, he wasn't kidding.

Johns recorded a video message for fans, posted on the band's website. 'I'm doing everything I can to get better,' he said. 'Sorry we can't be out there on the road at the moment. Thanks for all your messages to get well—I'll try to get well soon.' Yet touring, hardly his favourite pursuit in the first place, was a long way from his thoughts.

In September 2002, Johns and the band appeared on the cover of French music mag *Rock Sound*. Johns looked awful. Heavy make-up and a few rock-star accoutrements—shades tucked into a natty scarf, loads of hair product—failed to distract from his hollow eyes and the anguished look on his face. At least he was upright: that was a breakthrough.

As his body slowly started to heal, Johns decided to propose to Imbruglia, who'd stuck with him throughout the whole ordeal, helped him find the right treatment and even played nursemaid to Johns when he was wheelchair-bound.

'I knew [then] I wanted to marry her,' Johns said. 'She was strong about it all. We've been through a lot together, and we appreciate each other more because of it.' They made plans for a wedding sometime in 2003.

———◄○►———

By late 2002, Daniel Johns was a new man. He'd moved out of his parents' house and into a luxury Bondi apartment. Locals were surprised not just by the sight of him, but also by his new physique: he was buff and tanned; he looked like a million dollars. A paparazzo snapped him on his balcony, yapping on the phone, shirtless and seemingly carefree. Clearly, the therapy had done the job. Imbruglia was in Sydney, too, for dates at the Rumba pop festival. A year that had seemed to be the worst of Johns's life was now full of possibility.

And in an act of resurrection that would have impressed Lazarus, *Diorama*, like Johns, was also back from the dead. Many months after its release, sales had received a second wind through some shrewd marketing and two key appearances.

First there was Johns's 'comeback' performance at the 2002 ARIAs in October. Johns, who was still receiving treatment at the time, was unsure whether he should even be playing. I'd seen the band practise in a rehearsal space in suburban Alexandria a few days before the awards, and all he could physically manage was to play 'The Greatest View' a few times, at ear-splitting volume. Due to his arthritis, Johns was having trouble bending his fingers to play his guitar; if the band hadn't been so loud, I swear you could have heard him wince. Yet it didn't matter on the night. Johns and the band rocked 'The Greatest View' mightily, helped out by a five-man brass section and a grinning Paul Mac on piano, and the response was overwhelming—it felt as though the Sydney SuperDome might actually come crashing down on the crowd.

Later in the evening, Johns, decked out in a sharp waistcoat, a hippie bag slung across his chest, stepped up to receive the Best Group ARIA, the first of five gongs on the night, including Best Rock Album.

'I'd like to thank whoever organised Australian music's night of nights, erm, tonight,' Johns said, leaning into the microphone while Gillies and Joannou looked on. 'It's been pretty good. It's made even better because we've won something.'

Public speaking remained a challenge for Johns.

Second, there was the season-ending episode of *Rove Live*. Aware of the wide audience for the national television program, and keen to steer the band's music towards an even larger audience, manager Watson struck up a deal with the show's producers for an entire program dedicated to Johns and Silverchair.

On the set, Johns joked about the pills he took as part of his treatment ('lots of pills, actually'), which became a running gag throughout his sit-down with host Rove McManus, with sly references to designer drugs. Then there were his aerobics work-outs. 'My friends film me, and we put a soundtrack to it,' he said, straight faced. Johns had become the new Jane Fonda, apparently.

It hardly mattered that the bulk of the show was lifted straight from the *Across the Night: The Creation of Diorama* DVD; the boost to album sales was remarkable. The album—which had been floundering well outside the Top 40—raced back into the Top 10. By 20 December, *Diorama* had gone triple platinum (210,000 copies) in Australia and become the band's fastest-selling album in their home territory.

'Since we were fourteen,' Johns admitted to me after *Rove*, 'we've been told [of] the importance and value of promotion, and we've gone "bullshit". Now all we did was turn up on *Rove Live* and sell all these fucking records! I guess people are more liberal in their spending around Christmas. I've also bought a few thousand copies.'

Not only had the band kept their loyal Silver-fans, but mainstream Australia was also snapping up *Diorama*, as commercial stations such as Nova FM put their songs into high rotation for the first time. A hefty television advertising campaign and some high-profile Sunday news magazine stories—again, reaching a new audience for the band—didn't harm *Diorama*'s sales, either.

Silverchair were also, finally, set to return to the road, even if their 2003 itinerary wasn't as exhaustive as their promo schedules had been for their previous three albums. But that didn't mean that Johns had scaled-down plans. Far from it.

'Providing we have adequate financial support, I want to do something that's larger than life,' Johns said, as the band got back to rehearsals, 'that's visually surreal as well. It's going to be a sensory overload.'

———◄○►———

The upswing continued when tickets for all eleven Across the Night Australian shows sold out on the day they went on sale, 4 December. Their first hometown show, at Newcastle's Civic Theatre, since January 1999 sold out in a remarkable six minutes flat, grossing nearly $170,000. Tickets to the first Melbourne show were snapped up in nine minutes, generating almost $200,000; ditto a single show in Perth. Virtually all of the tickets for their two Sydney Entertainment Centre shows were sold on the first morning, raising more than $300,000 at the box office. By February 2003, with Johns's health very much improved, six additional shows were announced to meet the frenzied demand for tickets—they, too, were sell-outs. Offshore, 1000 pre-sale tickets were snapped up for their shows at New York's Bowery Ballroom in June. Extra dates were added to short tours of the UK and South America. Silverchair were a band in demand.

The Across the Night tour opened in Brisbane on 22 March. When the lights went up, Johns was alone, seated at a piano, wearing a striking red-velvet jacket, playing the sombre ballad 'After All These Years'. It was a song more suited to the night's end than the beginning, hardly the blitzkrieg of grungy days passed. The audience was caught off guard. *Was this a sit-down show? Surely not.*

With 'After All These Years' done, the first 'act' of the show—Silverchair didn't play sets, they now performed acts—formally began, as Gillies, Joannou and keyboardists Hamilton and new kid Stuart Hunter joined Johns and tackled the heavy emotions of 'World Upon Your Shoulders'. The first of the night's two acts was Johns's chance to totally immerse himself in the 'new Silverchair', including *Diorama* tracks such as 'Tuna in the Brine', 'Luv Your Life' and 'Across the Night'. He and the band also threw reconstructed versions of older songs—'Miss You Love', 'Paint Pastel Princess' and 'Ana's Song'—into a totally satisfying mix.

The lavish stage setting was alive with retina-wrecking fluoros and flickering video screens—it was almost as much a star of the show as the resurrected Johns, who kept his onstage rambles to a minimum, opting to let his lush, neo-psychedelic songs do most of the talking. He had to work a lot harder, too; these *Diorama* songs were tricky. Apart from a few mysterious hand signals during a stunning 'Luv Your Life'—and a hint of 'air conducting' in 'Across the Night'—he spent much of Act One with his eyes shut tight, concentrating hard. (When Gillies had asked,

'How the fuck are we going to remember that?' upon first hearing 'Tuna', he wasn't kidding.) But Johns did bust a few awkward moves during a freaked-out 'Steam Will Rise', which closed Act One. 'This song is made for dancing,' he told the crowd. It even came with a killer Gillies drum solo, a no-go zone back in the days of '95.

Fifty minutes in, the lights went up and the band headed backstage for a towel down and a quick change of outfit, leaving audiences to sift through the merchandise being flogged in the foyer. Silverchair PJs did a lively trade.

The band didn't intend to alienate the true believers who'd stuck with them ever since 1994. In Act Two, therefore, came more grunt, less Brian Wilson, with an extended 'Emotion Sickness' providing some great rock-and-roll theatre. Johns cut himself some slack, too, as he and the band swapped the intricacies of the night's earlier songs for sheer noise thrills and a few laughs. As the set progressed, he'd turn his back to the audience, shake his skinny butt and then mount his arsenal of amplifiers; he also gnawed on his guitar as if he was trying to floss his teeth with the strings. Every female in the house with a pulse screamed her lungs raw; this was sexy, primal stuff—and so what if Johns's tongue and cheek stayed close at all times? A near-naked Gillies and a highly physical Joannou didn't kill the mood, either.

As their long show turned for home, the two keyboardists exited and the stage was left to the three Novocastrian mates, stirring up memories of their early days in The Loft. Johns was clearly in the mood. 'Can everyone please

stand up?' he asked as they ripped into 'Israel's Son'—
and every arse in the house was duly raised. 'You've seen
the theatrics, now it's all vodka and light show,' Johns
yelled. 'Get the fuck up and let's rock and roll.' The
band then riffed and roared their way through 'The Door',
'Freak'—where Johns's guitar screamed like a dentist's
drill—and 'Anthem for the Year 2000', leaving the full
house satiated.

'If you're wearing sandals,' a vodka-slugging Johns
warned the Newie crowd on 20 April as he tore in the
'Anthem', 'you might as well take them off now, 'cause
they're coming off!' When a worse-for-wear bloke invaded
the stage, Johns warned away a hovering security guard.
'You take it, man!' he yelled at the crazy dancer. 'Take the
motherfucker! Take it!' The man did. Then he fell back
into the scrum down the front.

Those who weren't much for the fancy stuff at the start of
the night loved the rockers that ended it. Dripping sweat,
his eyeliner smeared across his face, by final curtain Johns
resembled a less creepy version of The Cure's Robert Smith.
Arthritis? Must have been another Daniel Johns.

Critics heaped praise on the band and the shows.
'The "Across the Night" tour shows a totally different
band from previous albums,' Robyn Doreian observed in
Rock Sound. Under the headline 'Chairman Wow', the *New
York Post*'s Dan Aquilante zeroed in on the reborn Daniel
Johns, describing him as 'incredible'. 'If Silverchair play
another NYC gig,' he declared, 'don't miss it.' Also amid
the heaving mass at their New York gig was long-time

Silver-fan David Fricke, who covered the show for American *Rolling Stone*. 'For Silverchair,' he announced, 'today is a lot more interesting than "Tomorrow".' The man spoke the truth.

Looking on from the side of the stage at a show in London's Shepherd's Bush was Natalie Imbruglia, now a familiar face in the world of Silverchair. Sucking on a lollipop—a post-arthritis Johns had also developed a sweet tooth—Imbruglia was electrified by the sweet noise her beau and his pals were creating. 'It was amazing,' she whooped after the show. 'The crowd was amazing.' Also in the midst of the Silver-scrum was *Diorama* producer David Bottrill. He, too, was impressed by the spectacle. 'He's a real star,' Bottrill said, looking towards Johns.

The Shepherd's Bush shows marked the end of the road for *Diorama*. Despite the heavy praise heaped on their few overseas shows—and the wild scramble for tickets to a single LA gig, which sold out in a heartbeat—their fourth album died a hasty death in North America, barely scraping into six-figure sales, terminating their relationship with Atlantic. Even though the poor US numbers shocked him, Johns grew to find the failure liberating. 'I really think it was for the creative good of myself and the benefit of the band that it wasn't a massive success overseas. It made us realise that we're not dependent on commercial success to be happy with our stuff.'

Johns had other, more pressing, matters to address. First up, he needed to plan an A-list wedding; Imbruglia had accepted his marriage proposal in January 2003 and now sported a hefty platinum and diamond ring from upscale jeweller Craig Leonard. Johns was also about to shock his fans by forming a new band. The whispers soon started up once again; maybe it really was all over for Silverchair this time.

11

I was trying to break something in my brain
[with pot]—and I think I did.
—Daniel Johns

IN ORDER TO MAKE THEIR RELATIONSHIP WORK,
Johns and Imbruglia lived like gypsies, bouncing between
homes in Sydney, Newcastle and London. 'It's a weird
lifestyle,' Johns once explained to me, 'but pretty exciting
as well. Like anything in life, it has its advantages and
disadvantages.' But Johns was especially partial to the
time he and Imbruglia spent at her palatial spread near
Windsor, located on the idyllically named White Lilies
Island (yes, she actually lived on an island). Elton John
was one of her few neighbours. Luke Steele, an occasional
visitor, dubbed it 'Nat's palace'. Steele, with his band
The Sleepy Jackson, had impressed Johns during a few
support dates on the Across the Night tour, and he had
become a close pal.

In the UK, Johns lived a relatively anonymous life. Occasionally he'd hear the words, 'I think that's Natalie Imbruglia's husband'. That was his cue to jump in his car and head home. But there were no photographers snooping outside his window, no lost and lonely teens camped on the front lawn, dreaming of exchanging just one word—a look, even—with Daniel from Silverchair. With the band on hold for the time being, Johns now spent much of his time in Windsor, enjoying the serenity.

It wasn't as easy for Imbruglia, of course, whose fame in the UK eclipsed even Johns's fame in Australia; she had, after all, starred in *Neighbours*. This meant that Johns was required to do most of the dealing with the outside world, as he explained in a 2004 interview with ABC television's Andrew Denton. 'I've been in shopping lines in Windsor,' he laughed, 'because I have to go buy the groceries. I'm just Captain Nobody over there.' Johns had established a relationship, of sorts, with 'my fellow 60- to 80-year-olds . . . that I only see at [local shop] Waitrose.' There was one local in particular whom Johns had befriended, with 'this amazing hat and cane . . . I would kill for it.'

'There's my old mate,' Johns would say when they met.

'Hello, my Australian friend.'

Johns fully embraced the English thing for eccentricity— Captain Nobody was just the beginning. While in Windsor, Johns re-christened himself 'Sir Whilliam Hathaway' (the extra 'h' his idea), an 'English statesman/poet'. He took to shopping in three-piece suits while holding a cane, even though he didn't need one to get around anymore.

Johns asked his friends to refer to him as 'Sir Whilliam'. Or just Will.

'This is a concept I've been working on for a couple of years,' Johns explained. But he then learned there was actually a real Whilliam Hathaway. 'Apparently, he's a prose writer from the 1800s, who also had something to do with the mass selling of gin, back when it was the worker's drink.'

'I'm not trying to run away from myself,' Johns insisted, although it was hard to imagine there wasn't just a hint of that at work.

Shopping and life as Sir Whilliam weren't the only tasks that soaked up Johns's time while living in the UK. At the end of the Silverchair tour in June, he'd put in a call to his buddie Paul Mac and invited him over to tinker about in the basement studio that Johns had set up on White Lilies Island. Over two weeks that Johns would recall were part of 'a beautiful English summer', The Dissociatives were born.

Ever since their collaboration on *I Can't Believe It's Not Rock* and Mac's increased involvement with *Neon Ballroom* and *Diorama*, Johns had planned to work more with the piano man, now his label mate at Eleven. Mac had great success with his first solo album, 2001's *3000 Feet High*, which won a Best Dance ARIA and sold upwards of 35,000 copies. He was no longer a sideman. The Dissociatives was a creative democracy.

'It was never about, you know, "I want to create a band to step up to the Silverchair mantle and take over the world",' Johns explained of his new collaboration with Mac. 'It was just about creating a band that had a completely different set of rules.'

Johns and Mac worked out some of those rules in the basement of Nat's palace. As a creative test, they would restrict themselves to eight instruments per track. They could only use the equipment they had at hand. This was no big-budget production; Johns had his fill of that with the problematic *Diorama*. If anything, this was the exact opposite.

'We just wanted to get ourselves in a dark, confined space, with all our own gear. Every single track we had to make sound different and interesting using these eight instruments. We were adamant that the best creativity comes from restriction; when the possibilities aren't endless.'

Johns wrote all the lyrics for the album's eleven songs— except for the breezy instrumental 'Lifting the Veil from the Braille', where he, quite literally, whistled while he worked— and the dynamic duo recorded the bulk of the album of cool, clean, digital-age pop in two weeks flat. There was a little outside input, mainly from drummer Kim Moyes, who, along with Julian Hamilton and James Hazelwood, would later make up The Dissociatives' live ensemble. A choir added their voices to several tracks, while Imbruglia sang on 'Thinking in Reverse'. (Johns would repay the favour by co-writing the track 'Satisfied' for Imbruglia's 2005 album, *Counting Down the Days*. A first for Johns, he found the experience, like many from this time, 'very liberating'.)

Having recorded all the music in Imbruglia's basement, Johns and Mac then shifted base to the former's home studio at his house in Merewether—re-christened 'Merry

Wether Forever' studios for the occasion—where they cut Johns's vocals.

A statement was released to the media on 11 December 2003, which simply read: 'Meet The Dissociatives'. By now, the album—which had more in common with Continental acts Air and Phoenix than it did with anything from Silverchair's back pages—was done and dusted, and a video for the lead single, 'Somewhere Down the Barrel', had been shot by animator James Hackett. The single was scheduled for a February 2004 release, with their self-titled LP set to follow two months later.

Not surprisingly, more whispers spread about the uncertain future of Silverchair. Johns and Mac gave the rumour mill a further nudge when they insisted that their band were 'more than just a side project'. But as usual, the restless Johns had little time to answer questions about where next for the 'Chair, because he was moving on again. He was getting married.

When Johns and Imbruglia announced their engagement in January 2003, I asked him what the obligation meant to him. Marriage seemed like an oddly conservative step for a nonconformist such as Johns.

'It's awesome, really good,' he insisted. 'It solidifies commitment, and I think that's pretty important if you want stability—and that's basically what everyone wants. [But] I haven't thought about having children or becoming an adult.'

At that stage, Johns jokingly suggested that they could tie the knot at Newcastle landmark Fort Scratchley. 'To scare off the paparazzi,' Johns figured, 'we could . . . point the cannons at them.'

But Johns had bigger plans: he wanted a romantic wedding in a beautiful locale. He also wanted to stop the paps from spoiling the party.

Throughout the week leading up to the New Year's Eve 2003 wedding, it seemed that every rag and mag in the country speculated on just where the wedding would be held. Yet the guests themselves didn't know. Those 60 guests, including the families of Johns and Imbruglia, Silver-pals Ben Gillies and Chris Joannou, Paul Mac, Julian Hamilton, Virgin impresario Richard Branson, Eleven's John Watson and Melissa Chenery, as well as producer David Bottrill, David Helfgott and his wife Gillian, actor Guy Pearce (who starred in the video for 'Across the Night') and pop princess Kylie Minogue, were given the most basic of instructions: pack enough warm-weather clothes for three days, they were advised. Air tickets to Cairns were included with the note. That was all they were told. Upon arrival, guests were transported by bus to a secluded beachside stretch just outside Port Douglas's very upscale Thala Beach Lodge, a five-star 'nature lodge' where the nightly room rates run close to A$500. A specially built marquee had been set up for the occasion, in a tranquil clearing between the beach—part of a two-kilometre stretch of pristine coastline—and the resort.

Despite the tropical heat, Johns wore a pale-blue vintage suit. Imbruglia rocked a V-necked silk chiffon wedding dress with a handkerchief hem from designer Monique Lhuillier, plus a Kaviar and Kind necklace and high heels—sand be damned—by Jimmy Choo. After a breakfast banquet, the formal ceremony took place, followed by a DJ set from Paul Mac, who still had to sing (or spin discs) for his supper. Kylie Minogue caught the bouquet.

Like most grooms, Johns's day went by in a blur of handshakes and toasts. 'I didn't get a chance to enjoy it, I was just so busy,' he said. 'It was beautiful, but it was just shake hands, shake hands, "thanks for coming, thanks for coming".'

Interestingly, rather than call on his rock-and-roll pals to supply the music for the day, Johns (with a little help from the PR manager for the event, John Scott, and wedding producer Marcus Francisco) took a far more sophisticated approach. An eighteen-piece ensemble breezed their way through a selection of classical and world-music standards. During a rare quiet moment, Johns took time to check out the band; he was impressed. 'Some of the musos we had were killer, playing sambas and things like that. I took away a couple of ideas.'

Not surprisingly, the couple had been offered serious dollars by the tabloid weeklies for exclusive access to their wedding snaps, but they knocked back all requests. It didn't interest them. They were famous enough. One unauthorised snapper did guess the right venue, and a heli-copter buzzed the wedding during the actual ceremony, but security managed to keep things very much on the quiet. As the reception progressed, the guests arranged them-selves in some kind of orderly fashion, and the one invited photographer, Adrienne Overall, who'd been shooting the band since the days of *Frogstomp*, took a group shot, which she immediately downloaded to her computer. The newly-weds agreed that any media outlet could buy the snap, but it would cost them A$5000, with the money going to the couple's charity of choice. Even that was kept a secret.

Those who attended were full of praise for the big day. Julian Hamilton described it as 'lovely'. David Bottrill said it was 'great, apart from the helicopter'. David Helfgott felt it was 'beautiful'. Johns's mood was captured precisely by Andrew Denton, when they spoke a few months later. When Johns opened up about his relationship with Imbruglia, Denton said, 'I think you're enjoying life now. Would I be right?'

'Yeah, definitely, I love life,' Johns replied without hesitation. 'It's the best thing in the world.'

A post-honeymoon Johns maintained his upbeat mood when the Australian public was given a sneak preview of The Dissociatives' first single, 'Somewhere Down the Barrel', on 6 February. The song was streamed on the EMI website three days later and was released to stores on 8 March. By this time, the highly hummable, keyboard-powered track would be one of the five most-played tracks on Australian radio and a Top 40 hit. 'It's probably the purest music that I've ever come up with,' Johns admitted. 'The idea of collaborating [wasn't] appealing to me until I realised the close musical connection I had with Paul. There's something about two people with equal passion for something that really makes magic happen.'

There was more than one partnership at work with The Dissociatives. James Hackett's excellent trilogy of inter-related videos for 'Somewhere Down the Barrel', 'Young Man, Old Man' and 'Horror with Eyeballs', part anima-tion, part live-action photography, would contribute hugely towards establishing The Dissociatives' Day-Glo identity. They were sort of an Australian Gorillaz (although they didn't like the comparison). Hackett had learned the anima-tion trade in London, where he worked on graphics for a variety of projects, including U2's Popmart tour.

'We wanted surreal stories . . . all about the band,' said Johns. 'We saved the world a couple of times, because that was our job!'

For the 'Barrel' video, Johns and Mac spent three days in a Sydney studio with Hackett, where he asked them to assume a variety of poses, which, with the assistance of numerous computer programs, would then make up the 'action' components of the videos.

Johns and Mac got more involved with the second video, for 'Young Man, Old Man', which was the best track on a very good record. Johns, in particular, grabbed the chance to mess with the 'serious young insect' persona he assumed for most Silverchair clips. By the end of the clip, he'd morphed into a bearded hillbilly farmer, slapping out hand jive on his back porch. It was hardly 'Ana's Song'. 'Daniel was right up for the idea' of destroying his Silverchair identity, said Hackett. Johns 'borrowed' a few visuals from Guns N' Roses' blockbuster clip for 'November Rain' during 'Young Man', a guitar solo among them.

Johns and Mac agreed that 'Young Man, Old Man' was a song that summed up their special relationship. Mac was fourteen years older than Johns, so it was pretty clear exactly who was who.

When The Dissociatives played at the Enmore Theatre in Sydney, Johns and Mac chatted between songs about their relationship. 'It's all avuncular, it's cool,' a smiling Mac said. He was perhaps having fun with whispers that as a gay-and-proud man he had somehow 'turned' Johns. Johns was also having fun with the rumours. 'Paul's more than my friend,' he told the crowd with a limp flick of his wrist.

Local critics gushed with praise for both 'Barrel' and the self-titled *The Dissociatives* album, which dropped in early April, debuted at number twelve and would go on to sell 60,000 copies locally. *Rolling Stone*, a long-time Johns advocate, gave the album a four-star rating; it also devoted a prized front cover to Johns and Mac. 'Music unlike anything ever produced by an Australian act,' its review declared. 'A pop/rock record for the ages to be placed alongside your Beatles and Beach Boys discs.' *The Australian*'s veteran music writer, Iain Shedden, was equally impressed by the album. '[It's] a beautiful work . . . [it's] stomping, brooding, anthemic and incredibly poppy.' The Dissociatives were compared to everyone from The Beatles to the Buggles, Radiohead to Brian Eno. When the album was picked up for distribution in the UK, Germany, France, Belgium, Sweden and Switzerland, the reviews were equally uplifting. *Mojo* mag stated that 'The Dissociatives lose touch with reality in gorgeous fashion', while *Q* magazine even likened the band to Antipodean pop treasures Crowded House.

Though few musicians admit to even reading their press, Johns confessed that all these favourable reviews came as a huge relief. He was gratified that he could be playful on a record and get away with it. It also proved to him that perhaps there was life beyond Silverchair.

'It was good for everyone involved with me, that record,' he said. 'It made me so much happier to know that people would still accept my music [even] if I wasn't slitting my wrists.'

And these reviews weren't blowing smoke; there really was a lot to like about The Dissociatives. Freed from the expectations of his day job, the obligatory big guitars and heavy emotions were relegated to the background, as washes of synths and a heavily processed mix of voices, bass and drums dominated. Despite some worryingly bleak song titles—'Horror with Eyeballs', 'Angry Megaphone Man' and so on—Johns's lyrical mood was overwhelmingly bright and breezy. And in the stark, wistful ballad 'Forever and a Day', Johns and Mac crafted a valentine to Johns's soulmate, Natalie Imbruglia. Until now, Johns had never been bold enough to croon such lines as: 'A thousand sunshines on rain clouds . . ./I don't see nothing if I don't see you.'

When we exchanged emails in 2004, I said to Johns that, surely, this was a straight-up love song for his wife. What else could it be? 'It could certainly be a love song,' he replied, a little cagily. But the truth was in the track; it was a heartaching standout on an album with more highs than a hemp grower's convention.

———◄○►———

Forming a touring band for The Dissociatives was easy—all Johns and Mac needed to do was sign up most of the players on the album. Their June–July 2004 Australian tour was soon announced, with Little Birdy, Perth contenders who were signed to John Watson's Eleven Records, opening each show, along with the electro-pop Presets. Their members included the hard-working Kim Moyes and Julian Hamilton, who'd be doing double time on the road, as they also played with Johns and Mac.

'I'm really looking forward to this tour, which is not something I'd usually say,' Johns admitted when the dates were announced. It seemed that life with The Dissociatives was more fun than working with Silverchair, which only helped nudge along rumours that perhaps the 'Chair were done. Needing a new look, Johns shaved his hair right back to the scalp and bought a collection of tight tops and cargo pants. Working-man's clothes. With that, Johns was good to go.

It wasn't a heavy itinerary. The Dissociatives were only scheduled to play fifteen dates over a month, beginning in Hobart on 8 June and working their way through most capitals, plus regional centres such as Tweed Heads, Coffs Harbour and Johns's hometown of Newcastle. The venues were more intimate than those Silverchair had filled on their 2003 tour. In fact, it was the type of back-of-the-Tarago tour that Silverchair had never undertaken in Oz. Their sets were shorter, concentrating on the album and a few whimsical covers. These included Johns's take on Tom Waits's 'Goin' Out West', a song he'd always wanted to growl, which gave the band the chance to wig out completely. And no Silverchair songs.

'Funnily enough,' keyboardist Julian Hamilton said about 'Goin' Out West', 'that was probably the most enjoyable song for me to play in the whole show.' Johns loved singing it, but quickly learned that his throat wasn't necessarily built for the tune. He was no Tom Waits. 'It didn't hurt to sing; by that stage I was pretty loose, in more ways than one. But the next hour I'd stop and clear my throat and go, "Tom Waits is getting to me".'

One thing that didn't change dramatically was the make-up of the crowd. The same screaming teens that had treated the Across the Night shows like some kind of second coming were there in numbers for The Dissociatives. And they were in equally strong voice. 'It was the same mental 'Chair fans at all the Dissos's shows,' reported Julian Hamilton. 'The 'Chair fans certainly are a special bunch. Every tour we do, there is always a group of kids who are at every show, every airport, every hotel. They must spend so much money following the guys around.'

It wasn't strictly business for The Dissociatives; it was perhaps the most laid-back road trip Daniel Johns had ever taken. Certainly, the most stoned. Johns freely admitted that he was out of it for pretty much the entire two-year life of The Dissociatives, which might explain why he took to wearing single-lensed aviator sunglasses. Maybe he didn't realise there was a lens missing. Johns's panda-bear eye make-up added an additional out-there touch.

'During The Dissociatives period I was excessive,' said Johns. 'I remember all of it, and fondly, but I was trying to break something in my brain [with pot]—and I think I did.'

According to drummer Kim Moyes, Johns 'smoked [pot] harder than Snoop Dogg'. Hamilton backed this up. 'There sure was a lot of it around on that Oz tour, let me tell you! The secondary smoke coming from Dan's joints in the tour bus got me pretty stoned.'

The great album reviews continued with their live shows. Street press mag *Brag* likened the band to Americans The Flaming Lips, currently one of the hottest live tickets on the planet. *Drum Media* was equally effusive, praising The Dissociatives' 'almost bizarre but amazing performance'. Other press was just as enthusiastic; *dB*'s critic claimed it was 'easily one of the best shows I've seen in the last couple of years'. But *Rave* magazine topped the list for smart observations. 'The Dissociatives pre-set their controls for the heart of the sun,' the reviewer wrote, 'with their happy, psychedelic pop.' Perhaps as a nod of recognition, when Johns and Mac sat down to host ABC television's *Rage*, they included Pink Floyd's wigged-out epic 'Set the Controls for the Heart of the Sun' among a set of favourite videos that also included the Muppets, The Beatles' 'I Am the Walrus', Sleepy Jackson, Radiohead, Mercury Rev, Spinal Tap and Kenny Rogers. A musical mixed grill.

Mind you, there were one or two hitches along the way to psychedelic bliss. Good business at the box office meant that additional shows were added in far-flung spots such as Tamworth, Blacktown, Port Macquarie, Byron Bay and Warrnambool, but two weeks along, Johns's voice started to show signs of wear. On 22 June, the band reached Sawtell, on the New South Wales north coast, and went as far as setting up and sound-checking when it became painfully clear that Johns simply had no voice left. The show was cancelled. The next night the band moved on to Brisbane, where they managed to get through their set, though Johns admitted from the stage that they'd also considered cancelling that gig right up until show time. Johns took a trip to the local rock doctor immediately afterwards, who advised him to cancel the next couple of shows and let his voice recover, which he did.

There were other hassles. Killing time before a gig at rural Warrnambool, the group soaked up a few hours at the local pub, but word got around that 'Daniel from Silverchair' was in the house, and an uncomfortable vibe started to build as a crowd grew around the band. Eventually, Paul Mac took the 'avuncular' step of driving Johns back to their motel. For those few brief moments, Johns was reliving the worst moments of Silverchair, when his celebrity eliminated any chance of a normal life. But in the main, just like the album they recorded, The Dissociatives' tour was a good time, pretty much all the time.

Paul Mac summed it up neatly after they played their final date at Byron's Splendour in the Grass festival, and readied

a DVD, *Sydney Circa 2004slash08*, for release. 'The Dissociatives' tour was really special,' he stated. 'Hopefully this
DVD will allow people who missed the gigs to get a sense of
how much fun they were.' To make the package complete,
the trio of James Hackett–directed videos—for 'Somewhere
Down the Barrel', 'Young Man, Old Man' and 'Horror with
Eyeballs'—were added to the DVD, rounding off footage of
the band's wildly received set at the Enmore Theatre.

But Johns's post-Silverchair odyssey wasn't quite over.
In mid-September, when nominations for the 2004 ARIAs
were revealed, Team Dissociatives (including video
director Hackett) scooped the pool, making the short list
for Best Pop Release, Best Group, Album of the Year,
Producer of the Year (a particularly sweet nomination for
the Johns–Mac team), Best Cover Art and Best Video.
They'd eventually win the latter two gongs. A subsequent
APRA award nomination, for Song of the Year, was sweeter
still. James Hackett would also go on to claim a Video
of the Year award for 'Somewhere Down the Barrel', at
the inaugural Australian MTV awards, with a proud Johns
looking on.

But just when it seemed that Silverchair may have run
their course, they made an unexpected return to centre
stage, coaxed back into life by a terrible disaster.

12

The great ones are the band who have been
together since they were kids, sorted out
their shit and kept going, and twenty years
later they were still killing it.
—Daniel Johns

STANDING ON STAGE at the Sydney Cricket Ground on 29 January 2005, just as the sun began to set, Daniel Johns looked amazing. The 25-year-old was stripped to the waist, his pierced nipples on full and erect display, a beard framing his face, his newly buffed, inked and tanned torso oozing rock-god sexiness. The old firm of Johns, Joannou and Gillies were plugged in at a fundraiser for the many victims of the horrendous 2004 Boxing Day Indian Ocean tsunami, which killed more than 230,000 people across fourteen countries.

As the body count rose, a new dilemma arose: how do you address a tragedy of this magnitude? The entertainment industry, to its credit, has a solid track record when it comes to helping those in need—Live Aid, Farm Aid,

Live 8 and many other large-scale events had done their bit to raise hard cash for the needy, and heighten awareness of various worthy causes. In the process, to many, Bob Geldof and U2's Bono had become modern-day saints.

The Australian music industry's reaction to the Indian Ocean tsunami was swift and efficient. Current hit-makers Powderfinger, The Waifs and Pete Murray, and veterans Nick Cave and the Finn brothers, all agreed to play and do their bit. Midnight Oil quickly signed up; this was to be the farewell gig for singer Peter Garrett, the recently elected federal member for Kingsford Smith. The concert, named WaveAid, would also mark the re-awakening of Silverchair.

In an official statement just prior to the event, Johns was pragmatic about his band's return. This was happening for all the right reasons. 'Obviously,' he said, 'anyone with a heart wants to do whatever they can right now to try and provide some help to all the people who are suffering. So, the cricketers play cricket, the TV people do a TV show and the musicians play a gig. It should be a really memorable occasion.'

But the trio came into the gig hugely underprepared, having rehearsed for just a week beforehand, and not having played together since June 2003. So Johns took a pragmatic approach to the one-off gig: there'd be no surprises. 'We decided not to be stupid, not to play "Tuna in the Brine". We decided to just try and sound like a great rock band. And the cause was the big thing, so it wasn't about showboating or making a big artistic statement.' Johns's MO for the day was simple: 'Just try and enjoy it'.

Johns, Gillies and Joannou duly tore through their brief set of signature songs, including 'Israel's Son', 'The Greatest View', 'The Door' and 'Ana's Song (Open Fire)'—which Johns dedicated to Midnight Oil ('But not in a love song kind of way'). The response was wild; the crowd totally engaged.

'This is a new beginning,' Johns declared at the start of 'The Door', perhaps with more intent than he realised. 'So, let's reach out and touch someone.' The massive SCG mosh pit went bananas.

A thought struck Johns as he left the stage: perhaps there was still a little life left in Silverchair. Then, when he and the others watched Midnight Oil tear it up for (supposedly) the final time, that idea started to really take shape. Maybe they could make one more album.

'After it, we thought, "Fuck, man, we didn't even try and people really responded",' he said. 'It was the crowd, and also playing together—we realised how easy it felt, it was so natural, the songs kept coming out. And then watching Midnight Oil, who were just absolutely killing it. We figured we only had one opportunity to be a great, great band.'

What, to Johns, defined a great band?

'The great ones are the band who have been together since they were kids, sorted out their shit and kept going, and twenty years later they were still killing it. So, we said, "Right, studio time".'

WaveAid didn't just mark the re-emergence of Silverchair, it was also a massive fundraising success, generating a touch over A\$2 million for the tsunami victims.

◄○►

But even though Johns began to think seriously about the next Silverchair LP as soon as he left the stage at the SCG, The Dissociatives still had touring commitments. They played shows in Europe and the UK during 2005, supporting their album's international release, shows that Johns felt were among the most satisfying of his life.

'We were in these packed little clubs and we were just going to town, doing these wacky, Frank Zappa–inspired gigs,' he said. This was a completely different experience to playing with Silverchair. 'I'm really inspired by playing with guys who have formal training. I feel so lucky to have worked with those guys. With Silverchair, I show Chris how the bass goes, then do the same with Ben and then say, "Right, just make this sound good". With The Dissociatives, they'd go, "Right, that's an A-minor inflection there," and I'm like, "Wow, don't overwhelm me with details!"'

Dissociative Julian Hamilton was equally impressed by Johns, especially when writing together. 'He would start singing these amazing melodies [and] I'm like, "Far out, I'm sitting next to Brian Wilson".' According to Hamilton, Johns possessed what he liked to call the 'sunshine', citing such songs as 'Ana's Song' and 'World Upon Your Shoulders' as proof.

'When you hear a song and the melodies and chords alone make you feel so positive—that's the sunshine. Dan's definitely got the sunshine, and it's something us trained writers and players would kill to have. Plus, he makes it seem so effortless.'

While still considering another Silverchair album, Johns, in the wake of these Dissociatives shows, had returned to Nat's palace, and by mid-2005 he had spent time writing with both Hamilton and Luke Steele (soon to hit paydirt with Empire of the Sun, an electro-pop combo not unlike The Dissociatives or The Presets). Johns's plan was to use these collaborations for a solo LP. The Silverchair album would happen after that.

Yet as these new songs began to come together during the UK summer, Johns had second thoughts. His mind flashed back to WaveAid and the sheer noise thrills that he, Gillies and Joannou felt when they turned the SCG into a seething, sweating mass of bodies. 'As usual, I got about eight songs in and started missing Ben and Chris,' he confessed.

Johns put in a call to his Silver-partners, floating the idea of using the songs he'd already written—alone and with others—for the fifth Silverchair album. His bandmates couldn't agree quickly enough, even though Gillies, despite a songwriting rebirth with a project named Tambalane, was still left out of the creative process. It must have stung Gillies to look on as Johns teamed up with others—Paul Mac, Julian Hamilton, Luke Steele—rather than suggest they try writing together again. As Gillies knew all too well, even a lone songwriting credit on a Silverchair album guaranteed handsome royalties. But Gillies never grumbled about this publicly.

Just before Christmas 2005, Johns returned to Oz. He, Gillies and Joannou rented two houses in the Hunter Valley, near the New South Wales Central Coast, and entered a period of personal and musical rejuvenation. Johns reported their progress to *Rolling Stone*. 'We just went to a little farm in the bush, and just lived and breathed and played music. [We] got back together, got to know each other again. It was great.'

By February 2006, they began readying themselves for a handful of shows over the next few weeks. Johns was changing things up again—taking a cue from the Radiohead playbook, this new album would be self-financed, using money generated by these gigs. They needed about A$500,000. (Radiohead had cut ties with their record company in 2005, becoming, in the words of *The New York Times*, 'by far the world's most popular unsigned band'.) Now there'd be no major label hassles for Silverchair, no repeat of the drama they'd had with Atlantic while making *Diorama*. This was going to be Johns's baby, for better or worse. They had eleven new songs demoed and ready to record; one of these tracks was so strong, in fact, that band insiders said it resembled '[U2's] "With or Without You" meets [Coldplay's] "Clocks".' That song, 'Straight Lines', was a sure-fire hit.

In order to raise the required cash, they opted for high-profile, big-payday shows, with gigs at the Rock It Festival in Western Australia on 19 March, the Clipsal 500 car race at Adelaide five days later and The Great Escape festival in Sydney mid-April. Crowds were big, ranging from 10,000 to 40,000.

Yet their warm-up gig for the tour couldn't have been any more low-key. Billing themselves as Short Elvis, the tag Johns and Gillies had used as schoolkids in the days of 'The Elephant Rap', they announced a 'secret show' at Sydney's Gaelic Club on 16 March. The few hundred tickets that were available to the public were, not surprisingly, snapped up within hours. The rest of the crowd of 700 comprised hand-picked true believers and music-biz tastemakers. Well before the doors opened at 7.30 p.m., the queue snaked for several hundred metres along inner-city Devonshire Street, with punters eager to get a rare close-up view of the band. To manager Watson, it must have felt like their first US shows back in 1995, just as 'Tomorrow' exploded. There was a tangible excitement to the gig, which clearly spilled over to the guys on stage.

After a quick 'hello', the newly stripped-back four-piece Silverchair of Johns, Gillies, Joannou and Paul Mac—who had signed on for a two-year commitment to the band— leapt straight into a new track, 'If You Keep Losing Sleep'. As was now the norm, they looked great: Johns wore a sleeveless vest, which didn't last long; Gillies didn't bother with a shirt. Joannou played with his sleeves rolled up, ready for business. As for Mac, he sported a top that read 'Yoko Ono', poking fun at his role as the person who kept dragging Johns away from his regular band for their own pet projects. Mac had called Johns beforehand, ensuring that he was okay with the gag.

Johns loved the idea so much that he replied, 'And it has to be better than a T-shirt that says Linda or Courtney.'

On stage at the Gaelic Club, the quartet offered up a 'greatest hits' set, of sorts, delivering such 'oldies' as 'The Door', 'Emotion Sickness', 'Paint Pastel Princess',

'Ana's Song' and a hefty serving of *Diorama* tracks—'Tuna in the Brine', 'Across the Night', 'The Greatest View' and the usual set-closing 'The Lever'. These were intermingled with a handful of new tunes-under-development, which included 'Waiting All Day', 'Mind Reader' and 'Straight Lines', the aforementioned blend of U2's 'With or Without You'—a reference that Johns loved—and Coldplay's 'Clocks' (which he wasn't so mad about). The rumours were true: 'Straight Lines' had hit written all over it.

Johns was clearly enjoying himself. When the requests for 'oldies' kept coming, Johns, instead, tore into a new song, and then sorted out a heckler in the crowd. 'You don't want anything from *Frogstomp* anymore, do you, mate? You've just seen the future.' And it didn't matter that the band were a tad rusty. When Joannou fluffed the opening bass line from 'Across the Night', Johns stopped, smiled at his old pal and told the crowd: 'It's okay, it's just a rehearsal—and you didn't pay full price, anyway'.

Johns had rarely been more open on stage, frequently thanking the crowd for simply showing up. When he suggested that someone shout him a drink, a vodka tonic hastily appeared from the bar, making its way, hand to hand, to a thirsty Johns on stage. The chatty frontman also passed his judgement on Surry Hills, the sleazy-but-chic Sydney inner-city suburb where the Gaelic Club was situated. 'Eez good,' Johns slurred. 'I like.' (These days, Johns was frequenting Sydney much more than Newcastle.) At one point, he even forewarned the audience about one of their more furious-paced new songs.

'This'll hit you like a truck,' he grinned. It did.

Johns was completely at ease, which might have had something to do with his rude new health. 'I just walked onstage at the Gaelic Club and immediately felt comfortable,' he said afterwards. 'This is what happens when you don't have anorexia and your bones aren't eating themselves. People got used to me being sick and then they said, when they saw me looking better, "What are you doing?" I told them I was simply not being sick.' Johns insisted that he hadn't become a gym junkie; this was just the healthy version of him. Maybe his new sense of onstage ease had something to do with the two-year-long pot binge he underwent while with The Dissociatives—perhaps married life had also mellowed him. Or it could have also been because he'd relaxed his attitude towards onstage drinking. (A few weeks later, at The Great Escape, he stumbled drunkenly about the stage, swigging heartily from a bottle of booze as he played.) Whatever the reason for Johns's new-found onstage freedom, it was infectious: Silverchair had never seemed so relaxed.

Half a million duly raised, sessions for album number five were set to start in April 2006. Even at this early stage, Johns had clear plans as to how the album would differ from its predecessor. 'If *Diorama* was like a painting, this is more like a sculpture,' he said, clearly getting into the discussion. 'It's not going to sound professional or nice. I'm really proud of *Diorama*, but this one I'd like to make more dirge-y and swollen and infected. I want it to be sprawling and unpredictable. If people like it, they like it. I know I'm going to like it.'

Many of his new songs had come to him during a restless few nights, when he wandered about Nat's palace, unable to sleep. 'It was a real "Across the Night" experience,' he explained. 'I didn't realise what I was writing about until I'd finished. Some of the lyrics are deliberately vague, whereas some are the most direct I've ever written. I'm really getting into the idea of trying to communicate to people who don't want to hear [Silverchair], as opposed to the music fans.'

As for his current musical sensations, Johns was citing Talking Heads' *Remain in Light* and Brian Eno's *Here Come the Warm Jets* as key influences on his new record, which would be called *Young Modern*. The title was inspired by his friend and collaborator, Van Dyke Parks, who was booked for new sessions with Johns and the City of Prague Philharmonic Orchestra. 'Hello, young modern,' Parks would greet Johns when they got together. The tag stuck.

Johns was also mad for Nick Cave and the Bad Seeds' two-album set, *Abattoir Blues/The Lyre of Orpheus*. ('It blew my mind to pieces.') Once he had pieced his noggin back together, Johns checked the production credits—the album was produced by Nick Launay, the same skinny expat Brit who'd worked the controls for *Freak Show* and *Neon Ballroom* and had gone 'egging' with the band back when they used to hoon around Newcastle in search of likely targets. Johns recruited Launay immediately.

'I didn't consider many others for this record,' Johns said to me, as the band started packing their bags for recording sessions that would take them from California's

Laurel Canyon to the UK and Prague and then to LA for the final mix. 'Fortunately, it was someone I knew.'

So why all the globetrotting? It was part of Johns's grand plan to record the songs in the same country where they'd been written. Sadly, he had to scrap plans to record in London's fabled Abbey Road Studios; that was a budget buster at A$4000 per day. Instead, they opted for a cheaper UK studio.

Unlike earlier albums, where major label needs and Johns's fragile health had made for tough times while recording, the only hitch during the making of *Young Modern* was of Johns's creation. It had been agreed that Launay would co-produce and mix the record, but after he'd completed four mixes in September, Johns took a week's break and decided that he wasn't satisfied with the results. It was a big decision, because the album was already running well over budget. (It eventually set them back close to A$1 million, almost twice their original estimation.) Citing the old classic 'musical differences', Johns fired a disappointed and slightly bewildered Launay. David Bottrill, Johns's right-hand man during *Diorama*, was brought in to do the mix, which delayed the album's release until early 2007. If nothing else, this insistence on getting it absolutely right proved that this record truly belonged to Johns. Everyone else was a hired hand.

Launay, despite his dismissal, gave the finished LP some high praise, describing it as 'more thematic than *Neon Ballroom*; it's quite conceptual. It's one of the most extravagant undertakings by any band in the world,' he said, 'more on par with [Queen's] "Bohemian Rhapsody"', for example.'

Behind the scenes, Johns was healthy and happily coupled; his personal life was as good as it had ever been. A Sydney newspaper report that he and Imbruglia were experiencing trouble in paradise prompted a simple (and as it would prove, prophetic) response from Johns: 'Those things give me the shits. We heard about it and just went, "Who is this source?" Time will tell if our marriage is on the rocks.'

Admittedly, their union could hardly be considered typical—Johns spent much of his time either on the road or locked away in a dark studio, while Imbruglia, the face of L'Oréal, was frequently called away to attend product launches and parties all over the globe, often without her plus-one. But Johns had found something that closely resembled domestic harmony. As for Joannou and Gillies, they were essentially the same likeable blokes from Newie, just worldlier—the BMW-driving Gillies had even developed a taste for Grange Hermitage. But Johns was a totally different dude from the surly teenager who glared at the world and snarled, 'Yeah, I'm a freak of nature' and taunted the cool kids with the lines, 'Come on, abuse me more, I like it'.

Julian Hamilton was one of those close enough to Johns to see the radical changes he'd undergone over the past few years: 'Sometimes I'll see a press photo or a billboard with him on it, looking all sad and troubled, and I'll have a laugh, because that's not the Dan that I know at all. He's just a regular guy. I think that most musicians are—despite the hype and spin and press photos, we're all just regular people.'

Of course, in Johns's case, the life of a regular guy meant living in a palace, 'smoking harder than Snoop Dogg', traversing the globe on a whim and having a bank account that ran deep into seven figures.

———◦———

Johns and the band launched *Young Modern* at Carriageworks in Sydney on 30 March 2007. With the addition of piano man Mac and a three-man brass section, the unit was as tight as a nut. Johns's all-black ensemble—with matching black headband—was equally sharp. The sophisticated, Mondrian-styled artwork used on the album's cover doubled as the night's vivid and vibrant backdrop. There'd be no more frogs or freaks for Silverchair.

While essentially a night of new music, Johns chose carefully from their back catalogue, playing 'Emotion Sickness', which still packed a weighty emotional clout, 'Luv Your Life', even golden oldie 'Freak'. And Johns was in total control from the first note of 'The Man That Knew Too Much' right through to the evening's barnstorming closer, 'If You Keep Losing Sleep'. He looked good, played great and was very much in charge. Aside from dropping to his knees for a blazing solo during 'Young Modern Station' and gnawing on his guitar strings in the midst of 'The Door', Johns spent much of the night working hard, getting these new songs right. His shirt didn't see out the night, though;

by the time of 'Ana's Song', Johns was topless. The partisan crowd didn't object.

It was a few songs into the night that Johns was feeling loose enough to order a drink. 'Is there any vodka?' he asked, squinting into the darkness. And then, after a beat, he delivered a joke at the expense of the industry-heavy crowd: 'Is it a free bar? You guys enjoying the fruits of our labour?' He duly dedicated 'Tuna in the Brine' to 'anyone who's had friendly relations with some kind of fish'. An album launch was serious business, but Johns hadn't forgotten the whereabouts of his funny bone.

Just before the launch, the band had convened for the usual on-air powwow (the event was screened on Channel [v]). 'Straight Lines' had already reached number one, hitting top spot on 19 February.

'So how did that feel?'

'Great,' Johns said without a moment's hesitation. 'We were really happy with the song, with the record, but we didn't think the response would be so accepting. We feel a bit overwhelmed.'

He'd come a long way from the time of 'Tomorrow', when he was almost urging the song not to go crazy on the charts, for fear of being seen as a sell-out. Success felt good. Great, even.

Somehow, talk turned to monogamy: was that a Silverchair trait?

'We're not gay, if that's what you're implying,' Johns deadpanned, as the others laughed hard enough to cough up a lung.

When asked about the lengthy downtime between *Diorama* and *Young Modern*—five years separated the two albums—Johns likened life in the band to a relationship. They'd needed some time apart; they'd needed to grow a little before making the new record. 'It wasn't because we didn't love each other,' he smiled. 'We just wanted to go out and experience other musical pleasures so we can enjoy what we have.' Silverchair still 'felt like home', he insisted.

Johns got into this with a number of journos while promoting *Young Modern*. He found himself regularly playing down any friction, repeating, almost like a mantra: 'We weren't fighting—we just weren't talking'. They each had their own thing: relationships, other work, family. And they were in different countries most of the time; Johns still preferred the gypsy lifestyle. 'I spend a lot of my time in London,' he told a writer from *The Sunday Telegraph*, 'but when we're touring, I'm never anywhere.' He lived out of two suitcases. 'That's it.'

———◆———

A high-profile American return had been arranged for Silverchair: a performance of 'Straight Lines' on Jay Leno's popular tonight show in mid-July. They couldn't have dreamed up a better US reboot, nor could they have had a better song with which to arm themselves. The jut-jawed Leno drew upwards of five million viewers every night.

But there was some high drama just before Johns left Oz. Speaking on Triple J, to rusted-on Silverchair supporters, he jokingly spoke about 'road-testing' *Young Modern* on a few famous friends.

'It was me and Natalie and Peter Garrett and Bono, laying on Bono's bed smoking joints listening to the *Young Modern* demo,' Johns said on air. Clearly, he was joking.

Johns had nothing but respect for Bono and Garrett— at the 2006 ARIAs, while tearing up a cover of Midnight Oil's 'I Don't Wanna Be the One', Johns had tagged 'PG for PM' on the set, a seemingly spontaneous gesture that the audience loved. Johns and the chrome-domed Garrett were close—Midnight Oil's fervent set at WaveAid had inspired Johns to get his own band back together. But all hell broke loose in the wake of his loose-lipped Triple J interview, ample proof of a conservative, humourless mindset infecting mainstream Australia. There were cries for MP Garrett to take a drug test, a particularly pointless gesture given that the alleged indiscretion happened back in November. Meanwhile, Tony Trimingham, the founder of Family Drug Support, took the highest possible moral ground. '[Johns] might see it as a joke, but he should realise that he is a role model.'

Johns was stunned—he'd made a joke about smoking dope, not shooting smack. And was he really a role model? As long ago as 1999 he'd rejected the notion completely. Nothing had changed for him. 'We're definitely not the kind of people you want to model yourself after,' he said. He was a musician, not a statesman like Bono or Garrett.

Johns swiftly cancelled all appointments and issued a formal apology, insisting that he was just having a laugh.

He also acknowledged that it wasn't his best joke. 'I really should just shut up and stick to singing,' he said in his statement. He sent messages to Garrett and Bono; both shrugged, accepted his apology and thought nothing more of it. Then he left town in a hurry, headed for the USA.

But even in LA he couldn't shake off the drama. Unable to sleep, feeling horrible about what had just gone down, Johns felt sick—and then he fell sick. He had contracted laryngitis just as he and the band were scheduled to make their big American return, their first appearance there since May 2003. Once again, his body had let him down. Two steroid shots in his backside helped him get onto the Leno set, but almost as soon as they powered into 'Straight Lines', a challenge for any singer, it was clear his voice was shot. It was painful to watch, and hear, as Johns searched for any trace of a voice, veering between a squeaky falsetto and a sandy growl. All live, coast-to-freakin'-coast. It was a disaster.

Afterwards backstage, Johns was close to crying—and quitting the tour. 'I am completely aware of what it was like, believe me,' he told a journalist once his voice had returned. 'I was bordering on humiliated.' (Johns wasn't the only one feeling let down; the video has since disappeared from YouTube.)

Two days later Silverchair were on yet another tonight show, this time with Roy Slaven–look-alike Craig Ferguson on the *Late Late Show*, but Johns's voice remained weak. The performance wasn't anywhere near as hard to take as that on Leno's show, but Johns continued straining for notes, not entirely sure if he should shout or whisper

'Straight Lines'. He settled on a bit of both, not really doing the song—an absolute American hit in waiting with the right push—complete justice. Clearly frustrated, Johns took out his angst on his guitar, giving it a solid pounding as the song built to a close.

On the morning program *Good Day Atlanta*, not only was Johns in better voice, but he was also feeling chatty. Looking dapper as always in a dark suit and skinny tie, he toyed with his guitar as he bantered with the bubbly host. 'The process of making that record was a lot more liberating than other records,' he said, wiping a little sleep out of his eyes, 'because we funded it ourselves. A lot of freedom.' (He decided it was best not to mention that they'd gone several hundred thousand dollars over budget; the album almost bankrupted the band.) When asked to give his definition of 'psychedelic pop'—it was a term being used to describe *Young Modern*—Johns thought about it briefly, smiled and said, 'I don't know if I can articulate that on morning television. I think it just means pop music that's not normal.' Then it was into 'Straight Lines'.

Yet *Young Modern*, like *Diorama* before it, wasn't a hit Stateside, peaking at number 70 on 11 August. (*Diorama* had stalled at number 91 and only lasted a fortnight.) By 18 August, it was at number 150, heading in the wrong direction, fast. The next week it stumbled to number 197 and then faded away completely. Their first three albums, by comparison, each spent upwards of six months on the US charts—*Frogstomp* had charted for almost a year. *Young Modern* was a bigger flop than *Diorama*.

As for 'Straight Lines', it did manage to make a dent on *Billboard*'s Modern Rock Tracks chart, a list of songs creating waves on radio. It peaked at number twelve (the Foo Fighters' 'Pretender' was *numero uno*) and hung about for ten weeks. But it didn't enter the Top 100 singles chart, which measured actual sales. It was a far cry from reaction to the song at home, where it had been their first number one since 1997's 'Freak'. By the time of its brief rise in the US charts, 'Straight Lines' was zeroing in on sales of 150,000 copies in Oz. It claimed second position on Triple J's taste-maker Hottest 100 chart and was also voted the APRA Song of the Year, the biggest accolade of all for Johns and co-writer Julian Hamilton.

Yet, still, it flopped Stateside, despite the band securing a spot at the influential Lollapalooza festival in early August and harbouring a genuinely strong ambition to succeed again in North America. Johns was eager to shake off the common perception of Silverchair as some 'grunge sensations from Down Under'. 'It's like we haven't done anything in thirteen years!' he said, clearly frustrated.

'Mainstream America remembers us as the band with the frog on the [album] cover,' Johns told a reporter in Fort Worth, Texas. '[But] it's a question of being known for what we are instead of what we were.'

That proved to be much easier said than done; it was as though they'd been set in stone as the kids in big shorts rocking 'Tomorrow'.

———◄○►———

Keen to put the American debacle behind them, Johns and the band agreed to a co-headlining Oz tour with Powderfinger, an undertaking called Across the Great Divide. It was no small enterprise, either: 33 gigs in 26 towns— many way off the rock-and-roll radar—requiring nine trucks, a crew of 65 and some 25,000 kilometres of travel, running from early August through to late October.

Johns was a little shocked when he saw the itinerary: 'I didn't know you could tour Australia for nine weeks,' he admitted.

The tour was a huge drawcard, pulling 220,000-plus paying customers through the turnstiles. The more extreme fans turned up to as many as a dozen of the shows, which were staged in venues ranging from the usual metropolitan superdomes to outback big tops—or in one instance, a not-so-big top. The gig in Ballarat in mid-September had to be rescheduled because of a massive hole in the tent.

Reconciliation was the theme of the tour, on a number of levels. Firstly, it brought together the two biggest Australian rock bands of the moment, a theme Johns took to with such gusto that he planted a wet one on Bernard Fanning's cheek during the pre-tour photo shoot. 'That's reconciliation for you,' Johns chuckled, searching for Fanning's sweet spot. On a more serious level, Reconciliation Australia, the country's key organisation in the quest for genuine reconciliation since being established in 2001, was a partner of the tour. (The bands donated $10,000 to the organisation.)

'I think we're drawing a lot of attention to a situation that a lot of people our age feel strongly about,' Johns told a reporter, in what might have been his last serious comment for the entire tour. In the past, he and the band had tended to keep their politics off the record—aside from his 'PG for PM' tagging at the ARIAs. But clearly, they felt strongly enough about Indigenous issues to sign on and speak out.

The odyssey began in Newcastle, on 29 August, with a secret show for just 200 punters, hosted by MySpace on the afternoon of the much larger 'proper' opening gig, when, as expected, queues stretched for hundreds of metres outside the venue. Judging by the mix of T-shirts and fans, it was hard to tell who was the bigger drawcard or the most in-demand frontman: Johns or Fanning. In the shared band room before the gig, there was a lot of high fiving and drinking, with the two groups mixing together easily. Both drinking and high fiving became tour rituals. Silverchair, in a honourable gesture, opened the night at Newcastle; Powderfinger returned the favour when the tour reached Brisbane, their hometown.

The love-in spilled onto the stage itself. In Sydney on 8 September, as a closer, both groups jammed The Who's 'Substitute'. It went so well they repeated the anarchic all-in at subsequent gigs. (Both bands—cheekily referred to as Powderchair—recorded a ringtone together, known simply as 'Jake', in honour of a crew member, for the tour's website.)

Johns was soaking up the bonhomie. This was way more fun than turning up on Leno without a voice. He even went as far as to submit to a 'meet and greet' before the Sydney gig, a recent entertainment phenomenon in which acts and their biggest fans (who've paid well for the privilege) stand awkwardly together in a soul-less room somewhere deep inside the venue and swap banalities.

'Playing any of your old stuff?' one eager fan asked Johns.

'Nah,' he replied, 'it's our day off.'

At that moment, Johns might have flashed back to a chance meeting that took place in Sydney's Hyde Park, when he was lying low, seated on a park bench, writing lyrics for *Young Modern* before its recording.

'Daniel, man,' a gushing fan shouted at Johns, who had his notebook in hand, scribbling away.

'Yeah?' replied Johns, a bit distracted.

'*Frogstomp*! What happened?'

Johns didn't say anything for a minute.

'Oh, fuck,' he eventually replied, 'you've ruined my day. What happened? Heaps happened.'

During the gig at rural Bendigo on 15 September, a local named Martin stepped up on stage in the midst of Silverchair's set and proposed to his girlfriend, Angie. Johns the MC hammed it up. 'I told my mother I wouldn't cry,' he said, choking back tears. Mac played the bridal waltz, the newly engaged couple snogged and the gig rolled on. (For the record, Angie said yes.)

As the roadshow progressed, the easygoing mood morphed into one long party, even while the on-tour-doco cameras were rolling. The old Latino pop chestnut 'La Bamba' had become the big backstage number, typically belted out by Johns and Fanning after several drinks—they even had a bash at 'Tomorrow' one night on the bus while lost on a dark highway between gig and hotel. Each band tried their hardest to out-do the other in the stitch-up department: Powderfinger erected a Silverchair shrine and Fanning was filmed kneeling before it, intoning the words of 'Tomorrow' like a sacred hymn. Seriously doctored band photos, always unflattering, became standard practice. Most ended up on the walls of the backstage portaloos.

In his downtime, Johns boned up on his local history, dressing in green for the Ballarat show because he found out it was once known as the 'green town' during goldrush days, when it envied its more affluent neighbour, Bendigo.

When the tour finally wound down in Wollongong towards the end of October, Across the Great Divide heralded an era of farewells: it was Silverchair's last lengthy tour of Australia, while Powderfinger would also split up, just one more album down the line, in 2010. The tour wasn't a bad way to go out, all things considered.

In the midst of Across the Great Divide, ARIA nominations were announced and, not surprisingly, the two bands split the spoils, sharing more than ten key nominations. Silverchair scooped the pool on the night, winning half a dozen trophies, among them Best Group, Album of the Year and Single of the Year for 'Straight Lines'. With twenty awards in total, they were now the most ARIA-d Australian group of all time.

But an equally big moment for Johns was inducting Radio Birdman into the ARIA Hall of Fame. After all, it was Radio Birdman's 'New Race' that Silverchair and Tim Rogers had furiously jammed at the ARIAs way back in 1995. Johns, in his prerecorded induction speech, made it clear that public speaking still wasn't his greatest joy. 'I hate it,' he said straight to camera, 'and I'm not good at it . . . I didn't give a speech at my own wedding. But it is a privilege; I feel honoured and proud to induct Radio Birdman into the ARIA Hall of Fame because they are a truly seminal Australian band.'

'I was born in 1979, the year after Radio Birdman split,' Johns continued, 'but as a kid growing up around the beaches of Newcastle, they were very relevant and real to my friends and I.' He revealed that Birdman's 'Aloha, Steve and Danno' was one of the first songs he'd learned.

During his induction, Johns recalled those 1995 ARIAs, and how their cover of 'New Race'—which culminated in Gillies doing a header into his drum kit—was 'our way of acknowledging' the trailblazing role Radio Birdman had played for them and dozens of other bands. 'And it was definitely a lot more fun than doing a speech.'

13

If I was gay, I'd say I was gay.
I wouldn't be ashamed of it . . . I'd headline
Mardi Gras and milk that puppy!
—Daniel Johns

JOHNS AND/OR SILVERCHAIR SIGHTINGS in the wake of the Across the Great Divide odyssey were rare. The band played two dozen US shows towards the end of 2007 but that didn't provide *Young Modern* with the jolt it needed. That ship hadn't sailed—it had sunk. It was a classic case of deja vu—just like *Diorama*, *Young Modern* had done good business at home, becoming their fifth straight album to peak at number one on the ARIA chart, but had stiffed commercially elsewhere. This wasn't for a shortage of good press: a four-star American *Rolling Stone* review laid on the praise with the proverbial trowel, describing *Young Modern* as 'aggressively modern', while *Entertainment Weekly*, in rating the album a healthy A–, noted Johns's knack for 'turning out memorable hooks', calling the album 'fairly astonishing'. Yet its closing observation—'Here's hoping Silverchair's second act is just getting started'—couldn't have been any further from what actually went down.

Johns and the band were stuck. While it was hardly the worst situation to be in—they could still make a handsome living at home, fill concert halls and be lavished with hefty praise—did they want to stay on this treadmill? Their next move, a spot on the 2008 Big Day Out, certainly felt like the act of a band in neutral. Johns told me once that festivals weren't his favourite thing; the shorter sets felt to him 'like infomercials'. Yet here they were again.

The Big Day Out itself had degenerated. It wasn't the taste-maker's delight it had been in the 1990s, a must-see festival that broke hot new acts and was renowned for big performances. It was now more a rite of passage for Gen Ys: rock and roll's answer to Schoolies' Week. Silverchair were playing their third Big Day Out, and they were among several return visitors on the 2008 bill—Rage Against the Machine, Billy Bragg and Björk were also enjoying another Oz summer junket. This definitely wasn't 1995, when Silverchair's wild mid-afternoon set inspired punters to leap like lemmings into the seething mosh pit. The mood of the event had changed; performers were now pretty much a backdrop for punters intent on having a mad day in the sun. Not everyone made it to the evening, when the big acts played.

For Johns, the journey must have stunk of recycling. To maintain his interest, he shaved his hair back to the skull, bleached it snowy blond and grew a moustache worthy of a pimp. At most gigs, he sported dark shades and a black-and-white ensemble, looking like a younger, leaner Blues Brother. The shirt didn't always stay; this was steamy mid-summer, after all.

Johns had fleshed out the band, too, adding backing vocalists and a brass section to the now standard two-keyboard attack. Daniel dubbed the ensemble 'the Silverchair Orchestra'. It definitely added muscle, but the effort seemed a little wasted in this environment. Most Big Day Out audiences merely wanted to get their rocks off and lose their black T-shirts in the chaos, yet Johns was asking them to work a little harder for bliss. He preferred to play 'Reflections of a Sound' than obvious party starters like 'Pure Massacre'. The masses really only went berserk during a trashy 'Freak' that closed the band's 50-minute-long sets, which would end with Johns, as always, humping both his guitar and his amp and dousing the crowd with hellish feedback. Then, with a theatrical flourish, he would bow and exit, stage right, another gig done.

Johns had some fun, admittedly, introducing most songs in the voice of a holy-rollin' southern preacher. 'Sydney,' Johns yelled, as the band tore into 'Straight Lines', 'sing it like you're on *Australian Idol'*. When his guitar failed briefly at the same gig, he toyed with the crowd, conducting them in nonsensical chants and chuckling at his own onstage misfortune. He instructed the masses to yell, 'Daniel, your guitar's fucked up!'—he replied with a plaintive: 'I know'. Paul Mac, too, enjoyed himself. He took to wearing a T-shirt emblazoned with the name David Furnish, a nod to Elton

John's hubby *and* the usual rumours about his relationship with Johns. ('They're not rumours,' Johns insisted with a mile-wide grin when asked by Channel [v]'s Jabba.)

After the final Big Day Out in early February in Perth, Johns and the band went to ground. They wouldn't emerge for more than two years.

———◈———

The second most common rumour relating to Daniel Johns—after the usual questions about the nature of his relationship with Paul Mac—dealt with the alleged rocky state of his marriage. There were frequent tabloid whispers: was it built to last? And when Johns did return to the news in 2009, it was because of exactly that: there *was* trouble in paradise. Big trouble. Divorce-sized trouble.

His marriage to Natalie Imbruglia had never been the easiest of relationships to maintain. Despite some minor overlap with their careers, it was unlikely you'd ever see Imbruglia on the main stage at the Big Day Out—nor was Johns going to score a cameo in *Neighbours*. They inhabited different creative worlds. And neither would have been crazy about being a plus-one, a handbag—they were both stars in their own right.

But it was the tyranny of distance, their careers constantly calling them in different directions, that proved to be the undoing of Johns and Imbruglia. Her film, fashion and music career was almost totally UK-centric, while Johns's core audience was in Australia (as the band's latest US sortie had proved conclusively). Imbruglia had her palace on White Lilies Island, which she was as unlikely to easily give up as Johns would his Merewether HQ (and his various Sydney boltholes). Imbruglia had been at Johns's side during his darkest days, when he was crippled by arthritis, which said a lot about their relationship when it was at its strongest. But now they'd drifted apart.

Hints of a rift had started circulating when Johns didn't mention Imbruglia during his various acceptance speeches at the 2007 ARIAs; nor did she rate a mention at the 2008 APRAs, when 'Straight Lines' won the Song of the Year gong. That raised eyebrows. ('I really love my family and really love my management and I really love everyone that I love. Umm, goodnight,' Johns said at the latter, looking the worse for wear.) Imbruglia was only with Johns for a short time during the lengthy Across the Great Divide tour, when the troupe reached Melbourne.

Most years, the couple would spend an extended New Year together in Oz. But in 2009, Imbruglia, who was in town for a commitment with department store David Jones, left on 2 January, leaving Johns behind. That was a surprise. And of course, there'd been ongoing whispers about Johns's sexuality. Normally he joked about this, especially when Mac was mentioned as his partner—after all, they'd agreed that Mac's role in Johns's life was purely 'avuncular'—but Johns did speak publicly, and seriously, about the suggestion during the Melbourme Big Day Out in 2008.

'I'm not fucking gay!' Johns said to the crowd between songs. He seemed annoyed, as if someone had dragged out the joke a bit too long. Mind you, Johns was adjusting a black lace garter on his leg at the time.

Whatever the true reason for the split, no celebrity uncoupling was complete without a press release, and one was duly dispatched to the media on 17 March 2009. It read, in part: 'Our career demands and our lives in different parts of the world have brought us to the point where unfortunately this difficult decision was necessary for both of us. We have simply grown apart through not being able to spend enough time together.'

But as recently as 2006, Johns had told me in an interview that their bond was strong. When I raised the subject of tabloid speculation about a rift, he laughed it off. 'Everyone knows they're a load of shit.' And in 2005, Imbruglia had said that she'd 'never let the distance or work get in the way of my marriage'. Still, the title of her album from that year, *Counting Down the Days*, made no secret of the fact they both spent so much time waiting for the other to return from their latest commitment. Johns, of course, had also documented this tricky part of their relationship in The Dissociatives' bittersweet 'Forever and a Day'. 'Forever and a day,' a forlorn Johns sang, 'so cold without you.'

'While we are very sad that our marriage has ended, we wanted to make it clear that our parting is amicable and we remain friends,' the March 2009 press release continued.

Perhaps one other factor that weighed heavily on their marriage was the idea of children. Imbruglia loved kids; most of her friends were parents. She was keen to have children of her own. 'I love babies,' she said quite freely when asked. Johns was a bit more guarded about the notion. 'I'm not scared of it,' he told me in 2006, when I asked if they had discussed the topic, 'but I don't want to do it yet. I'm not having kids until I'm about 70, and Natalie's happy with that. I've got no problem with the concept, I think it's very cool, but I have a few more years of having the benefit of not having to get up early . . . I need those extra hours in the morning.'

The former couple, to their eternal credit, said little about each other after the split. The most Imbruglia would admit, at least publicly, was that 'after my divorce I was doing lots of crazy stuff. That was one good thing that came out of it. You lose the fear.' She was duly linked with A-listers such as Prince Harry, *Friends* actor David Schwimmer and Harry Styles (even though the One Direction pin-up was a good seventeen years her junior), but Imbruglia remained resolutely single. And not a mother. But the former couple didn't remain friends: they stopped speaking altogether post-divorce. 'No, we're not really in contact,' Imbruglia admitted in a 2014 radio interview.

Johns began seeing 21-year-old Queensland-born Louise Van der Vorst, a waifish model best known for her 'alien chic' look. Their romance bloomed quickly; Van der Vorst moved into Johns's Newcastle hacienda after just two dates. Over time they'd bounce between Surry Hills in Sydney—the eatery Bills was a particularly favourite spot—and Johns's place in Merewether. When not modelling, Van der Vorst took over the task of giving Johns's home a decent makeover.

'It's pretty crazy,' she told a *Herald* reporter, 'stuff is everywhere, there are instruments, fabric, paint, crayons, food and cooking. It's all a big, crazy place.'

In early 2012, Johns and Van der Vorst posed together for a *RUSSH* magazine shoot at the house, looking impossibly cool together, a thoroughly modern couple draped around each other in a series of soulful, soft-focus embraces. 'Hidden away in a secret sanctuary,' read one wordy caption, 'Daniel plays the piano while Louise sews her own dresses. In ivory tones and with rough, frayed hems, he always loves the way they look on her.' It was hard to imagine that Johns came from an era of big shorts and flanno shirts.

When asked about Johns and their relationship, Van der Vorst said little. 'He is a private person,' was as much as she'd offer. And Silverchair? 'I liked some of their songs, but I never had a poster or anything.' As for Johns, he told those close to him that he was thinking about shifting to New York to support Van der Vorst and her flourishing career.

Life in Silverchair clearly wasn't great for maintaining relationships. Joannou had split with live-in partner Sarah McLeod in 2006. In 2009, Gillies had broken up with his fiancée, Hayley Alexander, and spent a week in 'detox' dealing with the emotional fallout. He married a friend from childhood, Jakica Ivancevic, in mid-2010, but his mother didn't attend the wedding. She'd told her daughter-in-law-to-be that her son was a drug addict and not in a fit state of mind. Gillies said that he'd simply been living a single man's life, 'running around, drinking, philandering, partying', when he met Ivancevic. It was ugly.

————◀◦▶————

But what of Silverchair? In June 2009, Johns and the band reconvened to begin work on a planned follow-up to *Young Modern*—imaginatively titled, at this early stage, Album No. 6. They spent three weeks together and, when those sessions concluded, made plans to continue later in the year, at home in Newcastle. Judging by the footage they released to their website, the new songs were still very much works in progress. Aside from the usual in- and near-studio hijinks—quad bikes were a current sensation, as was a homemade rocket launcher—and discussions of food (Gillies was a white-fish advocate), they didn't appear to spend much time actually recording music. It was fair to say they were having a high old time in the studio, though, if the constant giggling and glassy eyes were any gauge.

'Welcome to the future,' Johns said to camera, but without offering tangible evidence of what Silverchair's future might sound like.

Johns reported in to Triple J in early December 2009, talking up a new sound and talking down a recent spate of writer's block (his system had unclogged itself while he was in New York, apparently). So how would this new record, which he was producing himself, stack up against *Young Modern*?

'The main difference is there's a lot of experimentation with instruments and synths. I think there's only guitar on four songs . . . It's dirtier,' he explained. 'Surprisingly rocky, given that there aren't many guitars.' Two songs, currently titled 'Sixteen' and 'Machina Collecta', were nearing completion.

Johns hadn't lost his sense of humour, although he politely declined to get into any discussion about drugs. 'You remember what happened last time,' he chuckled, thinking back to the awkward Garrett–Bono drama. When asked to play DJ and choose a Silverchair song to play (the interview was live), he sounded a bit taken aback. 'Me? I've heard them all. It's up to you.' And what about hobbies: did he have any? 'My hobby became my job when I was really young,' Johns replied, which was surprisingly revealing, given the informal nature of the chat.

———◄o►———

Five months later, Silverchair re-emerged for half a dozen festival dates over three weeks, starting out in Bendigo in early May 2010. Once again, the gigs were undertaken to raise the necessary capital to keep recording their new album. And it didn't take a degree in psychology to determine that these gigs weren't rocking Johns's world. It was much like the Big Day Out 2008, playing the same songs to the same crowds, primarily to top up the coffers so they could return to the studio. They'd nearly bankrupted themselves while making *Young Modern*; that wouldn't happen again.

In Canberra on 9 May, as their set neared its end, Johns led the crowd in an *'Olé, olé, olé'* chant before taking a seat on his amp. For one nervous minute, it seemed as though the gig might end there. Finally, he leapt from his perch and tore into 'Freak', spitting out the lyrics with even more vitriol than usual. Despite the volume and his antics—he even took to Gillies' drum kit with his guitar and had earlier transformed 'Ana's Song' into the type of epic emotional purge that wouldn't have been lost on Jeff Buckley's *Grace*—in the main, he seemed to be going through the rock-and-roll motions. Just how many more times was he going to have to play 'Israel's Son'? And wasn't it ironic that even though they were working on a new record that virtually shunned guitars, here they were, yet again, playing the alt-rock, guitar-heavy faves for the concert dollar? The image on stage at the end of their Newcastle set, where Johns's guitar was draped like a hanged man over a microphone, bleeding feedback, pretty much summed up the state of his mind. He was done with rock. Maybe done with Silverchair altogether.

It wasn't for lack of enthusiasm from their die-hard fans. Every night when the group walked on stage and ripped into 'Young Modern Station', they were greeted with the kind of adulation usually reserved for boy bands—and there was plenty of action in the mosh pit. (Johns sorted out a fist-fight at one gig with a few well-chosen words. He was a lover, not a fighter.) The band also tried out the two new songs, 'Machina Collecta' and 'Sixteen', which they'd been tinkering with in the studio. 'Hopefully,' Johns told a reporter, 'this road-testing will help the recorded versions turn out better.'

The latter was out-and-out electro-pop, while 'Machina' sounded like a potential hit. One fan described it as the sound of 'Daft Punk fucking Optimus Prime', which seemed to be a positive.

During the band's opening-night gig at Bendigo, Johns reported to the crowd that they would love to stay in the town longer, but they'd been evicted from their apartment on the afternoon of the gig. 'Apparently, old people are sensitive to noise,' he said, rolling his eyes. Before playing 'Straight Lines', he told the crowd he was suffering from 'irreversible impotence'. He welcomed the crowd in Maitland with a generous, 'It's good to be home—thank you, you bunch of good-looking cunts'. Most nights, in the midst of 'If You Keep Losing Sleep', Johns would make crazy demands of the audience: 'Let me hear you scream eight and a half times!' He even went freestyle during the lead-in to 'Mind Reader', rapping: 'We like Melbourne/but we like Bendigo better'. 'I'm no Snoop Dogg,' he shrugged, drawing laughs from the faithful down front.

A shirtless, sweat-coated Johns tried this again in Darwin, at the end of the tour, improvising lyrics in the midst of 'Ana's Song': 'And I've been calling out your name/And you don't call me back/And you don't text me back/And I've been crying out just to meet you one more time,' he wailed, his tongue presumably pretty close to his cheek.

And that was it. Silverchair's final gig.

There were trickles of news over the ensuing months. Joannou was going to present an award at the ARIAs, and the bass he used at Rock in Rio had been auctioned online, with some proceeds going to his preferred charity, Nathan's Bequest. Johns had been tapped to compose music for a film with Newcastle-raised director Josh Wakely, named *My Mind's Own Enemy*. Gillies had put in some hours with the Starlight Foundation. Over time, there'd be more talk of their different acts of charity than of music. Johns would join forces with World Animal Protection and their 'Collars not Cruelty' campaign—the notion that 20 million dogs were slaughtered each year was all the motivation he needed to sign on. In lieu of performing at the next Big Day Out, Joannou raised awareness for Headspace, as part of a campaign called Rock N Ride, riding his motorbike from the Big Day Out Gold Coast to the event site in Adelaide. But, oddly, there was no more talk of Album No. 6.

—◄○►—

Like the rock star who cried wolf, Johns had been threatening to end the group pretty much from the time of their second album. If he had had a dollar for every time he'd told a reporter, 'I was seriously thinking about splitting the band,' he'd be an even richer man. Yet he always changed his mind. Typically, he'd drift into another project— *I Can't Believe It's Not Rock*, The Dissociatives—or take a long break and return to the others renewed. Then there were other motivators, such as seeing Midnight Oil go hard at WaveAid in 2005, that made him realise how good his own band could be, and how tough it was to replicate their special chemistry.

Yet as 2010 rolled into 2011, the situation was different—and serious. Johns and Gillies, in particular, had fallen out badly, the second key relationship in Johns's life to go south in recent years (the first being his divorce from Imbruglia). They were long-time friends, who together had been through a million things no Newie kid could ever imagine experiencing. They'd been as tight as two guys could possibly be in the pressure cooker that was a rock band. Yet now they were clashing, in part due to the direction Johns wanted to take the band, but also about personal matters that neither has been willing to divulge publicly.

Johns wanted to radically alter the band's sound; he didn't want guitars to dominate the sound as they had in the past. He said he was hoping to make a 'real weird arty album'. But when they returned to the studio, he simply wasn't feeling the magic. 'I felt flat,' Johns admitted. At the same time, he understood that if he pushed Silverchair too far creatively, he was committing 'commercial suicide'. 'I always felt like I had weirder music in me and wasn't allowed to do it,' he said. Johns sounded frustrated. He made it clear he had no outside pressure—Silverchair were now a truly independent entity—but the reality, as he understood very well, was that they needed to sell records to keep going. *Diorama* and *Young Modern* had struck a balance between the weird and the accessible—at least with Australian audiences— but Johns had a powerful urge to push his music further into the unknown. And it became clear that he couldn't do that as part of Silverchair.

As the end of summer 2011 approached, it became apparent to all of the band that Album No. 6—which Johns had envisaged as the band's swan song—wasn't going anywhere if they couldn't agree on how it should feel or sound, even more so if there was tension between two-thirds of the group. This, Silverchair's last LP, was feted to become one of the lost albums of local music history. Due to Johns's insistence on no guitars, no drums, no bass— he hadn't even cut any vocals—what remained was several hours' worth of what he called 'electronic noodling'. It was a mess, probably unsalvageable.

That was it for Johns. He was done. He wore some of the blame himself; he simply couldn't make it work. 'I just pulled the pin. I was firing myself.'

Gillies and Joannou reluctantly agreed.

Gillies, too, spoke about the end of the group. 'We hit a bit of a snag with the record we were working on,' he said, sounding like someone who wouldn't rule out a reunion in the future. He disclosed that they'd been trying to write in the studio, a first for the band. In Gillies' view, while making their aborted album, the band were operating 'by the seat of our pants to see what happened'. But it wasn't working. 'We hit a brick wall,' he said, and the sessions, and the band, were shut down.

———◄◦►———

Usually, whispers and rumours relating to Silverchair remained just that: whispers and rumours. But on 25 May 2011, a press release emerged that, for once, proved the rumours to be spot on. Silverchair were breaking up.

'We formed Silverchair nearly 20 years ago,' it read, 'when we were just twelve years old. Today we stand by the same rules now as we did back then . . . if the band stops being fun and if it's no longer fulfilling creatively, then we need to stop.' The official in-house term being used was 'indefinite hibernation'; there'd be no final lap of honour for Silverchair, as there had been for Powderfinger in late 2010 with their Sunsets tour.

'Back in 2009,' the Silverchair announcement continued, 'we went into the studio to start work on a record. Initially things were going well and as a result we did some shows in 2010 to maintain creative momentum. However, over the months that followed in the studio it became clear to us that we were moving in different directions. Despite our best efforts over the last year or so, it's become increasingly clear that the spark simply isn't there between the three of us at the moment.'

The band understood that some fans would be let down by the news, but believed the split was a good thing, a necessary move. They called their 'hibernation' 'a liberating and positive step for us'. Then came the usual sweet talk—'the three of us still really care about each other'— and mention of the various solo projects each had taken on. So, while Silverchair were taking a vow of silence, they'd all be working on their own new material. The press release was signed off with a simple, 'With Sincere Thanks for Your Understanding. Sweet Dreams. Daniel, Ben and Chris.'

And that was it. The most successful Australian rock band since INXS, who'd sold six million records, won more

ARIAs than even John Farnham and who'd constantly filled stadiums and their pockets—Johns's personal worth was estimated at A$20 million—were done. Officially.

◄○►

The news inspired a round of headlines. Some were clever—'No more tomorrows for Silverchair', announced *The Sydney Morning Herald*—and others not so. 'Johns toasts the Silverchair split', crowed news.com.au, as he ducked one of their snappers while drinking at an inner-city Sydney pub a few days after the news broke. The implication was all wrong: while he felt liberated by the decision, Johns also understood how much Silverchair meant to a lot of people. He might have been boozing, but it was hardly a celebration.

Johns never held back when asked the right questions, and he was forthcoming when asked about his new, post-Silverchair life. 'Some die-hard group of fans will be massively offended by what I choose to do next,' he admitted, politely declining to add that those fans were probably the ones he could happily live without. He stressed that he was proud of what Silverchair had achieved, but didn't want to find himself at 50 with the band his only claim to artistic merit. Heaven forbid he end up like one of The Rolling Stones. 'I didn't want it to be my thing forever.'

Though Johns mightn't have intended any insult, his former bandmates would have been within their rights to feel offended: Silverchair *had* been the biggest thing in their lives and probably always would be. This was reflected by their post-band life—soon after the split, Joannou gave up music altogether and bought into an upscale Newcastle venue, The Edwards. Gillies formed a new band named Bento but became better known as the partner of Jackie Gillies, a regular on television's schlocky *The Real Housewives of Melbourne*.

In later discussions, Johns would confess that he was 'just sick of being the guy who had to be louder than the cymbals, and louder than the distortion, and like a rock'n'roll lead singer'. He categorically ruled out any kind of Silverchair reunion down the line; he was adamant that would never happen. This was despite all the talk of putting the band into 'deep sleep' and going into 'indefinite hibernation', the two terms bandied around in the official statement announcing their split.

Johns did have a plan, of sorts. Not only was Silverchair in hibernation, but he, too, was about to go to ground. He wanted simply to sit in his living room and 'noodle and manipulate shit and get a bit more techno'. He wanted to teach himself how to make music differently; he'd had enough of guitars and amps and volume. There had to be another way. And mixing with the music-biz crowd had little appeal for him, either. 'I just like chilling at home with my girl [Van der Vorst] and my dog,' he told a journo, when he did bother taking someone's call. A perfect day for Johns was spent on the couch, in his PJs, playing with his favourite bit of gear, a vocoder, and smoking like a chimney. He wanted to 'develop my skills, not release anything, *not be famous*'.

Johns, who at the turn of the century didn't even own a computer, let alone a mobile phone, was now embracing the digital age with gusto. When he learned that he could order groceries online, he was in. 'Man,' he exclaimed, 'I don't have to leave the house.' For the next few years, he'd be all but a recluse. One writer went as far as to tag him 'the Howard Hughes of Oz rock'.

Johns also thought about getting back into painting, which he had enjoyed as a kid; he was even toying with the idea of acting. Whatever new music Johns made would be on his terms. If anyone wanted to collaborate with him, they'd have to do the legwork. 'I'd prefer people fly to me.' He rarely left the house, apart from time he spent with producer and friend Chris Townend, who'd been in the studio with Silverchair during their aborted album sessions. Townend owned a shack in the mountains. Johns described how he and Townend headed there to 'smoke and listen to the weirdest, most hectic electronic music'.

Johns was convinced that rock and roll was a no-go zone. He had a new mission statement: 'I'm going to go full Scott Walker: go fucking nuts, sample the weirdest shit'.

————◦————

Johns had hoped to move as far away from Silverchair as possible, and he definitely achieved it when he did finally return to the spotlight, in the most unlikely of scenarios.

'I had a slight brief,' Johns admitted in May 2012 when asked about a new piece of music he called 'Atlas'. This was a first in a series of firsts for Johns: he'd never written to a brief before (despite the demands of Atlantic around the time of *Diorama* to come up with a radio hit). And he'd never composed an ad before—'Atlas' was to be used as branding for Australia's national airline, Qantas, as part of a campaign called 'You're the reason we fly'.

That brief requested a composition that sounded 'international'; this was a global airline, after all. Johns interpreted that as 'big' and set to the task with the Australian Chamber Orchestra, which was a personal dream fulfilled. This was one collaboration for which he was willing to leave the couch. 'It seems to have come out pretty well,' said Johns, as he gathered with the ACO in May to record the track, which was premiered two months later.

Johns didn't want to write a jingle. There were no lyrics; instead, he crooned some Beach Boys-esque harmonies over the top of a broad musical palette that ranged from epic and orchestral to scratchy and electronic. 'Atlas' encapsulated everything he'd been trying to do on the orchestrated passages of *Diorama* and *Young Modern*, all in a few crisp minutes. His time with Van Dyke Parks, clearly, had been well spent. He'd learned from a master. It was a striking piece of music—if Johns's goal was to provide a modern flavour far removed from the homesick jingoism of 'I Still Call Australia Home', which the airline had milked since 1998, he'd nailed it.

Silverchair fans' take on 'Atlas', as noted on the song's YouTube page, was mixed. They ranged from the blunt— 'Don't get it'—to the irate ('This made me want to hijack every Qantas flight I ever caught just to make it stop'), to the accepting: 'I think it sounds like Australia: modern, a little lighthearted and easy-going'. Unfortunately, 'Atlas' didn't last long: in July 2013, Qantas replaced it with a new campaign, and quietly slipped 'I Still Call Australia Home' back onto its playlist. Perhaps 'Atlas' had been a little too progressive.

But Johns's role with Qantas didn't end there—it extended into the area of mentoring. A few months after 'Atlas' was unveiled, Johns and music producer Lee Groves met with three finalists from the Qantas Spirit of Youth awards program. Among them was Melburnian Courtney Barnett, who'd soon explode onto the international music scene with her distinctive, chatty take on the singer-songwriter form. Barnett grew up with Silverchair. She was thrilled to meet Johns.

'It's kind of a little bit strange to have him in the room,' Barnett confessed, as she unveiled a new song called 'History Eraser'. Johns eased any tension by laying on the positive feedback to this and the other pieces he was exposed to; he hadn't forgotten what it felt like to be starting out. It probably helped that Johns slugged from a beer while playing mentor—he looked pretty relaxed.

But it was Johns's private life that seemed to be garnering the most interest, especially from Sydney's ravenous social reporters. Johns had reason to wonder whether the paparazzi had him under surveillance; there seemed to be a camera nearby every time he took a drink. 'Wait til tomorrow: Silverchair star Daniel Johns pictured drinking vodka at 3pm on a TUESDAY [caps deliberate] at a Bondi pub then sitting on a park bench alone to roll a cigarette', screamed one headline, typifying the 'outrage' that seemed to accompany every mention of Johns in the press. It may have also been the longest headline in tabloid history, courtesy of the *Daily Mail Australia*.

Around the time of 'Atlas', Johns, having recently split with girlfriend Van der Vorst (who duly took up with the son of Oz rock great James Reyne), was spotted kicking back at The Star casino in Sydney. Another breathless headline, this time in *The Daily Telegraph*, omitted nothing: 'Daniel Johns partied with girls and a man across Sydney after breaking up with girlfriend Louise Van der Vorst'. (Phew.)

'Daniel Johns has wasted little time breaking into the bachelor lifestyle,' barked an anonymous reporter, 'with the newly-single rocker spotted partying his way across Sydney at the weekend with a string of ladies—and even one guy.' The story went into some detail about Johns's big night out, pointing out that he was 'not short of any female company' yet was also spotted in a tight huddle with Simon Hancock, a promoter at the casino's nightclub, Marquee. 'They were pretty much all over each other,' revealed one clubber. The paper went as far as to contact Hancock, pressing him for details: what was going on between him and Johns? Was it another Paul Mac situation?

'We're mates,' Hancock said, 'that's it.'

Johns's sexuality seemed to be a constant source of fascination for society reporters. Interestingly, if he was gay, he certainly chose the most beautiful women to conduct relationships with: Natalie Imbruglia, Louise Van der Vorst and his next girlfriend, raven-haired fashion designer-model Estelita Huijer.

'If I was bisexual, I'd say I was bisexual,' Johns insisted, when asked that question once again. 'If I was gay, I'd say I was gay. I wouldn't be ashamed of it. I'd celebrate it. I'd headline Mardi Gras and milk that puppy!'

In time, Johns would credit Huijer with being his 'muse', 'Not like a Yoko thing,' he hastened to add, when the subject came up with a news.com.au reporter, 'but I was seeking that approval.' For fun, he and Huijer would dress in disguise—Johns developed a liking for what he called a 'North Shore mum' wig—and meet startled friends for drinks. It was one way to stay off the paps' radar.

In these various reports of Johns's movements in Sydney's lively drinking-and-snorting circuit, there appeared to be an underlying sense of shock. Reporters seemed genuinely amazed that 'Daniel from Silverchair' was now an adult, living a fully grown-up life. It was as though many people thought he was frozen in time at the age of fifteen, never allowed to grow up, growling 'Tomorrow' in that ungodly voice he'd long discarded. 'Dan does what he wants, and he's always been like that,' replied a rep from John Watson's company Eleven, when contacted about Johns's nocturnal adventures. 'This is not a big deal.'

14

I'm not going to let [the past]
affect me like it used to.
—Daniel Johns

WHEN NOT OUT ON THE TOWN, Johns had finally completed another project, *My Mind's Own Melody*, his collaboration with film-maker Josh Wakely. Wakely described the short film as a 'cinematic musical'.

Again, like the orchestral 'Atlas', this was a long way from rock and roll, a chance for Johns to tap into his love of film and visual artists such as Brett Whiteley. Johns and Wakely had a unique way of collaborating: Wakely would leave Johns phone messages explaining what he was trying to say with his script, then Johns would call him back and play pieces of music down the line, along with his own interpretations of how this music and the storyline worked together. After a few of these creative calls, Johns said, 'Enough'.

'Let's not do this on the phone anymore,' he told Wakely. 'Roll up to my house, and let's see what happens.'

Together at Merewether they'd 'jam'—Wakely would read aloud from the script while Johns conjured up ideas on the piano. It was a radical new way of making music. Gradually the project came together; the film, completed in 2013, featured old stagers such as Max Cullen and emerging actress Kate Beahan. Golden Globe–winner Lisa Gerrard also contributed to the movie.

Johns had previewed some of the music from the arthouse film at a TEDx talk at Carriageworks in Sydney during May 2011. The last time he had played there he was premiering *Young Modern* and being shouted vodka tonics by the audience, but this was a vastly different crowd, the Sydney arts community. They were older, a little harder to please, more demanding. Just what Johns needed if he was to bust out of the rock-and-roll stereotype. He handled it well.

At TEDx, Johns, alone on the piano, played a reworked version of 'Those Thieving Birds' from *Young Modern* and *Diorama*'s 'After All These Years'. He then riffed on the piano as Wakely read from his script. 'Daniel isn't just creating the score,' Wakely emphasised at TEDx, 'but creating the film with me. We're both storytellers.'

Yet aside from a screening at the prestigious New York Film Festival in 2013, the film didn't garner a formal release. Still, it was yet another new sensation for Johns. He had tweaked his master plan; he said he was now attempting to 'delete [himself] and start again'.

All this time, Johns was gradually working his way towards his 'proper' solo debut, a full album of new music. In 2012, he'd invited Julian Hamilton to his house to listen to some music he was working on. Johns told Hamilton he was in 'a bit of a crisis'—he'd grown to hate the sound of his singing voice. So instead of 'regular' songs, he'd assembled wild sound collages, without a vocal or a guitar in earshot. *Was it even music?* Johns wasn't sure.

'It's good,' Hamilton said diplomatically after a listen, 'but you need to get back to writing songs.'

This was backed up by another friend of Johns's, who said: 'Dude, there's no songs. It's all these hectic noises!'

While harsh, this was exactly what Johns needed to hear. He'd been so busy clearing his head of everything Silverchair-related, getting so far away from anything that remotely resembled guitar rock, that he'd overlooked the very thing that made him successful: his ability to write great songs. He'd forgotten to bring 'the sunshine', to use Hamilton's description.

A week later, his shit finally together, Johns sat down at his piano and began writing songs again. He shared the first of these new tunes with Sydney-based, Dutch-born producer Louis Schoorl—collaborating with unfamiliar people was very much part of his new MO—and the record that would become *Talk* had begun.

———◄o►———

Johns returned to Sydney's Carriageworks on 24 March 2015 for the APRAs. The event was a favourite of Johns's, who'd now won the coveted Songwriter of the Year award three times (a record in itself). R&B was his new thing, and the signs were everywhere as soon as he stepped onto the stage: from the pimp-y bling draped around his neck to his new singing voice, a soaring falsetto, Johns was all about the groove. Premiering his song 'Preach', Johns was surrounded by three backup singers, a harpist, plenty of laptops and a noticeable absence of guitars and amps. Johns seemed a little confused as to what to do with his hands, given that he wasn't packing an electric guitar, but that didn't make his performance any less mesmeric. The four-minute spot was soulful and haunting, and it completely overshadowed anything else that happened that night, with all dues to the likes of Thelma Plum, Jimmy Barnes and M-Phazes. Johns owned the APRAs. And 'Preach' couldn't have been further removed from the rattle and hum of Silverchair; Johns had truly reinvented himself. The industry taste-makers looking on seemed a little stunned: the final note of the song hung in the air for what felt like minutes before they burst into applause.

Was this the same Daniel Johns?

Johns looked happy to be back in the spotlight; it was certainly an improvement on recent events in his increasingly troubled private life. On the night of 28 October 2014 he was driving along Morgan Street in Merewether in his black Jag when he was clocked at somewhere between 70 and 80 kilometres an hour in a 50-kilometre zone. He'd also had a few glasses of wine. When he was pulled over by the law, he blew 0.126, more than twice the legal limit. A few months later, a very contrite Johns copped his punishment in Newcastle local court: an $880 fine and his licence cancelled until June 2015. He also had to undertake a traffic offenders course. 'It will never happen again,' a solemn, stony-faced Johns told reporters outside the court. When the old 'role model' question was raised— 'any message for young people who might look up to you, Daniel?'—Johns turned on his heels and walked away, his lawyer close behind him. He'd had enough of that during the Garrett–Bono fiasco.

In May 2015, during a night at one of his favourite hangouts, the Low 302 bar in Crown Street, Johns fell and cut his head. He lay sprawled on the footpath as a crowd gathered, wondering who was being stretchered into an ambulance for a ride to St Vincent's hospital's ER. When a photographer tried to jump into the back of the ambulance, a friend of Daniel's intervened, telling him to 'fuck off'. Daniel casually dismissed it as 'one of those dumb kind of falls'; he reported that he was in and out of the ER in 30 minutes. But the photos from the scene were worrying.

Soon after, a paparazzo snapped a thongs-and-singlet-clad Johns on the way home after another bender, his friends protectively throwing a coat around him.

By the time of the APRAs and his various inner-city misadventures, the *Aerial Love* EP, from which 'Preach' was lifted, was already number one on the Oz iTunes chart. The provocatively raunchy video for 'Aerial Love' was shot, partly by drone, in the Sahara-like wilds of Newcastle's Stockton Sand Dunes. Johns compared the vision to 'the desert scenes from *Star Wars*'—and he did carry a little Hans Solo–like swagger during the clip, in which couples happily humped in the dunes while he walked and crooned. Johns may have lost his driver's licence, and his private life was being played out a bit too publicly for his liking, but with 'Aerial Love' he was back in business. Sexy business.

The APRA spot was merely a warm-up for Johns's big coming out—two headlining nights in late May at Vivid LIVE, a highlight of the Sydney arts calendar. The 3000 tickets for each of the two Sydney Opera House shows, running at around $100 each, disappeared in minutes.

Johns may have looked the worse for wear in recent pap shots, but he looked just fine at the Opera House, as he emerged amid a dizzying arsenal of lights and other visual effects to launch his show with the slick 'Aerial Love'. Given the fact that it was his first time in public as a solo act (the APRAs was an industry bash), Johns and band opted for virginal white; he wore a long sleeveless top draped over what looked oddly like drop-crotch pantaloons. A white bandanna covered his close-cropped hair. His seven-member band also looked effortlessly cool, seriously stylish. His two female backing vocalists, both sporting wide-brimmed hats, seemed dressed for the races—if the races were being held in Milan, that is.

As the gig progressed, Johns reached for his guitar during 'Going on 16', but it was more a prop than a weapon. Occasionally he wrung a note or two from it, but the song, like so much of his new material, was driven by beats and deep grooves—and his pet vocoder. Johns wasn't kidding when he said that he hoped to sound like Janet Jackson, although you'd also have to factor in the likes of new kids Flume and James Blake. (Darth Vader, as well; that vocoder could do strange things to his voice.)

Nerves now calmed, Johns started talking after a few songs. 'Is it too early for a singalong?' he asked. 'You're beautiful people,' Johns exclaimed during 'Too Many'. And he meant every word. It wouldn't have been beyond the realms of possibility for the crowd to boo him off the stage—after all, this was Daniel Johns from Silverchair, the rock guy, and here he was crooning nu-soul ballads like Australia's answer to D'Angelo. There'd be no speaker humping or roaring feedback tonight. Who needed it? Johns was tired of all the old noise. The audience, fortunately, were down for the ride—at least until Johns told them to get out of their seats.

'Come on, come on, get the fuck up, it's Friday!' The faithful did as they were instructed.

Johns didn't completely neglect his past. But these brief flashbacks were not quite what anyone in the Opera House expected. Included in his hour-long set was 'Straight Lines', which he transformed into a relentless techno-groove, his drummer standing upright, thumping the tubs Salvation Army–style. Makeover be damned, the song still inspired a singalong; everyone in the Opera House was out of their seats and into the moment. Johns clearly loved the interaction; he wound the crowd up, encouraging them to get even more involved, as the song grew and grew into a wild rave-up. Also included was 'Young Man, Old Man', The Dissociatives' track Johns wrote about his relationship with Paul Mac. But again, the song underwent some major tweaking; Johns had stripped it of its hummable melody and turned it into another heavy groove.

Then there was 'After All These Years', the heart-on-sleeve ballad that he'd used to open most nights of the *Diorama* tour. But this was a different beast altogether, slowed down to almost a crawl, Johns's voice twisted and distorted by his ever-present vocoder, faithful sidekick Julian Hamilton conjuring up some magical shapes on his keyboard. As Johns sang the line 'I'll be home again', its significance struck him: he was home, in Sydney, back on a concert stage for the first time in five years, and the audience was right there, in his hands, loving his every move. It was a big moment in what might well have been the bravest night of his career.

Then came the biggest surprise of a gig that didn't scrimp on shocks: a sincere rendition of the old *Wizard of Oz* chestnut 'Over the Rainbow', a serious throwback for a night of futuristic sound and vision. A hefty layer of synths and harmonies provided an almost hymnal feel—at least until the band kicked in and a dance rhythm took over. As that happened, Johns stood stage front, pulling some poses for the crowd, flexing his muscles, extending his heavily inked arms like some sort of preacher of groove. It was the perfectly over-the-top conclusion to a night that totally redefined Daniel Johns, musician. Anything was possible for him now. That sense of freedom was written all over Johns's face as he bowed, blew kisses to the crowd and left the stage. Johns was the wizard of Oz.

Johns's Vivid shows were huge, a genuine breakthrough. The closest a local artist had come to such radical restyling was when Michael Hutchence teamed up with Ollie Olsen and became part of underground dance act Max Q back in 1989, but even then Hutchence and INXS had always been funkier than most rock bands. You couldn't dance to Silverchair, unless you wanted to get thumped by some mosh-pit bruiser. It's true that Johns's buddy Luke Steele had also taken a vastly different approach with tech-pop duo Empire of the Sun, but he wasn't risking much: his former day band, The Sleepy Jackson, didn't sell too many records.

Critics were as taken by Johns's performance as the Opera House audiences had been. 'The only thing you need to know,' said *The Daily Telegraph*'s Kathy McCabe, 'is that Johns looks and sounds sexy as hell. Landing somewhere between Bowie and Timberlake with a ridiculously healthy dose of Prince, the performance and its state-of-the-art lighting were world class.' Over at *The Sydney Morning Herald*, an almost-completely-won-over Bernard Zuel, another long-time supporter of Johns, name-checked everyone and everything from David Bowie to *Blade Runner*, LCD Soundsystem to *The English Patient*, in his glowing review. And his reaction to 'Over the Rainbow'? 'Given a spray of skittish beats and some swelling sounds, it was unexpected and diverting, played wholeheartedly but ultimately unsuccessful. Most of us were wondering not so much "why?" as "wha?"'

Johns's Vivid performances almost overshadowed the album *Talk*, which emerged at the time of the two shows. Trimmed of, say, five tracks, *Talk* would have been the perfect reimagining of Johns's career. (Who knows how long it might have run had Johns not lost a phone containing around 200 musical ideas just before recording began.) Still, *Talk* was vastly different to *Frogstomp*, another universe altogether. Who could have ever imagined the kid who yelled 'Tomorrow' teaming up with cutting-edge people such as Joel Little (who'd hit major pay dirt as producer of Lorde's 'Royals'), local hip-hoppers Styalz Fuego and M-Phazes and writer-producer Louis Schoorl? There wasn't a rock dog among them (although Little, truth be told, had messed about in a pop-punk band in the past). Johns's thing for collaborations—he'd also recently worked with The Veronicas and rapper 360 and was set to work on ZHU's 'Modern Conversation'—gave *Talk* the sound and feel of a modern-day R&B album. The studio code for Daniel Johns was open house: everyone was invited.

Johns was asked by writer Everett True what he'd say to hardcore Silverchair acolytes when they heard the new record. He had a one-word answer: 'Sorry'. And some long-time devotees *were* very critical of the new record; they felt that Johns had somehow betrayed them by hanging up his guitar. 'I'm sorry,' one fan wrote online. 'The person once responsible for some of the most thunderous riffs and heavy cacophony with meaning has descended to the level of elevator music.' It didn't sound much like an apology.

Johns genuinely didn't care. He was moving on, and if the old fans didn't like that, well, that reflected poorly on them, not him.

'I definitely feel like this new record is me protesting and spray-painting the wall, and putting a wall up and saying from now on I'm not going to let [the past] affect me like it used to.'

How would he feel if he'd opted to make a 'big heavy rock record?', Johns was asked. He didn't have to think too hard before responding.

'That would have been a safe and pathetic move.'

◄○►

The Vivid audiences were luckier than they realised: they'd witnessed the only live shows Johns would play in support of the album. Johns cited stage fright as his reason for not going on the road, yet judging by the way he owned the Opera House, that seemed hard to believe. Still, he was insistent: there'd be no tour. It would have been an expensive tour to mount, with the large band and space-age production. Perhaps that might have been another reason for the second 'indefinite hiatus' in Johns's recent career— first Silverchair, now playing live.

Reviews of the album were almost uniformly positive. In a four-star rave, *The Australian*'s Iain Shedden cited trip-hoppers Portishead as a key reference, while noting that *Talk* sounded very much like the beginning of Johns's journey into the future. 'The closing, arty ramble "Good

Luck",' he wrote, 'hints at how Johns might be feeling about his future direction: "I don't know where I'm going/ But I know what to do" ... Upwards and onwards, one would suggest.' Australian *Rolling Stone* writer Annabel Ross spotted a Savage Garden echo in 'Dissolve', one of two co-writes with Julian Hamilton. Prince, too, was name-checked. Despite admitting that it did run overtime, Ross concluded that '*Talk* is an exciting and rare example of an artist refusing to be shackled by their past'.

Over at *The Sydney Morning Herald*, Bernard Zuel drew an interesting parallel between Johns's new moves and country king Garth Brooks's failed attempt to reinvent himself in the mid-1990s as singer-songwriter Chris Gaines. But Johns, unlike Brooks, succeeded. As Zuel explained, 'He has burnt down the house but built another for occupation'. He bracketed Johns circa 2015 with Lorde, Frank Ocean and James Blake. '*Talk* is R&B and soul, imbued with falsetto and hushed singing.'

Yet with no live support, *Talk* did lukewarm business by Johns's standards, selling fewer than 10,000 copies. Johns jumped into a new project, Shot By Sound, for David Jones, his ex-wife's former employer. And within a year of *Talk*'s release, Johns had not only left the stage, but also the country, as his public misadventures kept piling up—and continued to be captured by Sydney's ever-alert paparazzi. Some of his moves weren't the smartest: he and girlfriend Huijer were spotted at an Indian restaurant in northern Sydney soon after his DUI charge, their table awash in wine bottles. Johns hosted a birthday lunch for Huijer at flashy east Sydney eatery China Doll, where he mingled with surprised patrons, posed for selfies and admitted that he was 'utterly wasted'. When Johns spotted some News Corp photographers, his mood changed: he leapt from his seat and chased the snappers away, while a crowd gathered at a nearby pub cheered him on. He managed to grab one lens man; Huijer intervened, persuading Johns to let him go. Johns flopped onto a nearby bench, his head in his hands, clearly distraught, as Huijer tried to console him. The only good thing to come from it was that no one managed to photograph Johns while he was grappling with the pap.

Industry insiders leapt to Johns's defence, citing the '25 years of intense fame and all the ridiculous pressure that goes with it' as the root cause of his recent melt-downs—this latest drama, his DUI charge, the trip to the ER for a head wound and the rest of it. While he should have been more discreet, there was a lot of validity in this claim: the type of scrutiny that Johns had lived through would have been tough for an adult, let alone a suburban teenager growing up very much in the spotlight's gaze. It now seemed as though Johns was trying to make up for all those years he'd spent under close watch by his parents, management and the media. He was letting himself go, living large. Unfortunately, falling down in public places wasn't the best way to go about a personal rediscovery.

Johns was sufficiently together to realise that he needed to get away from Sydney, at least until the smoke cleared from his latest indiscretion. By mid-June 2015 it was made known that he'd left for LA, where he hoped to 'lose himself' in the music scene there. (Hardly the best place to recover from a bout of overindulgence, it should be noted.) Yes, it was another in a series of 'indefinite hiatuses'.

Yet when Johns returned towards the end of the year, local photographers were back in business when they caught up with him after what was clearly a very long lunch with his new buddy, fellow musician Joshua Mullane— it appeared that Huijer wasn't on the scene anymore. A pale, drunk and shirtless Johns stumbled and fell in full gaze of startled Eastern Suburbs matrons in ritzy Double Bay. The blurred lipstick and eyeliner look that Johns was now favouring gave him the appearance of a bedraggled drag queen, wandering the streets the morning after Mardi Gras. Not a great look.

Local media, of course, had a field day. A *Daily Mail* headline snickered: 'Having trouble walking in a straight line, Daniel?' He was keeping sub-editors very busy.

Soon after, Johns took to Instagram, posing in increasingly bizarre selfies, usually with hard-to-fathom captions. 'A lot of you have been mean to me lately,' Johns wrote in one, probably referring to his recent assault by paparazzi. 'To that I can only say I love you.' 'There's something bigger than all of us,' he wrote in another, 'so love another like a paper aeroplane that will land in a palm tree.'

Johns deleted the account soon after—a wise move— only to reactivate it for more personal revelations. (Not so wise.) In May 2017, he released a happy snap with Michelle Leslie, an interior designer and Sydney socialite, best known for a 2005 drug conviction in Bali that resulted in three months' gaol time—and a conversion to Islam. The caption that accompanied the new couple's photo— and no couple is legitimate until their love is announced on Instagram—quoted philosopher Friedrich Nietzsche: 'Without music, life would be a mistake'. It was the sagest thought Johns had shared for some time—and not a bad take on his own journey. At least this time he posed with a guitar.

◄o►

Amid this whirlwind of social faux pas and new loves, Johns hadn't completely forgotten about music. There was ongoing talk about his much-discussed project with Empire of the Sun's Luke Steele, in the works for nigh on a decade. In 2016, Johns insisted it was inching closer to completion, even though he accepted that the project had by now become some sort of 'urban myth'. Perth duo Slumberjack confirmed that Johns had agreed to join them in the studio, having spent time with them at the FOMO festival in suburban Sydney. (Their collaboration was the smooth 'Open Fire'.) Daniel had also been linked with Sydney muso Jake Meadows and had completed work on an animated kids' series named *Beat Bugs*, a creation of Josh Wakely, who'd worked with Johns on *My Mind's Own Melody*. *Beat Bugs* premiered on Netflix in late 2016; in his role as musical director, Johns produced and arranged 30 Beatles songs for the program's star-studded soundtrack. Vocalists included Eddie Vedder and P!nk.

'It's a dream job,' self-confessed Beatles nut Johns said. As well as being MD and working on the animated show's score, Johns brought in locals such as Joel Little and Louis Schoorl—both of whom had worked on *Talk*— and fellow Aussie Alex Lloyd as guest music producers. And while voicing a large blue slug named Walter, Johns had the chance to sing the timeless 'I Am the Walrus'. Great work if you could get it, although singing about sitting in an English garden might well have reminded him about his time in the UK with his former wife.

It seemed that the process of collaboration, such an integral part of *Talk*, was a concept that Johns wanted to keep pursuing. What wasn't going to happen next was a repeat of the eight-year gap that separated *Young Modern* from his solo debut. In late 2016, Johns posted a typically cryptic message to Instagram, accompanying a photo of him at work in the studio: 'Kitchen is hot, no pressure cooking just slow burnt and pin cushioned. BOOM TISH.' Clearly, he was back at work on another record.

And Silverchair—was there any likelihood they'd ever emerge from their 'indefinite hiatus'? Not bloody likely, according to a comment Johns made around the time of *Talk*'s release. He insisted there was no way he'd get the band back together, 'not even for a million bucks'.

As disappointing as this was for the band's legion of fans, it made perfect sense. Johns had begun growing apart from the others back in the time of *Neon Ballroom* and, unless his financial stocks took a major battering, there was no need for him to return to the past. And more importantly than commerce, it would hardly be the smartest step for a guy completely focused on moving on, changing things up and pushing himself towards a brave new sound. *An explorer.*

CODA

IT WAS IN KEEPING with Daniel Johns's recent flair for large gestures—most notably at Vivid 2015—that his long-overdue live return in 2018 was on the stage of Coachella, possibly the biggest and certainly the most attention-grabbing festival on the planet. Why fuck around with small scale when you've got a potential online audience of millions, plus however many could squeeze into the Mojave tent at Coachella on the night of 13 April?

Months before the festival itself, online whispers started to spread, asking who, exactly, was DREAMS, and why were they being billed as one of Coachella's surprise guests? The savvier punters knew it was the new moniker of Johns and Luke Steele—there'd been a series of far-freakin'-out Instagram posts dropping the heaviest of hints and Johns even had the word DREAMS tattooed on his chest—but that still didn't stop some lively speculation.

'Maybe,' pondered one online post, 'it's some kind of collab project . . . Maybe a French duo of robotic entities?'

It became clear that this was not Daft Punk when Johns (now going by the moniker Dr Dreams) and his buddy Steele (aka Miracle) finally premiered the collaboration they'd been whispering about for years. Their Coachella set had been preceded just four days earlier by a new single, 'Silence', which was anything but.

'"Silence" is a song which came to us after the Charlottesville riots,' Steele said in a press release. 'It broke our hearts to see the violence and hatred that occurred. We wanted this song to elevate the people, let their voices be heard, inspire them with courage and bravery.'

Fine intentions, to be sure, but the video was almost unwatchable; it was so manic that it actually contained a health warning that announced: 'This video may potentially contain seizure triggers for those with photosensitive epilepsy'.

So, while they may have named their outfit DREAMS, their sound was hardly ethereal. It was no random decision to use a scorpion as their logo, because this was music with bite: intense, driving, very 21st-century music, as relentless as a piledriver—with the exception of one song, 'Love to Live', which radiated the same glacial pop cool as Steele's wildly popular Empire of the Sun, or Johns's 2018 collaboration with Sydney electronic artist What So Not, entitled 'Same Mistakes'. At times, they came on like a digital-era version of The Clash circa 'Rock the Casbah' and 'Radio Clash'—with an added whiff of the industrial grind of Trent Reznor's Nine Inch Nails.

It was not to everyone's liking, though. 'DREAMS will be more readily accepted by Empire of the Sun fans,' noted the *LA Weekly*, 'but that doesn't take anything away from the polished, hyper-catchiness of the songs.' An earlier single, 'No One Defeats Us', which had been first aired on Triple J on 15 March, copped a serious bagging. Silverchair fans, in the main, hated everything about it—the music and particularly the gritty yet flashy video, shot in LA, in which Steele and Johns committed various crimes of fashion while wandering through an apocalyptic wasteland. 'This is beyond cringe,' screamed one blogger. 'The worst part is that they don't seem to realise how truly awful this is,' wrote another. Then this: 'Somebody casted [sic] a curse on DJ. It looks like everything he touches outside Silverchair is bound to be mediocre'. Or this more measured response: 'The curious case of Daniel Johns. A rebel teen at 40 years old and an amazing artist at 24.'

But no one mentioned this peculiarity—Johns wasn't the biggest star in this band; he hadn't been a commercial force in the USA since the days of *Frogstomp* and *Freak Show*. The LA-based Steele, as one half of platinum-plus-sellers Empire of the Sun, who'd had hits across North America, Europe and Australia, was now the big attractor. The tables had turned since the two began toying with the idea of a collaboration all those years ago in 'Nat's palace' in London, when they'd actually completed an album's worth of material, but in a very stoned act of solidarity buried the tape and promptly forget where it was. The dynamic between the pair had shifted.

As far as Daniel Johns was concerned, his former band were old news, way off in his distant past. It was time for him, and the 'Chair's rusted-on fans, to move on. He'd also moved on from his long-time manager and advocate, John Watson, choosing to now work with his brother, Heath. And to hell with anyone who didn't appreciate his new direction. Better to fail boldly than tread water, or, even worse, to recycle the past.

On stage at Coachella, Johns was back to his buff self. His thigh-length fur coat didn't last long, and he went shirtless for much of their set, aside from a black, lacy something-or-other that covered his neck and little of his nipples. His feet were squeezed into the type of stacked heels that would have done Kiss's Gene Simmons proud. Steele, too, had undergone a hefty makeover, having shaved his hair into a fierce semi-mohawk. When he, too, was done with a coat—in his case a cream-coloured stormtrooper number—he spent much of the set in a loose singlet top, thrashing the strings of his transparent guitar. Johns, too, did his fair share of shredding during their time on stage. So much for the alleged stage fright that had kept him from properly promoting *Talk*.

They were an impressive-looking pair.

DREAMS' first set (there was a second on 20 April) was squeezed in between Soulwax and Black Coffee and the headliner Jamiroquai. But the white-boy's funk of Jay Kay seemed desperately dated by comparison with the fierce tribal rhythms cooked up by Johns and Steele. Okay, so DREAMS' live debut may have been overshadowed by

Beyonce's very theatrical reunion on Coachella's main stage with her fellow Destiny's children—and the 100-odd musicians and dancers and who-knows-what with whom she also shared the stage—but their set left a hefty impression. Minds were duly blown.

'This is the end of our extensive American tour,' Johns deadpanned from the stage at the close of their second set. 'Thanks to all those who followed us around the country.'

But this was no throwaway jam session for Johns and Steele; this was serious business, with more DREAMS shows at Vivid 2018, a welcome return to the Sydney Opera House for Johns. Once again, Daniel Johns was moving on, striking out for unfamiliar sonic territory, and damn the freakin' torpedoes. Their debut album, *No One Defeats Us*, appeared in September.

Johns had laid out his new MO when he spoke with Australian *Rolling Stone* upon the release of *Talk*. 'I can never imagine playing [Silverchair] songs again. I don't listen to that kind of music. My sole purpose,' he added, drawing a breath, 'is consistently seeking the future.'

ACKNOWLEDGEMENTS

Many thanks to Jane Palfreyman at Allen & Unwin and my trusty agent Jo Butler for giving me the chance to revisit Daniel Johns's past and to bring his story kicking and screaming into the now. It's not often a writer gets that opportunity, so thanks hugely. And, as ever, love and sympathy to my wife, Diana, and children Elizabeth and Christian and the cat without a name. Thanks also to Samantha Kent, Susan Keogh and Luke Causby for bringing the book together so well.

Comments and quotes that appear in the text, unless otherwise noted, were derived from interviews conducted by the author with the following people: Daniel Johns, Chris Joannou, Ben Gillies, Tobin Finnane, John Watson, John O'Donnell, Nick Launay, David Fricke, Elissa Blake, Van Dyke Parks, Robert Hambling, Tracee Hutchison, Matt Lovell, Peter McNair, Craig Mathieson, Paul Mac, Phil McKellar, Gerald Casale, David Helfgott, Julian Hamilton, James Hackett, Kevin Williamson, Kevin Shirley, Luke Steele, David Bottrill and Phil McConville.

NOTES

Chapter 1: 'They thought they had a crazy son, but after eighteen months they realised they had a normal boy like everyone else.' Andrew Denton, *Interview*, 2018.

Chapter 2: 'I didn't really like ['Tomorrow'].' *Rolling Stone*, 1996.

Chapter 3: 'People give us shit. It's good in some ways . . . If people hate you, it makes you want to keep going, 'cause you want to prove them wrong.' *Rolling Stone*, 1995.

Chapter 4: 'I got stitches and everything . . . It was so funny. It was heaps good fun. Everything went wrong.' MTV 1997.

Chapter 5: 'I was just like, "Fuck this, I'm just gonna sit in my room".' *Rolling Stone*, 1999.

Chapter 6: 'There's a lot of good people in the industry and there's a lot of dicks. So, you've just gotta live with the dicks and get on with the people that are all right.' *Cleveland Scene*, 1997.

Chapter 7: 'I couldn't leave my house without thinking something terrible was going to happen. I was really freaked.' *Enough Rope with Andrew Denton*, 2004.

DANIEL JOHNS
SELECTED
DISCOGRAPHY

Frogstomp, March 1995

'Israel's Son'/'Tomorrow'/'Faultline'/'Pure
Massacre'/'Shade'/'Leave Me Out'/'Suicidal
Dream'/'Madman'/'Undecided'/'Cicada'/'Findaway'

Freak Show, February 1997

'Slave'/'Freak'/'Abuse Me'/'Lie to Me'/
'No Association'/'Cemetery'/'The Door'/'Pop Song
for Us Rejects'/'Learn to Hate'/'Petrol &
Chlorine'/'Roses'/'Nobody Came'/'The Closing'

Neon Ballroom, March 1999

'Emotion Sickness'/'Anthem for the Year 2000'/
'Ana's Song (Open Fire)'/'Spawn Again'/'Miss
You Love'/'Dearest Helpless'/'Do You Feel the
Same'/'Black Tangled Heart'/'Point of View'/'Satin
Sheets'/'Paint Pastel Princess'/'Steam Will Rise'

I Can't Believe It's Not Rock, December 2000

'Rain'/'Take Her Out'/'3'/'Staging a Traffic Jam'/'Home'

Diorama, March 2002

    'Across the Night'/'The Greatest View'/'Without You'/'World Upon Your Shoulders'/'One Way Mule'/'Tuna in the Brine'/'Too Much of Not Enough'/'Luv Your Life'/'The Lever'/'My Favourite Thing'/'After all these Years'

The Dissociatives, April 2004

    'We're Much Preferred Customers'/'Somewhere Down the Barrel'/'Horror with Eyeballs'/'Lifting the Veil from the Braille'/'Forever and a Day'/'Thinking in Reverse'/'Paris Circa 2007slash08'/'Young Man, Old Man'/'Angry Megaphone Man'/'Sleep Well Tonight'

Young Modern, March 2007

    'Young Modern Station'/'Straight Lines'/'If You Keep Losing Sleep'/'Reflections of a Sound'/'Those Thieving Birds (Part 1)—Strange Behaviour—Those Thieving Birds (Part 2)'/'The Man Who Knew Too Much'/'Waiting all Day'/'Mind Reader'/'Low'/'Insomnia'/'All Across the World'

Talk, May 2015

    'Aerial Love'/'We Are Golden'/'By Your Side'/'Preach'/'Too Many'/'Cool On Fire'/ 'Imagination'/'Dissolve'/'Chained'/'Sleepwalker'/ 'Faithless'/'Warm Hands'/'Going on 16'/ 'New York'/'Good Luck'

No One Defeats Us, September 2018
'Movies'/'No One Defeats Us'/'Numbers on the Board'/
'Silence'/'Young Minds'/'Dreams'/'California'/'Love to
Live'/'Odd Party'/'Always'/'Into the Wild'

For full details of Silverchair albums, EPs and singles
go to www.chairpage.com/releases/. For a list of
Daniel's collaborations, see www.allmusic.com/artist/
daniel-johns-mn0000567824/credits